IN THE TRACKS OF THE
WEST CLARE
RAILWAY

IN THE TRACKS OF THE
WEST CLARE RAILWAY

EDDIE LENIHAN

MERCIER PRESS
WHAT YOU NEED TO READ

MERCIER PRESS

Cork

www.mercierpress.ie

Trade enquiries to CMD Distribution
55A Spruce Avenue, Stillorgan Industrial Park,
Blackrock, County Dublin

© Eddie Lenihan 1990, reprinted 1991
Revised edition 1999; this edition 2008
ISBN: 978 1 85635 579 7

10 9 8 7 6 5 4 3 2 1

TO ALL THOSE, LIVING AND DEAD, WHO
SERVED WITH THE WEST CLARE

The author and publisher would like to thank Herbert Richards of the Irish Railway
Record Society for the use of photographs; the National Library of Ireland for the use of
photographs from the Lawrence Collection; Michael Lenihan for his illustrations, and
Roy Denison for his permission to use his collection of photos of the railway from 1961.

A CIP record for this title is available from the British Library.

Mercier Press receives financial assistance from the Arts Council/
An Chomhairle Ealaíon.

Printed and bound by J.H. Haynes & Co. Ltd, Sparkford

Contents

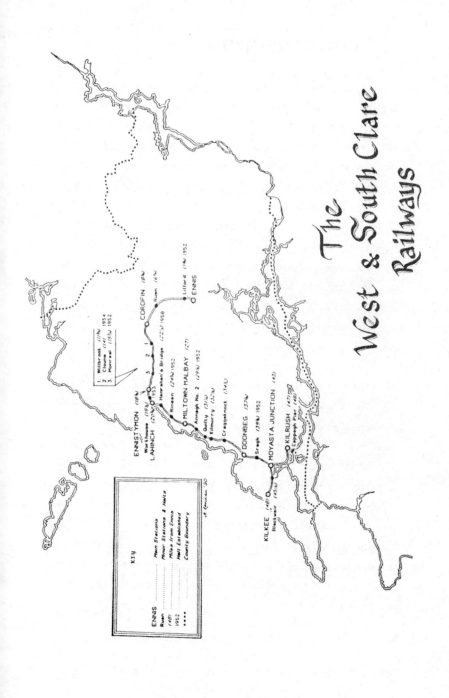

The
West & South Clare
Railways

KEY

ENNIS .... Main Stations
Ruan .... Minor Stations & Halts
(48) .... Miles from Ennis
1952 .... Halt Established
•••• .... County Boundary

H. Fayle '50

1. Willbrook (11¾) 1954
2. Cloona (14¼) 1949
3. Monreal (15¾) 1952

ENNISTYMON (18¾)
Workhouse (20¾) 1953
LAHINCH (22¼) 1953
3 2 1
CORofIN (8¾)
Ruan (6¾)
Hanrahan's Bridge (22½) 1958
Rineen (24¾) 1952
Lifford (1¾) 1952
ENNIS
MILTOWN MALBAY (27)
Annagh No. 2 (29¾) 1952
Quilty (31¾)
Kilmurry (32¾)
Craggaknock (34½)
DOONBEG (37¾)
Sragh (39¾) 1952
MOYASTA JUNCTION (43)
KILRUSH (47)
Cappagh Pier (48)
KILKEE (48)
Blackweir (45¾)

Acknowledgements

A composite work such as this cannot possibly be brought to satisfactory completion without the help and interest of many people. Perhaps my greatest debt of gratitude is due to the ordinary men and women of Clare who, almost without exception, informed, fed and encouraged us in our task. But there were others whose expertise in particular fields of knowledge solved many problems which would otherwise have bedevilled progress. I cannot hope to mention them all, but the following are particularly deserving of my thanks: Colm Casey, whose mastery of maps was indispensable; Mick Lenihan, for map and drawings; Paddy Hanrahan, driver of the last West Clare train into Ennis Station, who allowed me to use the documents and memorabilia in his possession; Seán O'Donoghue, stationmaster at Ennis, who patiently explained to me the names and uses of various pieces of railway equipment; Jim O'Neill and his wife Bridie, who helped me track down many ex-West Clare workers; Seán Spellissy, Martin Breen, Martin Boland, Mary Moroney, Fr Ignatius Murphy and Bríd Doohan, all of whom went out of their way to verify numerous historical and archaeological details and clear up some problems of chronology; Joe Taylor, for allowing me to consult the manuscripts of the late Patrick M. Taylor; Capt. J.M. Feehan, who suggested the enterprise in the first place.

Nor must I fail to acknowledge explicitly my debt to Keith, whose young curiosity so often prompted the questions that I might not have thought of, and to Mary, whose life was considerably brightened and simplified during those dark winter days by having us out of the house for protracted periods of time. To all of them, *míle buíochas*.

Eddie Lenihan

Introduction

To the men who closed the West Clare branch of CIÉ in 1961 it must have appeared that their decision was a sensible one, the only one possible in the circumstances. It was losing £23,000 per annum, much of its rolling stock needed replacement, its gauge was outlandish, needing specialised replacement parts and involving double-handling of all goods carried. In economic terms, plainly it did not make sense and if strict economics are a justification for anything, the government of the day did the correct thing in terminating its services on Tuesday 31 January 1961.

But one thing they did not reckon on: that forty-seven years later it would not have died. Rather it would be remembered larger than life, whereas they, if they were remembered at all, would be seen not as men who did the country a service but rather as a short-sighted cabal of bunglers who tried to destroy a legend – and failed.

Far more people have heard of the West Clare Railway than ever travelled on it. Far more talk about it than have ever seen any part of it. For this, Percy French's famous song 'Are Ye Right There, Michael' is chiefly responsible. Born out of a commonplace mishap in 1896, this song has gone round the world and given to this little branch line of the southern Irish railway system a mythical aura out of all proportion to reality. For the reality was that the West Clare was a slow, sometimes annoying, yet homely affair. But the song certainly goes to prove the truth of Patrick Kavanagh's assertion: 'Gods make their own importance'. Else why are all the other railway lines closed in the same era as the West Clare not as famous? Where now are the Tralee and Dingle, the West Cork, the Cahirciveen lines? Who now remembers the Kenmare, the Waterford–Tramore, to go no further than the confines of Munster alone?

This book is a record of a walking journey along the West Clare line from Ennis to Kilkee/Kilrush undertaken in the winter of 1987 and the spring of 1988 in the company of my son Keith, and also a tribute to the people and county of Clare.

Anyone with even a superficial acquaintance with Clare will know what a wealth of varied scenery it contains, together with abundant archaeological sites and historical remains spanning 5,000 years and more of human habitation. What may not be so obvious is the character of the people: friendly yet by repute reserved, helpful though not demonstrative. Outsiders who have lived for maybe half a lifetime in Clare will freely admit that it has taken them all of that time to get to know the county and the subtleties of its populace, but I must confess that I found no such reserve on this journey, even though I met, on every day of it, with people who were complete strangers to me. Perhaps a few did not invite us 'in for the tea', but there were others whose kindness surpassed all that might reasonably have been expected. On three occasions during the dark evenings of January and February when we should have had to face long, exhausting walks to where we had left our transport in the morning, people who had received us into their homes offered to drive us all the way back, at inconvenience to themselves, and did so. Words can do little to express our gratitude to these; I can only hope that this book will be accepted by them as a tribute to their generosity.

It may well be asked why such an undertaking as this should have been attempted in the darkest season of the year, when days are short and weather uncertain. The answer must be that every season has its advantages and disadvantages. If it had been done in summer the weather might be fine but foliage and undergrowth would have reduced visibility along large sections of the line. Travelling in bare winter conditions ensured that the land for a good distance around could be examined for whatever of interest it might contain. And, on balance, it seemed that a wide-ranging description of the countryside was preferable to any narrow emphasis on the railway line only. For the sad truth is that what remains of the line today, little less than half a century after its closure, is not, for most of its length, impressive. Perhaps it never was, but people's expectation is that it should be something out of the ordinary – after all, Percy French's picture of the line as an audacious anachronism in its own time still remains vibrant today, and the memories of those who travelled it have already begun to play the rosy tricks that memory so frequently does.

But facts, so often bare and unromantic, must be stated. All the usual instruments and machinery one associates with a working railway are long gone. One of the most noticeable things about our journey over the 54 miles of the West Clare's length was the almost total absence of metal debris of any kind larger than the odd bolt or fencepost. What remains is a skeleton of what once was, moreover, a skeleton with many bones missing. Only when one looks at photos of the line in its working days does it become apparent how much has changed. What was a railway is now a disjointed succession of pieces linking not just places but in a way two worlds, one unhurried, traditional, the other brash, frenzied and modern.

A time will come when parts of the West Clare Railway line will be preserved as national monuments. There are still wonderful embankments and cuttings that will survive simply because it would require too much effort to obliterate them. Cut-stone facings, bridges, the more sophisticated end of the achievement that was the physical line will be first to vanish – plundered for short-term gain as building stone or scrap metal, but, as in the case of earthen ringforts, the bulk works will remain to remind a future generation of what once passed through this countryside: not just the trains but the gangs of sweating workers who preceded them in laying down the line. If, at that future time, an observer should manage to come upon some of the surviving photos of the line in its heyday, he will be as little able to associate them with the visible remaining fragments as we are now able to do in the case of 'fairy forts' and the artists' impressions of them in their days of habitation which we sometimes see in books.

For even now, hardly five decades after its demise, the greater part of the West Clare needs a considerable effort of imagination to bring to life the coherent and complicated system that operated here.

In spite of this, there are many who persist in the belief that the line could be, and will one day be, reopened and that tourism in West Clare will prosper as a result. This is a pleasant dream. No doubt tourism *would* benefit – especially in the scenic Kilrush–Kilkee stretch where, as one person I met with on my travels said, 'The slower it'd go the better they'd like it. They could make a day-excursion of the 8 miles.' But those who harbour such fond notions are invariably people who do not know the line as it is today. To walk it would cure them of their illusions and give them a more realistic notion of what might be achieved. For, as this account will show, the line has come to be used for many purposes never envisaged by its builders: rubbish tip, septic tank, cattle feeding-place, site for buildings, etc.

These various uses to which it has been put illustrate the constant change that is occurring in the physical landscape, change that has accelerated rapidly with the proliferation of heavy earth-moving machinery. This we found to be especially true of areas in the vicinity of towns and villages. Good examples of this would be Ennistymon, Lahinch and Quilty, and in the case of Ennistymon it has to be said that much of the development seems to have been haphazard and to have taken too little account of the possibilities presented by the undulating landscape surrounding that town. But Ennistymon alone need not be singled out, as the same applies to many areas.

In the light of a widespread casual attitude of large numbers of people to their own surroundings, it seems strange that many of the same people should so vehemently decry the 'vandalism' of Todd Andrews in terminating the service in 1961. Illogicality aside, they are entitled to their opinion, and moreover are determined that it will be heard. We heard it expressed dozens of times in the course of our journey. Even the staunchest of Fianna Fáil supporters, those for whom the party could do no wrong, would consider themselves not at all disloyal in claiming that the Fianna Fáil government of the day made a bad mistake. One of the more forgiving I spoke with,

a man in Kilrush, put it succinctly: 'Brilliant men gone astray.' The
implication is clear: Clare would today be in some way a better place
if the railway were still in existence.

Whether it would or not is debatable, but the feeling certainly
grew on us as we tramped the line south from Lahinch that much of
that part of west Clare is now relatively isolated from the rest of the
county, a feeling that persisted until we got to the main east–west traffic artery at Moyasta. The intervening country, with its succession of
once-busy stops – Rineen, Quilty, Annagh, Kilmurry, Craggaknock,
Sragh – is now a backwater.

All this we observed, and it is there for anybody to see. To have
discovered this alone would have made our journey worthwhile, but of
course there was much more, not least being our personal satisfaction
at completing the journey, meeting with interesting people, visiting
new places and the acquisition of much railway lore and terminology.
So basic was my knowledge of this latter at the time of beginning
our walk that I had difficulty distinguishing the 'up' and 'down' lines,
never mind being able to differentiate between a block-post and a
flag station, or between running roads, passing-loops and sidings.

But almost all things are possible to those who wish to learn
– and who are blessed with generous teachers. And ours were of the
best. I only hope I have thanked them sufficiently elsewhere.

Part I

Historical

In the 76 years from the turning of its first sod by C.S. Parnell at
Miltown Malbay on 26 January 1885 to its closure on 31 January
1961, the West Clare – 'Kate Mac', as it was affectionately known by
many Clare people – became one of the mainstays and shapers of the
agricultural and social life of its hinterland, and part of Clare's legacy
to all of Ireland.

Practically, it served the people of Clare well during two world
wars, but that part of its function has long passed away. Emotionally,
however, it still lives on, and it needs no saying by me that wherever
Claremen are gathered, one or other of two subjects – Biddy Early
or the West Clare – will sooner or later be remembered nostalgi-
cally. But the West Clare did not always arouse such fond emotions.
During its construction and for much of its working life it was to
provoke reactions ranging from annoyance to outright hostility from
widely differing groups of people. On more than one occasion the
clergy had to be called on to restore a semblance of calm.

All this, however, was far in the past by the time the fatal termina-
tion order was put into practice in January 1961, and its closure was
felt by persons of all ages and classes. There were the ritual petitions
and denunciations by interested parties, of course, but by and large
the feeling among the public in general, and politicians in particular,
seems to have been one of resignation, powerlessness, even apathy.

It was, after all, mainly a pre-lobbying age, a time of depression and high emigration, when political loyalties were still unshakable.

But there was genuine regret also. The *Clare Champion* was probably voicing a general sentiment when it stated that 'Tuesday, January 31st, will long be remembered in west Clare as the day they lost a railway – and a friend'.[1] The writer of the article was not pleased with CIÉ's handling of the closure, claiming that it had sought to 'hoodwink' the public about the time of the last train's departure – presumably to forestall any popular show of displeasure. The national daily papers of the time were even more forthright in their disapproval of the company's callousness in depriving loyal customers of a trip on the last train.[2] Overall, CIÉ is not fondly remembered for its actions during the closure and the years immediately preceding it, particularly by ex-railwaymen. Constantly, during many conversations with these men, several questions were thrown at me: why were the rails raised with such unholy haste after the closure? Why was other rolling stock allowed to run down so lamentably even after the purchase of railcars and diesel locomotives in the 1950s? Why were these same locomotives, which had cost over £80,000 each, allowed to stand rusting for a year after the closure when the whole line was making a loss of only £23,000 per annum? Why were bus and train scheduled to leave Kilkee at the same time each day?[3] What kind of management could possibly imagine that the few alternative trucks made available could do the work of the goods' trains?

A strong suspicion persists among many of them that a deliberate policy of undermining the West Clare was operated by the company, reinforced by lack of knowledge and foresight at the top. This is followed by claims that most of them preferred working for 'The Southern' (Great Southern Railways) because the feeling among the staff was that those who made decisions in that organisation knew what they were doing – since the majority of managers had come up through the ranks – whereas in CIÉ there was too much political interference.

Whatever the truth of all this may be, one positive fact does remain and must be answered by critics of the company: CIÉ *did* invest heavily in dieselisation and other upgradings of facilities very late in the day. Why?

The answer is probably simple enough. There was no positive plan for the future of railways in Ireland at that time, and an easy option was taken: cut losses and run.[4] That, combined with lack of sufficient will to make the system work, ensured the end of not just the West Clare but of many other small lines also.

But all this was a long way from the saga of the coming of the railways to Clare – and I use the word 'saga' advisedly, because merely to get the first train moving took almost four decades and labyrinthine proposals, counterproposals, false starts, politicking, bankruptcy and natural disaster. It certainly reads like a saga, and, for good measure, it was largely a family affair between the people of Clare, Catholic and Protestant, landlord and peasant, priest and layman, town and country, with a few important outsiders thrown in to lend spice to the mixture.

To bring to some kind of order not just the complicated dealings which led to the establishment of the railway but also its subsequent history, I have picked out sixteen dates which I consider to be crucial to any reasonably complete account of the line. They will also provide a convenient reference point for the reader. They are:

1. 1845: First Kilkee–Kilrush/Cappagh rail link proposed by Col. Vandeleur.
2. 1858: First scheme to reach the stage where ground was actually broken to lay a railway in west Clare.
3. 31 July 1871: Ennis and West Clare Railway receives Act of Incorporation and is authorised to build a narrow-gauge line (the first company in Ireland to get such permission).
4. 24 August 1883: Tramways Act passed by Parliament.
5. 15 December 1883: West Clare Railway Company registered.
6. 9 June 1884: South Clare Railway Company formed.
7. 26 January 1885: First sod of West Clare Railway turned by Parnell at Miltown Malbay.
8. 2 July 1887: West Clare Railway opened for regular services.
9. 9 October 1890: First sod of South Clare Railway turned by Mrs Reeves at Kilkee.

10. 23 December 1892: South Clare Railway opened for regular services.

11. 1 January 1925: Amalgamation of West Clare Railway and Great Southern Railways.

12. July 1927: ETS signalling introduced on Ennis-Miltown sections of the West Clare line.

13. 1945: CIÉ takes over the West Clare line.

14. 1948: Milne Report. First official mention of possible closure of West Clare branch of CIÉ.

15. 1952–55: Dieselisation.

16. 31 January 1961: Closure of West Clare line.

In the years after the Famine a sort of railway fever gripped Ireland, but it was merely an extension of the tremendous upsurge in railway construction in Great Britain in those years.[5] In the four decades from 1845 to 1885 no fewer than a dozen railway-building schemes were mooted for Clare alone, as well as various plans for tramlines. The large population of the time may have justified such proposals, but much of the impetus certainly came from landlords whose travels abroad demonstrated to them the advantage of fast and comfortable transport, and emphasised the shortcomings of their own home areas.[6] But other possible advantages would not have been lost on them – the boost to their status and the enhancement of their incomes. A glance at the proposed schemes shows the main movers to have indeed been a combination of landed proprietors and businessmen.

All these plans were similar in some vital respects: they all included as their terminus points Ennis, Kilrush and Kilkee. At that time traffic on the Shannon was considerable, and Cappagh pier had to figure large in any route that hoped to be profitable, but how Cappagh might be made accessible was the subject of widely varying proposals. Essentially, though, there were three routes: from Limerick to Foynes by rail, then to Kilrush by steamer; from Ennis via Kildysart, Killimer and Carrigaholt or Querrin to Kilkee; from Ennis via Ennistymon and Miltown Malbay, then southward.

The various plans formulated in the 1840s and 1850s foundered on one common rock: finance, and this largely because they proposed crossing Poulnasherry Bay rather than going round it. Certain progress was made in each of these early schemes but all failed to reach the construction phase. The first to achieve this distinction was the Cappagh–Kilkee line, for which discussions began in 1858 and on which work actually commenced in 1863. From its remains today it can be seen to have started on the western end at Lisdeen cutting, extended for 400 yards south-eastward before coming to a dead end facing slob-land in a tidal valley approximately 1¼ miles long (for a description of this, see p. 276). It continued on the higher ground in the townland of Termon West, north-east of where Termon school stands today, and ran along the southern shore of the bay through Termon East, Leaheen and Kilnagalliagh, passing through a deep cutting to reach the tide at the mouth of the bay.[7] From here it was intended to link the two shores by an embankment, with a bridge in the middle to allow the passage of turf-boats up to Moyasta, Bohaunagower and Blackweir quay. Across the channel on the eastern shore, in Carrowncalla South, the remains at Ilaunalea make it clear that this would have been the main junction of the Ennis–Kilkee and Kilrush–Kilkee lines – in effect, what Moyasta Junction was to become on the 1887 line – had not bad planning and even worse weather intervened to bring to nought the whole venture. For, after repeated stoppages during the mid-1860s, the embankment across the bay was almost completed by the winter of 1868–69, and the two sides had even been linked by a boardwalk. But though it was advised that no more should be done until the bank had solidified and the winter passed, this was not heeded, the various gaps were closed and a violent storm later that winter destroyed much of the earthworks, bringing the whole scheme to a halt not just for the time being, but for nearly twenty years.[8]

During these twenty years there were very many meetings and proposals, both for the Kilrush–Kilkee section and for the Ennis–Miltown route, including, in 1871, one for a line from Ennis to Miltown via Corofin, Ennistymon and Lahinch – exactly the route later taken by the West Clare Railway. But practical developments had to await the passing of the Tramways Act in August of 1883, a measure that allowed the interest on capital to be guaranteed by the baronies through which a railway passed.[9] On 15 December 1883 the West Clare Railway Company was registered, and shortly thereafter W.M. Murphy, one of the foremost contractors of the day, and later to achieve notoriety for his part in the Dublin Lockout of 1913, was appointed contractor and the scene was set for solid progress.

An Order in Council of 26 May 1884 authorised construction of a railway from Ennis to Miltown of a gauge of 3 feet,[10] and a contract between the company and Murphy was signed on 3 November.[11] On 26 January 1885, at Miltown, C.S. Parnell, in the presence of a huge crowd, turned the first sod of the line and afterwards was presented with the ceremonial barrow and shovel, which can be seen today in the De Valera Library in Ennis. Work commenced in late February from both ends, and by October 9 miles had been ballasted from Lifford crossing to beyond Corofin, and Drumcliff road-bridge, fourteen culverts and nine level crossings were also completed.[12] But progress was not uninterrupted. During the summer there was a strike, and towards the end of the year the company was overtaken by interrelated financial and political difficulties that almost brought about a repeat of the 1860s debacle. During these months the possibility of Home Rule was uppermost in the minds of those who might have provided the money necessary for the work of construction, and as a newspaper of the time put it, 'no capitalist would advance any money … after the fatal blow had been struck by the [Home Rule] Bill at the value of the security'.[13] An application was made to the Board of Works for a loan to complete the line and this at last was sanctioned, but with many strings attached and only after months of ill-tempered wrangling.[14]

However, by May 1886 the crisis had been overcome, and with £54,000 obtained from the Board operations continued.[15] On 28 October the *Clare Saturday Record* could report: 'on Saturday Mr William Murphy, MP, constructor, and Mr Wilson, head engineer … made an inspection of the works now in progress and are satisfied with their inspection. The works are in an advanced state and it is expected that the line will be open for traffic in the early months of 1887.'

Early in the new year locomotives nos. 1 and 2 arrived, and no. 3, *Clifden* and no. 4, *Besborough*, had been completed by their builder, W.G. Bagnall of Stafford, and all seemed fair for the completion of work in a short time.[16] But in March the Athenry and Ennis Junction Railway Company brought an action against the West Clare Company to try to prevent it from trespassing on certain of its lands through which the West Clare would have to pass (i.e. the 1¼ mile length from Ennis Station to Corrovorrin). In handing down his decision, the judge sought to acknowledge the rights of both sides, for though the A&EJ Company was awarded compensation, the WCR Company was allowed to finish its line.

But a last obstacle had yet to be overcome. On 18 May, at the road sessions in Ennis, W.R. Kenny, one of the company directors, made a speech containing serious allegations concerning the quality of the work and the reliability of the contractor, and predicted dire consequences for the taxpayers of the county. So thoroughly did he alarm his hearers that it was decided to forward a copy of the speech to the Board of Trade before the government inspector should be sent to inspect the line.[17] In spite of this, however, the inspector, Major-General Hutchinson, arrived at the beginning of June to put the line to the test. He was not immediately satisfied but did comment that this was in many respects the best of the railways that he had inspected under the 1883 Act. After a second and final inspection on Wednesday 29 June he allowed it to be opened, and notices immediately appeared in the newspapers that regular services would commence on Saturday 2 July with three trains each way daily, to be synchronised with arrivals and departures on the broad gauge at Ennis.[18] Also mentioned in the advertisements was a linking car service to Lisdoonvarna, at a cost of one shilling, which could be arranged by notifying the stationmaster at Ennistymon.

On Sunday 3 July the first excursion train left Ennis for Miltown Malbay, and thus began a summer service which proved immensely popular from the very beginning and which was to bring prosperity to Lahinch and later to Kilkee.[19] In fact, for Limerick people as much as for the inhabitants of mid and east Clare, this yearly trip to the seaside was to become an institution in its own right (the 'Sea-breeze' special) over the next seventy-odd years.

Though the South Clare Railway Company was formed in June of 1884, it was not until six years later, in June 1890, that work actually started. During that time it was by no means certain that any south Clare line would be a continuation of the line from Miltown. An influential group of people was entirely opposed to the narrow gauge, and in 1885 they had obtained sanction from the grand jury for a broad-gauge line from Ennis to Cappagh via Kildysart, Kilmihil and Cooraclare, then across the bay to Kilkee. The contractor, W.M. Murphy, would not agree to any project which included a crossing of the bay, but the grand jury was just as vehemently determined on this route, and so the impasse continued until 1890. In March of that year a semblance of agreement was finally reached and the line sanctioned in the form favoured by Murphy (i.e. by Moyasta and Blackweir, avoiding any crossing of the bay). The necessary bill was passed in parliament in August, and the first sod turned at Kilkee by Mrs Reeves on 9 October amid general rejoicing that despite all obstacles the South Clare Railway was at last set to become a reality.[20]

It was intended that construction work should not start until the spring of 1891, but because of hunger in west Clare that winter due to potato failure Murphy was persuaded to begin work immediately at various points along the line (for example, at Kilrush on 10 October and at Miltown on 1 November). At first all went well and there was rapid progress, but soon labour problems surfaced and there were a number of strikes early in 1891. These were eventually settled through the mediation of local clergy, and by March the consulting engineer, Mr Barrington, was able to report steady progress on all fronts – part of the section between Moyasta and Kilrush actually being ready for ballasting. He also reported difficulties in the boggy section at Sragh, a place which was to cause some embarrassment the following year when the line subsided during a trial run and the engine was overturned in the bog.[21] But on the whole he was convinced that things were going as well as or better than could be expected. By May the iron bridges had arrived from their manufacturer, Matthew Shaw, London, and work to set them in place continued throughout the summer. But in August there was more trouble at Miltown and Mountrivers, this time between railway employees and farmers who were dissatisfied with the terms they had obtained from the company, and the police had to provide protection for the workers. Operations eventually proceeded but only after court appearances had guaranteed undertakings of non-interference by the protestors. It appears that another reason for the poor relations with some farmers may have been the insistence of the latter that they get work in the construction, while the same demand was being made by the unemployed in every town and village along the way. This led to bad blood and resentment, which could all too easily be translated into attacks on workers, and later attempts at derailment. It is remembered even today that Mr Griffin, the chief engineer, had to accompany the driver and fireman with a shotgun on some sections, and had to enlist the help of Fr Quinlivan, parish priest of Kilkee, to speak to the people in order to allow work to proceed.[22]

Engineer Barrington, in his report in November, again announced good progress, and in his final report, on 1 May 1892, declared that all the rails had been laid and the final touches were being put to buildings, sidings and signalling arrangements.

Some of the rolling stock had arrived, and inspection by the Board of Trade would soon be possible. Before this inspection took place a round trip from Miltown to Kilrush/Kilkee was made on 11 May, the train being hauled by one of the new, more powerful 0–6–2 engines, no. 6, *Saint Senan*.

On first inspection, at the end of July, Major-General Hutchinson did not sanction immediate opening, but after a second visit on 11 August the go-ahead was given though there were still minor problems to be righted, and the Kilrush—Kilkee section was opened to traffic on 13 August. (However, a number of passenger specials had been run as early as 3 July. On that day a derailment was narrowly avoided at Lisdeen, near Kilkee, when a man with a red flag waved down the train to give warning that the line ahead had been tampered with).[23]

Inspection car, 1953. (Photo: Irish Railway Record Society, no. 10600)

A third inspection at the end of October allowed the Miltown–Moyasta section to open for goods' traffic, and this service commenced on 11 November, but it was not until Hutchinson's final visit on 20–1 December that the line was passed as fit for all services, and accordingly it was declared open on 23 December, with two trains each way daily, increasing to three early in 1893. From its inception the South Clare Railway was operated by the management of the West Clare, which by now had over five years' experience to its credit, and for the next thirty-three years until the amalgamation of 1925, services ran regularly if not always punctually.

It was, of course, lack of punctuality which was, through the agency of Percy French, to bring a wholly unlooked-for fame to the line, but there were practical enough reasons for this recurring annoyance. Cappagh caused problems right from the beginning since trains from Kilrush had to be scheduled to meet those on the broad gauge at Ennis while at the same time the arrival of steamers at the pier-head depended on the vagaries of tide and weather.[24] The almost inevitable result was the continual stranding of passengers, with all the ensuing bad publicity.[25] Matters were not initially helped by the lack of a siding on to the pier for the transporting of heavy luggage, but the deficiency was soon made good, and a second siding was later added by the GSR.

But an even greater cause of delays to goods and passengers was recurring mechanical failures, especially in the first four locomotives, of the 0–6–0 type. This was because they were not powerful enough for the work required of them. And also, no doubt, because they were the first passenger locomotives to be produced by their builders, there were teething problems still to be overcome.

Improvements were made under the Superintendency of George Hopkins (1891–1902), and a new, more powerful type of engine introduced – the 0–6–2 class – which provided much better traction on the steep gradients of the West Clare line, such as Clouna and the Black Hill; for although the three engines of this class (no. 5, *Slieve Callan*, no. 6, *Saint Senan* and no. 7, *Lady Inchiquin*) were built for the South Clare Railway, they were in fact used with the four West Clare engines throughout the whole system.[26]

Due to the experience gained with these locomotives, further refinements were introduced into the next two engines delivered, no. 8, *Lisdoonvarna*, in 1894, and no. 9, *Fergus*, in 1898. By now Hopkins was planning to replace the four original engines that had caused so many problems, and a new no. 2, *Ennis*, was built in 1900 as well as a new no. 4, *Liscannor*, in 1901, the old engines bearing these numbers being withdrawn from service simultaneously.[27] However, his departure the following year left the original engines no. 1 and no. 3, *Clifden*, in service for a number of years more, thus ensuring further maintenance problems. Only three more locomotives were acquired up to the time of the First World War: no. 10, *Lahinch*, in 1903, no. 11, *Kilkee*, in 1909 and no. 1, *Kilrush*, in 1912. After the war a further two were built: no. 3, *Ennistymon*, and no. 7, *Malbay*, in 1922, and these had the distinction of being the last steam locomotives built for an Irish narrow-gauge line.

Shortly afterwards, on 1 January 1925, the rolling stock and locomotives became the property of Great Southern Railways, and the names were abolished, the prefix 'C' being added to the running number instead. Romantic notions were even now giving way to hard facts! But changes extraneous to the railways were already making survival more difficult. The demise of Cappagh pier in conjunction with the decline of steamer traffic on the Shannon made the direct loop at Moyasta almost redundant, and by the 1920s it could be said that rail traffic in Clare had seen its best days, for as motor transport became more common the railway suffered accordingly, and the line, which had been quite profitable in the early years, now began to accrue deficits from which even its faithful service during two world wars could not save it.

Certainly, efforts were made from time to time to modernise the system, and to make it safer and more cost-effective – for example, by the introduction of ETS working in July 1927 and the purchase of two Drewry railcars in 1928.[28] But the inescapable fact was that effective control had now moved to Dublin, where there was far less tolerance of inefficiency or understanding of local sentiment. A large part of the Ennis carriage-building works and maintenance depot was closed down, and ballast ceased to be quarried locally, all supplies now coming from the GSR quarry at Newbridge, Co. Kildare.[29] The only link with tradition preserved in this regard was that the 1908 decision of the West Clare Company to ballast the line annually in May, June and October was adhered to until the time of the closure of the system in 1961.

A proposal was made in 1936 to widen the gauge from 3 feet to the standard 5-foot-3-inches so as to avoid the necessity for transfer of all goods at Ennis Station, but this came to nothing in spite of a lively debate on the matter in the local press which lasted well into the 1940s. The cost would have been out of all proportion to any prospective benefits.

By the end of the 'Emergency' the West Clare was in dire straits. Lack of proper fuel and spare parts during the war years had taken their toll and the Milne Report mentioned it as a 'line which CIÉ is considering closing'.[30] However, it was given a final chance. The old steam engines, which were an average of fifty years old, were withdrawn from

West Clare rolling stock at Ennis, after closure, 7.6.61. (Photo: Roy Denison)

passenger services in 1952 and replaced by four diesel railcars, nos. 286–9 (later renumbered 3386–9), specially built by Walker Brothers of Wigan. Frequency of services was increased and five new halts opened: Lifford, Ruan, Rineen, Annagh no. 2 and Sragh, with another at Monreal later in the same year. Three more were to be opened before the closure of the line: Workhouse Halt near Ennistymon in 1953, Clouna in 1954 and, finally, Hanrahan's Bridge, close by the Black Hill, in October 1958.

Meanwhile, the steam locomotives, supplemented by two 2–6–0Ts from the defunct Tralee and Dingle line, continued to haul goods' trains, though more and more falteringly, until, in October 1955, they were superseded by three diesel mechanical locomotives of the 0–4–4–0 variety, (nos. F 501–3), thus making the West Clare the only narrow-gauge railway in Ireland and Britain to be fully dieselised.[31]

The last steam passenger train left Ennis on 15 March 1952, and the locomotive on that occasion was no. 5C, the former *Slieve Callan*. One last glimmer of fame awaited her, for, in May 1956, she was called on to haul a number of coaches and wagons from Kilkee to Moyasta during the making of the film *A Minute's Wait*. She was officially withdrawn from service only in October 1959, and stood for years, ever more weatherbeaten, outside Ennis Station until she was removed to Shannon for refurbishment at the end of 1989.

In spite of this last injection of new locomotive equipment and
the consequent increase in passenger numbers the line still continued
to make a loss of over £20,000 per annum, partly because of the run-
down condition of much of the other rolling stock and also because
the government of the day had perhaps by then decided that many
of the small branch lines had no longer a useful purpose to serve.[32]
This is partly evidenced by the fact that some time before the final
closure order came into force a community-development group in
Lahinch invited Mr Andrews to see for himself how inadequate the
available coaching stock was to the demands of the tourist season.
On the day of his visit crowds of people were being left behind at
Lahinch Station for want of adequate accommodation, but he was
quite non-committal and would give no assurance that anything
would be done to improve the situation. It was obvious to those who
accompanied him that the writing was on the wall. And so it was that
on 27 September 1960 the death sentence was pronounced: it was
declared publicly that the line would close on 31 January 1961. This
time there was to be no reprieve and the axe duly fell as scheduled,

Engine 5C, Slieve Callan. *(Illustration: M. Lenihan)*

bringing to an end all passenger services on the narrow gauge in Ireland.

But there is a little postscript to the story. If the West Clare was now dead in its original home, at least part of its equipment continued to work on, for Bord na Móna bought the railcars and they went on giving an efficient service for years in the Bord's bog railway system.[33]

And who knows, but maybe somewhere in Nigeria, to which the rails were exported, a slow, homely little train wends its way through stations with names unpronounceable to Irish tongues, all the time travelling to the tune of 'Are Ye Right There, Michael, Are Ye Right'!

Part II

The West Clare Railway

Day 1

Ennis Station to Ballygriffey Castle

It would seem logical that anyone who intends viewing the West Clare Railway line at first hand should visit its main terminus and point of departure, Ennis Station, to find what may be gleaned there. That, at least, was the approach I had decided on long before Keith and I ever set foot in the station yard on 27 September 1987. On entering the station grounds one sees immediately on the left a little park in the triangle of ground between the access road, the Limerick–Sligo railway line and the public road to Quin. This is the Percy French Memorial Park, and here, on a raised platform, was displayed until recently the South Clare Railway 0–6–2T engine no. 5, *Slieve Callan*, first of the three new locomotives bought for the opening of that line in 1892. A short distance away, on a plinth, is a little sculpture executed in bronze and depicting, it seems, episodes from the life of the West Clare and particularly Percy French's association with the line. Close by is a tourist map containing a brief summary of the history of the line. Little else remains that might remind one that here,

Ennis Station, 1952. (Photo: Irish Railway Record Society, no. 10136)

scarcely more than a quarter of a century ago, trains of that famous railway came and went at least five times daily.

The lie of the station and car-park has been much altered since 1961, so it is difficult to imagine that where there are now flower beds and footpaths the West Clare line then ran. Parallel to the broad gauge and separated from it by the present platform, it proceeded from the station, under the Quin road-bridge and out into the busy yard beyond, the site now occupied by the ESB. But today all such facts are merely history. As one walks along the platform (which was rebuilt by the famous Limerick masons, the Kemmys, for the coming of the diesel trains in the early 1950s) on the first steps of the 54-mile journey to Kilkee, one sees ahead only a narrow pedestrian passage underneath the roadway. A closer scrutiny of the high road-wall will show that there was once a bridge here and that it has been completely blocked – but with concrete, not stone, so the original outline is still clearly visible. Hard to believe now that two lines of the West Clare ever ran through here, linking the station proper, the West Clare engine shed, turntable and carriage works (which were situated where the little park now is) with the engine shops, goods' shed, loading bays and the transfer bank with its 3-ton crane, all in the large compound on the far side of the bridge. The diesel locomotives were left unprotected here for over a year after the closure in 1961.

Before proceeding further, pause for a moment, observe and listen. The quietness and lack of activity are striking. The passenger service on the broad-gauge has been discontinued for some years now, and even goods' trains are infrequent. Apart from the coming and going of occasional buses, nothing seems to happen any more at Ennis Station. But it was not always so. Up to a thousand people at a time milled about on this platform in the early years of the West Clare, when the summer specials were in full swing, and even within the memory of people by no means old it was a hive of frenzied coming and going as passengers from places west came to town on Saturdays to do their week's shopping, on Sundays to watch hurling at Cusack Park, or to catch 'The Southern' for pilgrimages to Knock or 'The Reek'.

It saw its share of tragedy, of course. A short newspaper report on 26 March 1888 states that the widow and family of a Michael Buckley were seeking compensation from the railway. He had been killed two months previously. Three years later, in 1891, a young man was crushed to death by a moving train.[1] And there were others.

But the lighter side of life, never very far away from the operations of the West Clare, got its fair share of coverage, too, as in the case of the businesslike Limerick lady returning from Lahinch on a fair day in 1896. While hurrying along the platform to catch her connecting train for home, she was knocked down and injured by a donkey which rushed out of a carriage of a West Clare train. The ensuing court case was reported blow by blow in the local press and makes hilarious reading. The company, however, was not amused when a decree for £16 plus £6 0s 10d expenses was given in favour of the plaintiff.[2] At the same quarter-sessions sitting, a second action against the company was decided – none other than the famous Percy French case. It also went against the West Clare, but at least the £10 decreed was money well, if unwillingly, spent. For such a paltry sum was immortality bought!

Diesel railcar about to leave Ennis, 25 July 1954.
(Photo: Irish Railway Record Society, no. 11009)

The shenanigans were by no means confined to daylight hours, however. The 'coffins' episode is even today recalled with much mirth by West Clare men and shows something of the friendly rivalry that existed between themselves and those who worked on 'The Southern'. A consignment of eight coffins bound for an undertaker

Diesel locomotives at Ennis Station.
(Photo: Irish Railway Record Society, no. 83602)

in Kilrush was left on the platform overnight, ready to be shipped out on the morning train. The West Clare gang on night shift, knowing the time at which their 'Southern' counterparts would be passing, were kneeling and to all appearances praying devoutly when their victims arrived. The 'Southern' gang, taken aback by the strange and eerie sight, stood amazed only to be told 'Kneel down an' say a prayer, wouldn't ye. Or what kind o' pagans are ye?' Sheepishly, they did so, completely taken in until they realised minutes later that they had been had when the pranksters, no longer able to keep straight faces, burst into giggles. Needless to say, the affair was long a source of embarrassment to the 'Southern' men. Harmless fun it was, though, and a sense of humour was a necessary thing, for wages were low and the work often gruelling. This was especially so at the 'West Clare bank', the transfer bank at the northern side of the Quin road. Here, not alone porter, foodstuffs and cattle had to be transferred from one gauge to the other, but also heavier cargoes such as coal and phosphate. This latter arrived on specials from Ennistymon and had to be shovelled across the intervening space to the 'Southern' wagons, a much disliked operation since it was extremely demanding physically.

An equally tough and even more responsible job was that of steam-riser, for he had to be out of his bed at 3 a.m to clean out the fire-boxes of as many as six engines and have them ready to roll at 8 a.m Especially busy was the sugar-beet season, when up to three 'Southern' engines from Tuam would be in Ennis together to collect cargoes of beet. The large fire-boxes of these locomotives might contain thirty shovelfuls of cinders each, and these had to be cleaned out with a clinker shovel and a long poker called a 'dart'. Next, the steam-riser went down into a pit beneath the engine to empty the ash-pan of two to three barrow-loads of ash, and then, finally, cleaned the smoke-box (another barrow-load, this time of soot). The ash and clinker were taken to a siding and used at a later date for packing sleepers, etc., along the line.

Once the fire had been lighted it might take anything up to two hours to get up 75 pounds of steam, sufficient to move out the engine, so there was little leisure time on this particular job. Even worse than usual would be the morning when a 'light special' was due to leave for Ennistymon, or wherever, for a cattle fair. On top of his normal duties on such a day, the poor steam-riser might have to head off on his bicycle into the dark countryside to call up the driver, fireman or guard.

And what of the boilermaker's mate? His job was dirtier still, for he had to climb bodily *into* the fire-box whenever the copper tubes began to leak, in order to clean and prepare them for the boilermaker, who would then caulk them. The necessity for this became more and more frequent as the steam locomotives aged, and matters had become so bad by the 1940s and early 1950s that each driver carried a bag of bran in the cab as a temporary sealant. A couple of fistfuls of this in the water tank would allow him to travel the few extra miles to a station, where the ailing tubes might receive professional attention.

But let us walk on and see for ourselves the site of all this former activity. You will note when you emerge from the narrow little underpass that you are in an area which has a distinct air of being run-down. The broad-gauge line is here, but to its left, between it and the ESB yard, lies a jumble of rail-yard bric-a-brac: fenceposts, rails, sleepers and all the other paraphernalia of a working line. Where, though, is the West Clare? Look closely as you may amid all these distracting bits and pieces, you will find few remaining traces. Only the low cut-stone boundary wall and a few steps, now leading nowhere, signify that here was once a complex of thriving industry.

Having obtained permission from the stationmaster, we proceeded along the Sligo line, past the sites of the 'north cabin' and its equivalent, the West Clare signal box, which was on the down side at the junction of the two lines. Between this point and Shaughnessy's Bridge, 1½ miles further on, we were, with a growing sense of incredulity, to ask ourselves this question time and time again: 'Where can the West Clare have gone?' For all except a few scattered remnants of it have disappeared along this stretch. Later, to put my mind at rest, I asked the stationmaster at Ennis to explain this and he did so quite simply: when the narrow-gauge line was raised in 1961 the space it occupied was used to allow more room to the broad-gauge. This latter has been slightly centred several times since, especially on the high embankment which carries the line onto the Fergus no. 1 Bridge at Clonroad and off in a dead straight line to Corrovorrin Bridge, half a mile beyond.

After a walk of perhaps 800 yards and several glimpses of Doora and the low-lying marshy land to the east of Ennis, it is a pleasure to pause for a moment at Clonroad Bridge. We did not cross by the main bridge but walked instead over a somewhat rickety foot-bridge which has been erected on the metal piles that once supported the West Clare line. The Fergus is at least 50-feet wide here, so a substantial structure was required. But was it necessary'? Was this whole separate 1¼-mile section to Corrovorrin level crossing really needed? William Kenny did not think so, for as early as May 1887 he ventured to say that 'if this railway is to continue as a working concern it must be eventually turned into an ordinary gauge line'. If it had been a broad-gauge line in the first place, he said, there would have been no need of the duplication necessary all along here, such as this extra bridge across the Fergus, which had cost about £7,000 – an enormous sum in 1887.[3] Also avoided would have been the unseemly brawl with the then owners of the main line, the Athenry & Ennis Junction Railway Company, which eventually ended in court proceedings. However, such was not the thinking of contractor Murphy and the West Clare Company, and so the work was pushed on, this bridge being completed in May 1887. Stories are still told of the two trains racing each other over their respective bridges, watched by people on the road-bridge 500 yards upstream, but this is probably only the fanciful imaginings of those who happened to catch both trains crossing the river simultaneously and concluded that some competition must be in progress.

One may get a reasonable view of Ennis from here, but it is better to travel on 300 yards more, for then, from the continuous high embankment, one begins to appreciate the true lie of the land. To the east is a veritable sea of reeds in a low marshy valley. Here runs one channel of the Fergus, and we would certainly have missed

Twin bridges at Clonroad, 1 mile north of Ennis Station, 1953.
(Photo: Irish Railway Record Society, no. 10426)

it, so still is the surface, but for two swans peacefully going about
the business of their day. Some way further along this valley is a
river junction, and we began to see where 'Inis', the Gaelic name for
Ennis, comes from. For this was once a maze of little waterways,
marsh and mud – the origin place of the town as we know it today.
Clonroad is now accepted by most historians as the site of the first
O'Brien stronghold in these parts, dating from the early thirteenth
century. The fortification protected the only ford across the river in all
this marshy area, and it continued in the possession of one or other
branch of the family for a further four-and-a-half centuries. Quite
recently a reminder of this long-vanished history was the discovery of
some subterranean passages at the rear of Clonroad House, which is
just to the left of and beneath the railway embankment leading to the
bridge.

Turn now from right to left and you will note a strange contrast,
indeed, for it is as if the embankment forms a dividing wall between
the swamplands to the east and the town of Ennis, built on solid, dry
land. From here, the skyline of the town appears to good advantage,

Diesel railcar and steam train pass at Ennis Station, 1954.
(Photo: Irish Railway Record Society, no. 10855)

and one might say that it is totally dominated by its clerical buildings: the cathedral, with its 170-foot spire, St Flannan's College and
the old Franciscan friary, crowned with odd pinnacles which give it
a distinctly Protestant appearance. Founded originally by an O'Brien
in the 1240s, the present building dates from the early fourteenth
century and has had a turbulent existence. The community was
suppressed in 1542, but the friars continued to live here for many
years after. In the early seventeenth century part of the building was
being used as an inn, and some years later Church of Ireland services were taking place in the transept. On at least two occasions in
the eighteenth and early nineteenth centuries the tower was struck
by lightning, which necessitated extensive repairs. The pinnacles
and battlements date from this time. With the opening of the new
Church of Ireland premises in Bindon Street in 1871 the friary was
abandoned and later came into the possession of the Board of Works,
which still cares for it today.

   The two other prominent buildings – the cathedral and St Flannan's
College – date from the 1840s and late 1870s respectively. The only

non-clerical influence on the skyline is the O'Connell monument in the square, but it is not visible from this part of the railway line. The one commercial structure of any stature – the red-brick chimney of Bannatyne Mills – was demolished in October 1984 despite strong protests from those who felt that something of the industrial heritage of the town should be preserved.

The courthouse – another of those imposing nineteenth-century limestone buildings bequeathed to the town by British rule – stands only a short distance away, but, once again, is out of sight. Completed in 1850 for the sum of £16,000, it still serves its original purpose.[4] Walking through the town today, one is struck by the number of large stone buildings, most of them from that same age. The conclusion must be that the nineteenth century was a reasonably prosperous time for Ennis. No doubt this prosperity was greatly aided by the completion of the line of railway from Limerick in 1858–59 and the building of the station.[5] However, it took a further decade to carry the line northward towards Galway, and the company that did so, the Athenry & Ennis Junction Railway, we have heard of before – none other than the concern that brought the West Clare to court in 1887! Even from its beginnings it was a rickety organisation, and by all accounts had a hard time even protecting its rolling stock from seizure by the sheriff.[6] No surprise then that it should have been the subject of a takeover by the Midland Great Western Railway scarcely two months after its court case. If newspaper reports of the time are to be believed, a great service was done to humanity by putting the Athenry & Ennis Junction Company out of its misery. For example, in the debate relating to the bill to purchase the line, it was stated in evidence that it took four hours to get from Galway to Ennis, a journey of only 49 miles, that the rain came through the roofs of carriages and that oil leaked from the lamps onto the hats and clothes of passengers.[7] And there was more in a similar vein, so much so that the chairman of the inquiry became thoroughly disgusted with the litany of complaints and terminated the proceedings.

If the West Clare directors thought that their problems were over, though, they were mistaken, for less than a year later they were embroiled in another dispute, this time with the Waterford and Limerick Railway (the unsuccessful bidder against the Midland Great Western for the Athenry & Ennis Junction Company). The W&L was at this time working the West Clare's traffic at Ennis Station, and the argument concerned the proportions of the running expenses to be paid by each company.

The sound and the fury of those altercations of a century and more ago is now a faint memory only, preserved in yellowing newspaper files, and as we walked on towards Corrovorrin road-bridge, our attention was taken up wholly by developments of the present day, especially the long line of new houses still furiously a-building, flanking the line all the way to the Tulla road. No doubt whoever walks along here in a century's time will have a very different vista to describe. At Corrovorrin Bridge the embankment suddenly seems to narrow, the reason being that the present Sligo line uses only half the capacity of the original structure. The deck on the left side, where the West Clare ran, has been removed and a protective barrier blocks the way. We crossed hurriedly by the other section, closely watched by several curious pedestrians below.

The Tulla road, which passes here beneath this bridge, runs north-east as far as Spancilhill crossroads. That celebrated place needs little by way of comment, but along the way to it there are some items well worthy of note. One of these is Newpark House less than a mile away. Dating from the mid-seventeenth century, it is one of the oldest inhabited houses in Clare and was once the property of the family of The O'Gorman Mahon, a flamboyant character who helped Daniel O'Connell win the Clare election of 1828. It is said that on at least one occasion O'Connell stayed here as his guest.[8]

A mile further on, standing on a small eminence at the right of the main road, is the gaunt skeletal ruin of Tooreen House, residence in the nineteenth century of the Hynes family. The execution in Limerick Jail in 1882 of Francie Hynes, a son of this family, caused a huge stir by virtue of the odd circumstances of the case, and is remembered even yet in folklore and ballads.

A short distance away stood, until recent years, the withered remains of an ancient tree called 'The Bile'. Several monks were reputedly hanged from its branches in Cromwellian times; as a result it became the object of some veneration among the people about, and no one would cut it or interfere with it in any way. Stories abound of how those who attempted to do so were quickly brought to see the error of their ways, and even when it eventually fell it was allowed to decay without any hindrance.

Three hundred yards beyond the bridge, the line disappears round a gentle curve to the right, but less than half that distance away, a stream – an unlikely branch of the Fergus – is crossed by a fine stone-arched bridge. A little way upstream is the corresponding road-bridge, surrounded on all sides by a new housing estate. We were beginning to get worried by now. We knew that the divergence point of the two lines must be close at hand. The map told us so much. But where? One thing was obvious: the Sligo line curved off northward ahead, and since we knew that the West Clare passed close by Our Lady's Hospital, and that building was clearly visible less than a half mile to the north-west, we decided to leave the main line at the first opportunity and begin our search for the lost narrow-gauge. Our chance came a hundred yards further on, at Corrovorrin level cross-ing, where the old road to Ballycoree crosses. It is now practically disused but was formerly one of the main roads out of Ennis, and along it passed a large part of the vast crowd of 700,000 people who gathered at Ballycoree in June of 1843 to attend one of O'Connell's Monster Meetings. At this very crossing, a century ago, an attempt was made to shoot the keeper on duty.[9] Intimidation seems to have been the motive, for, a short time before, a previous keeper had been fired for neglect of duty and had, by all accounts, taken the matter very much to heart. The new man, however, refused to be frightened off and held on to the post despite all threats.

As for us, we had gone 1¼ miles and still we could show not one solid bit of evidence that we had walked on the West Clare line! We set off between the houses, beginning to wonder just when we might make a definite breakthrough. Attempting to estimate distance or direction in a modern housing estate is usually a futile business, but here at least we had the distinctive limestone hospital tower to guide us, and at the edge of the estate, though we were faced with rough waste ground, we had little hesitation about our route. And our faith was quickly rewarded, for a short way into the wilderness we came on a small river and the remains of a bridge, unmistakably a railway structure. Nothing stands except the abutments, but crossing here is easy since the stream bed is cluttered with the cut-stone debris of the demolition or collapse. This was Shaughnessy's Bridge, no more than a stone's throw from Our Lady's Hospital boundary wall, and the curving section of line through what is now the housing estate was known as the Tank Curve, from the huge hospital water tank, supported still by its stone pillars.

Across the stream we could congratulate ourselves on standing for the first time on the West Clare line proper, for plain to be seen beneath our feet was the clinker, ash and ballast peeping through the overlying grass. Clearly demarcated from the swampy ground on either side, the line stretches on here between two thick hedges which give a sense of privacy and quiet. Round another little curve and the view as far as the main Galway road, 500 yards off, is unhindered. For the line is dead straight along here. But even this quiet place saw its share of carnage, for on a number of occasions patients from the hospital were killed or injured by passing trains, the most recent such accident occurring just after the introduction of the diesel railcars. Imagine the shock of the driver, on rounding this bend, to see the man standing on the line, the frenzied but unavailing efforts to stop in time, the look of terror on the face as the train bore down. Such incidents were to occur at many points along the line, and if they make grisly reading for the uncommitted bystander it can safely be said that for the drivers involved they were the very stuff of nightmares.

St Clare's Special School now uses over half of this straight section as an access road, so its preservation is assured. In a matter of minutes we arrived at the main road, the site of Lifford Halt – the 'Asylum crossing', as it was called – 1¾ miles from the station. Apart from the crossing cottage at the western side of the road and the strip of darker-coloured tar on the roadway which marks out the former route of the rails, no trace remains of the line here. The road has been widened and an ESB sub-station now stands outside the cottage where trains passed several times a day. This was one of the most important road crossings on the whole system, and in early May 1952, with the coming of dieselisation, it was made a halt, and the railcars could be stopped at the gates by flag or by notifying the guard in advance.

The occupant of the cottage could tell us nothing about the railway since she had lived here for only a short time. Luckily, I was later able to track down the supervisor of one of the 'per-way' gangs, and his recollections of a job done here over forty years ago throw an interesting light on the working conditions of the time. Let him tell the tale himself: 'We were replacing the rails there at Lifford Halt, an' d'you see, it had to be done at night for fear o' the traffic. We quit at half-past five in the evening an' I had to cycle home after that, 12 miles, an' be down there again at four o' clock in the morning. The pair o' rails were prepared, bolted an' everything, just waiting to be fitted into position. The rails were measured so that they'd fit at both sides o' the crossing. An' we had to break the road, tear up the place completely to put 'em down. An' by God, didn't there a car come. Wouldn't you think, now, that at that time o' the morning there'd be no one stirring. An' since I started out in the morning above at home until I arrived down there 'twas raining the same as you'd let it out of a riddle. An' we closed up that road, an' worked on again until half-five that evening. Wasn't that slavery? Good God, I'd cycle anywhere that time. I'd come up the Cliffs o' Moher for you.'[10]

After a cursory glance about, we took to the adjoining field and quickly found the line again in a little cutting to the rear of the cottage. I had already decided that I should walk every step of the journey literally 'in the tracks of the West Clare', and so got down among the thick growth of briars and whitethorn, intending to batter my way through. Keith, suffering from no such purist obsessions, sensibly took the easier option of walking in the open field beside the cutting, where I was forced to join him after repeated futile efforts to claw and tear a passage through the thorny horrors. The decision made sense for I would have seen nothing of our surroundings had I continued my imbecile struggle. Now I could observe. Not that this quarter of Ennis provides much in the way of scenery. But at least there was Cois na hAbhna on the other side of the stream which we had earlier crossed at Shaughnessy's Bridge. This, the county headquarters of Comhaltas Ceoltóirí Éireann in Clare, was built in 1981 to a very singular design, modelled on the plan of an Iron Age circular house, such as may be seen at Craggaunowen, near Kilkishen. Much frequented throughout the year by lovers of Irish music and dancing, it has added greatly to the cultural life of Ennis. Close by it is Brookville, an eighteenth-century house still in good repair, and beyond, stretching along the Galway road, lies one of the mainstays of the town's economy, the new industrial estate.

A walk of no more than ten minutes brings one to Fergus no. 2 Bridge, or Lifford Bridge as it is called in the *Clare Saturday Record* report of 20 August 1887, which describes an attempt to blow it up that very week. The job was bungled, however, and the bridge still survives, though somewhat the worse for wear. All that remains is the skeleton of girders which once supported the metal deck, and these have not weathered the years well since their laying down in 1886. They are seriously corroded at many points and gave us several heart-stopping moments as we picked our way carefully across. Testing our luck and our balance, we hopped from girder to rotten girder, while under us the Fergus flowed fast and deep. No person in his sane senses would wish to fall in here, but the children of the town often thought otherwise, for on hot summer afternoons the more daredevil among them, bent on mischief, would climb onto the last carriage as the train pulled slowly away from Lifford Halt, ready themselves as it approached this bridge, and then jump off into the river as it crossed. Some of them (middle-aged now) still delightedly claim that this was how they learned to swim. We, for our part, had no great desire to take to the water, and as we looked back from the safety of the far abutment, we decided that no matter how long the journey home might be by road that evening, we would take it and suffer in preference to trying to negotiate our way across here in the dark.

Before moving on, we had a final leisurely look back at the scatter of houses that is the northern part of Ennis, and noted how relatively little development there has been in this area. At this point, one is in open countryside, and yet only a short walk from the town. To come on more concentrated building, one has to go a mile further north, where a new luxury suburb of the more prosperous sections of the middle class is taking shape beside Ballyallia Lake.

After a brief space, the line curves and rises out of the river valley, and soon we were walking a wider section, beautifully straight and open. This is the beginning of hazel country, and on all sides that handsome bush, regarded by many as mere scrub, begins to crowd in on the walls bordering the line. Nuts there were in great abundance so that anyone who chooses to walk here at this time of year need never go hungry, but the other side of the story was that we no longer had much of a view of the country round about. In any case we were soon too busy crawling, for we had come to the first of those sturdy fences that were to plague us all along the way to Kilrush and Kilkee. It was pointless to try to climb over it for a combination of interwoven barbed wire and briars is a formidable obstacle indeed. We had no desire to break it down, since a cardinal rule with anyone engaged in a walk such as this should be to leave boundary fences and gates exactly as one finds them. Having walked even the shortest distance along the remnants of the railway, it becomes all too obvious that there must be fences. But we, when we began, had not even considered the possibility, and so it is better to mention it here in order that anyone attempting a similar walk may be warned and so come prepared. Strong boots and padded clothing are a must, and nowhere more so than on this craggy section to Ruan, where the limestone promotes luxuriant growth of all our native wild plants, especially the ones that can tear a person to shreds.

But as for the fences, they are there because CIÉ, anxious after 1961 to be rid of the line – and the possibility of insurance claims as well as responsibility for upkeep of fences, drains, etc. – sold it off in lots at very low prices to the farmers through whose land it passed. These, naturally, were then forced to extend their boundary markers across the line itself in order to prevent cattle from wandering freely from one farm to the next. And so came into being probably the main obstacle to any reopening of the West Clare, as well as the bane of every walker's life. After that first fence, our progress began to slow alarmingly, and we came to have serious doubts then that we would ever get to Drumcliff road-bridge that day, even though the map, consulted as we rested on a telegraph pole collapsed across the way, showed us that it was a mere quarter of a mile ahead. What it could not show us, though, was what might be lurking in the intervening thickets. However, there were no thickets, only a farmyard wall which blankly accompanied us on the left. The line had become a well-used boreen, and before us was a flock of noisy geese, ready to defend their territory against intruders like us. They changed their minds when we armed ourselves with long sticks, and so we passed unmolested. Beyond, at a shed built corner-wise to the line but forming no obstruction, we peeped over the wall, curious to know what might be hiding there. We were surprised to find ourselves looking down on a house, its chimney on a level with where we stood. Without realising it, we had been on a high embankment for some time and we soon saw why, for Drumcliff Bridge lay directly ahead, its flat iron parapets inviting the traveller to sit awhile and rest.

Many tracks worn up and down the embankment just overlooking the road show where children and animals use it frequently nowadays, probably for peaceful purposes; but it has seen a number of malicious visitors, too. For example, shortly after the line opened, an attempt was made to derail a train here by the removal of some rails. No one was injured on that occasion, and one would hope that the same might apply to the present-day users of this airy place, for though a fine view of the road may be had from here, it is dangerous that children should have such free access to it. After the first tragedy, horrified parents will predictably raise an outcry and ask indignantly how such a thing could be allowed to happen, and weren't the county council or whoever most remiss in not foreseeing the danger.

On the deck of the bridge is the moss and grass of a quarter-century's disuse, but the whole structure is in remarkably good condition. From here, one can look north and glimpse Drumcliff old cemetery rising on its steep hill where the stump of one of Clare's five remaining round towers still keeps its stolid vigil over the dead. Of the history of this ecclesiastical foundation little is known; even the name of its founder is disputed. Nowadays the site is known almost exclusively as the main burial ground for Ennis, an importance it took on only in the 1830s when the original small graveyard around the church and tower was expanded owing to demand for graves during a cholera epidemic. Three hundred and forty people, we are told, were buried in one mass grave here at the height of the contagion.[11] Along this road beneath us have passed the high and the lowly of Ennis since that time, all on their last journey. In stark contrast to the hasty burial of all those poor pestilence victims a mere half-century before was the pomp and ceremony of the funeral of Stephen Joseph Meaney on 11 March 1888. A noted journalist and patriot, he was born near Ennis about 1822, and having worked in newspapers in Scotland and Ireland began to accompany Daniel O'Connell to the Monster Meetings, eventually becoming known as 'O'Connell's reporter'. He later joined the Young Irelanders and in 1858 went to the United States. He was appointed a delegate to the Fenian Congress in Philadelphia in 1865, and two years later was arrested while on a visit to Ireland. As with many of the other Fenian prisoners, his treatment in jail was atrocious, so much so that he lost 7 stone in weight. He returned to America after his release, but visited Ireland several times after, including Clare, to report on the Irish problem for American newspapers. Again in 1882 he was arrested in Ennis and had the mortification of not being recognised in his home town. But some amends were made after his death in February 1888, for the occasion was used by the National League as a showpiece of solidarity against the authorities. The Ennis branch issued a notice: 'Irishmen! Assemble on Sunday next and pay the last tribute of respect and honour to the remains of one who risked everything in the cause of Irish liberty. Come in your thousands, and march in processional order to Drumcliff churchyard. If you admire Irish patriotism in the purest form stand shoulder to shoulder with our friends. God save Ireland."[12]

The crowds did assemble on 11 March but not in as large numbers as the organisers had hoped for. This was blamed on the very bad weather that day. Yet a special train from Miltown Malbay was hired to bring a contingent from the west, and a similar arrangement was made with the Waterford & Limerick Railway – though the company displayed a certain mistrust of the whole proceedings by demanding £10 payment in advance, a condition which was promptly met.

Today the grass grows around the S.J. Meaney monument, and he has been largely forgotten, one more casualty to time, but no doubt he would be pleased to know that scarcely half a mile away from where he lies the men that he championed in his writings all those years ago are still recalled in the name 'The Fenian Grove', a conspicuous group of trees on a hill overlooking Ballyallia Lake.[13] It is said that they once secretly drilled here.

Ballyallia Lake, one of the largest on the Fergus, is now widely known as an amenity area, and is much frequented by townspeople and tourists alike for its pleasant adjoining walkways and tame waterfowl. A credit to those who developed it, it has of late fostered the growth of a veritable chain of mansions, some imposing, some merely grandiose, on the opposite side of the road – a development that has made Ballyallia the most desirable new address in Ennis. The new, however, are merely travelling on the swallow tails of the old, for it is the nearby Ballyallia House with its many surrounding historical remains, plus the natural beauty of the landscape, that gives the area its real interest. The present house dates from the eighteenth century, and has been associated with some of Clare's best-known landed families – Cuffes, Stackpooles, O'Briens, etc. Its woods of handsome mature trees are a landmark in the region, though much damage has been done to these by storms in recent years – a sign that replanting cannot be forever neglected, and that most of the surviving timber from the landlord era is now in its old age and urgently in need of renewal.

Even the most casual visitor to this place will quickly realise that it has been a centre of human habitation for centuries. The *crannógs* in and beside the lake are witness to this, as are the ruins of Ballyallia Castle. These are close to the lake but in a very decayed condition. Built in the sixteenth century, it was besieged twice by the Irish Confederate Army in 1642. The Cuffe family, who were in possession at the time, were finally reduced to eating rats and other such morsels, and surrendered soon afterwards. They do not seem to have been harmed, in spite of the annoyance they caused the besiegers. Maurice Cuffe, one of the defenders, wrote a very detailed account of their time under siege, and it remains today a useful description of the warfare of the time as well as a much-studied example of the written English of Ireland in that age.[14]

There is so much of interest within a 2-mile radius of Drumcliff that any description by me can only begin to do it justice. I would strongly recommend, therefore, that it should be visited personally and savoured at leisure.

Indeed, I had become so engrossed in my own reminiscences that Keith had given me up for dead and had begun to explore at the far side of the bridge. That was when the sound of furious barking startled me into attention, for at the new houses which have been built beside the embankment, various guard dogs had begun to do their duty at sight of him. All we could do was face them and try to pass by before they became too excited by their own barking. Luckily for us, the steep stonework at the foot of the bank prevented them from getting up to our level and so we escaped unharmed. As we passed we could not help noticing that at least one of the gardens has been partly created by excavating the line, but no major damage has been done to the fabric of the bank.

Our headlong hurry away from the dogs came to an abrupt halt 400 yards from the bridge. The land had been drastically disturbed here, and the line was, quite simply, gone. Common sense, as well as a glance at the map, suggested that it once continued straight ahead, but it is easy to be sensible in retrospect. How were we to know then that this was the first of those huge land-reclamation spoil heaps

that litter the countryside from this point to Corofin and beyond?
No doubt if we could have seen this place from the air all would
have been as clear as day, but we were all too obviously at ground
level and in trouble. We cast about us for a while, searching for some
other possible route, and at length decided that the line must have
curved to the right here, continued across the low land and out near
Drumcliff – though the map clearly showed otherwise. We set out,
uncertainly, exploring these fields, but of course nothing came of
it. After a wide detour we returned to the huge mound of rocks.
From the top, we could see a wood several fields ahead – probably
Ballygriffey Wood, we concluded. But of the railway there was not
a trace. We were travelling blind now, merely hoping to come on
it again by accident. At the wood, our way was solidly blocked by
a stone wall, as we thought, but a closer examination revealed it to
be a well-finished heap of stones, the clearings of the surrounding
fields. After much exertion, we got by it, only to find ourselves on
the edge of a huge drop down into the unknown. It certainly seemed
like a railway cutting, but we could not be certain since we were now
looking down on a roof of hazel. More careful manoeuvring at last
brought us to ground level and into a gloom that was positively green
and luminous. So taken aback were we by this strange place that we
stood in silence for a moment to peer ahead along a dimly lit tunnel
of foliage.

We set off, delighted to be able to make real progress again, the
chippings crunching underfoot, quite as clean as on the day they
were laid when the line was ballasted for the last time in the summer
of 1960. For as far ahead as we could see, our way ran straight as a
rule and quite clear and passable – more so, indeed, than many of the
so-called roads of the county. But the flatness of the line is deceptive
in that it leads one into an expectation that the surrounding land
should also be level. This is by no means the case, as was quickly
brought home to us, for at one moment we would be walking along a
high embankment and on a level with the tops of surrounding trees
maybe 20-feet tall; then the land would again be towering over our
heads as we picked our way through deep cuttings where rocks jut

out from the steep sides, and beyond that again level green fields would be all around, with cattle going about their business.

In all this changing landscape only the wood on the left is constant. Sometimes it approaches to the very boundary wall, sometimes it falls back sufficiently to give up, grudgingly, a little open patch of scrubby field; but always it is there, like one's shadow. Because of it, there is little to be seen along here. Even the occasional gap in the trees gives no clue to the lie of the land. We were completely dependent on our maps for information, and they showed us little. But though it might be thought that rocky country like this would have little to yield in the matter of history – and certainly there are no Big Houses here, as in the more fertile land nearer to Ennis – a journey through the hazel and scrub can be a wonderful eye-opener. For here, in the most inaccessible of places, along pathways long since grown in, one will come across the *cabhails* of little houses, often of one or two rooms only.[15] It was to places like this that the poorest of the Irish were consigned, scraping out whatever living they could, until the terrible scourge of famine and disease swept them away in the years after 1845. The census returns for 1841, 1851 and 1986 make for sober reading in this regard:

Census	1841	1851	1986
Population of Clare	268,394	212,440	91,334

Only these hidden crumbling walls are left to tell of the misery that emptied whole districts like this of their people a century and a half ago. Their loss has never been made good, as the census figures show. Even the town of Ennis has not recovered, its population in 1986 being only two-thirds of what it was in 1841: 6,106 as against 9,318.[16]

The limestone boundary walls are in excellent condition all along here, a tribute to the masons of a century ago, and also perhaps to the owners of the land on either side. We knew that we were still in Drumcliff townland, but we were anxious to get to a house now, since directions from a native of the place would be of more use to us than what we might glean from any map. But there were no houses, only a fast-flowing stream passing through a culvert under the line. But at least this pinpointed our position: we were at the boundary of Drumcliff and Ballymacquiggin townlands. From the map we were able to determine the source of the stream as Lough Cleggan, a short distance away, but the lie of the land did not allow us a view of it. What we did see, away to the west, was the large quarry worked by Whelan Brothers at Fountain – a well-known landmark – and from this we took our bearings.

Shortly thereafter we noted a gable ahead and a wall blocking the line. In fact, we were at a public road but could not see it until we were almost on it. Only then was it obvious that this was a level crossing, the first since Lifford Halt. We were at Erinagh crossing, in the townland of Reascaun, 3½ miles from Ennis. The only vestige remaining of the original crossing is one cut-stone pier and a short length of wall, and this seems to confirm what one old ex-railway-man told me: that no matter how many times a train broke the gates, he had never seen a pier fall as a result, so sturdily were they built. The adjoining house no longer looks like a crossing cottage. It has been too much modernised and altered to be recognisable as such, and our enquiries brought us no information except that the last railway occupants were Conways but that they were long gone.

As at Lifford crossing, a short detour and we were on the line again at the rear of the building. The limestone pokes through the thin topsoil in many places here, but this has not prevented the building of several new houses nearby. The tracks of the bulldozers were still fresh where they had been engaged in scraping together heaps of precious soil, leaving nothing except the bare rock. Of the line's foundations little more than this same rock survives, and as we surveyed the desolate scene, an unusual-looking formation in the limestone caught our attention. Box-shaped, 4 feet by 1 foot by 2 feet deep, it looked like a burial chamber that might have been lined on three sides with smooth flags, but without any means of identifying it more accurately, we could do little more than note its presence and press on.

Much destruction has been wrought to the line beyond this point and for some distance; in parts it has even disappeared altogether. But always there is something or other to guide one onward. Yet only when we came to a stream on the left, flowing in our direction, could we say that we were again on unbroken line, this being emphasised by a row of sleepers stretching out like silent soldiers on sentry duty in the swamp. A crane, rising heavily, slowly, showed off its dull blue back and held our attention for a moment on the verge of an embankment that still carries itself aloof through the wetland, as proudly as in the heyday of the West Clare. Halfway across, we noticed off to the left a large stand of reeds at least 6-feet tall – an indication of a river course – while, on the right, mossy boulders jutted like balding heads out of the sodden ground. Past another culvert – one finely preserved and as functional as on the day it was built – Whelan's Quarry, now almost 2 miles behind, showed itself again. But closer to the line, two oddly-shaped boulders confronted us, the larger set in a frizz of bushes, the smaller bare and looking remarkably like an anvil. Very probably a legend once attached to these, or still does. A similar pair 8 miles away, in Crusheen parish, are known as the Coffin Rock and Hearse Stone.

Marshy ground on both sides of the line here ensured that there would be no escape should we meet any tough obstructions, but the worst was a palisade of sleepers and barbed wire which we crossed carefully and did not damage. But now Keith had caught a glimpse of a moving van to our right, and our spirits rose somewhat, for though the light had not yet begun to fade, we knew that we could have no more than forty-five minutes left before it became too gloomy to move safely. We would call a halt, we decided, at the next most convenient spot. But before ever we reached such a place, we found that we had a problem on our hands – for in our way it seemed that every blackthorn bush in Clare had gathered to bring us to a spiky halt. There was no possibility whatever of passing through the dark mass. We took to the fields, which were like a boggy patchwork being gradually repossessed by nature as ever more bushes encroached. There is no easy way from field to field here, and a detour on either side of the line is likely to be a painful experience. Heavy clothing and much perseverance are a must. Care should be taken also not to get too far from the line here – something that can easily happen since all one's attention is likely to be focused on the immediate problems of walls and thorns.

By now we had worked our way back to the edge of the line, only to find that we were looking down into a deep cutting. So overgrown are the fields we had passed through that we had not noticed that we were climbing. But from this vantage point we were able to see, on the left, a useful landmark, Ryan's Quarry on the Ennis–Corofin road. A cause of even more jubilation was the clear view of Ballygriffey Castle, since we knew that the line ran directly to the rear of it. We began to believe that we might even get as far as the castle that day.

But it was not to be. As the crow flies it was no further than a half-mile off, but we were no crows. It took us several false starts down the sheer 20-foot face of the long cutting to even get onto level ground, and when we emerged at the Ballygriffey end, it was to find that the land had been massively disturbed by reclamation. Nothing, not even the foundations of the line, could we find. It was the final straw, and since a road and some houses were near to hand, we decided it was time to seek advice.

A man in a nearby cowshed kindly gave us a brief picture of the line and the area around. He and two other neighbouring farmers reclaimed this land five years ago, and so up to a quarter of a mile of the line no longer exists here in the townland of Licknaun. Among his fond memories of the railway were the many efforts of children to make pennies out of halfpennies by placing them on the rails for the train to roll over. Before we moved off he pointed out to us a large fort nearby with an unusual feature: a deep hole containing water at a depth of about 40 feet. It still retains its Irish name, Poll Phocáin.

As for the castle, it was pointless to try to visit it now; the prospect of the journey back to our car at Ennis Station was quite enough to be going on with, so we turned right at the next crossroads and walked the mile to Ballyhea Bridge in the semi-darkness. We were still in time to see from this bridge one of the finest engineering

works of the nineteenth century, not just in Clare but in all of Ireland.
This is the Ballyhea cutting. Excavated in the years 1848–52 to lower
the level of nearby Cloonteen Lake and prevent flooding over a wide
area of low-lying land, it stretches for half a mile at depths of up to
45 feet, and drains water into Ballyallia Lake and so to the Fergus.
Hacked out with pick, shovel and crowbar, as were the cuttings on the
West Clare, it gave much-needed employment in the hungry years
after the Famine, and remains today a testimony to those terrible
times and to the labourers who toiled here for ten pennies per day.[17]
Some of the folklore of its construction is still to be found in the locality,
and what is said to be one of the workmen's crowbars, still embedded in
the rock, is even today pointed out. The bridge was built at the same time,
and south of it – surrounded by its graveyard – stands the fifteenth-cen-
tury Templemaley Church from which the parish partly takes it name.[18]
It is a plain building with no especially noteworthy features.

By the time we were passing the graveyard gate, it was quite
dark and some of the tales associated with the place leaped to mind,
particularly that of the rabidly anti-religious lady from a local Big
House who, to show her contempt for the cross, wore two crucifixes
embedded in the soles of her shoes so that she might trample Christ
as she walked! She lived to a ripe old age and was buried within these
walls, and it is said that afterwards, whenever workmen cleared the
graveyard, they took care to burn the scrub and bushes on her grave-
stone. A reminder to like-minded persons, perhaps, that such deeds are
not forgotten, even in this world. Nothing was stirring, however, as we
padded past, and we were glad. It had been a hard day and we needed all
our energies for the 3½-mile walk back to Ennis Station.

When we came to the high rear wall of Ballyallia Estate, we were
even less inclined to delay than at Templemaley, for this was a notorious place in days gone by. Otherworldly lights were seen many times
along here, at the part of the road known as the Brown Hill, and not
only lights; the story goes that a man returning late at night from
card-playing was met here by a spectral figure on horseback, two huge
mastiffs hanging from his ears. He spoke: 'D'you see them dogs?'

'I do,' stammered the man.

'If you were where you should be you wouldn't see 'em.'

Needless to say, the gambler mended his ways, glad to have escaped so lightly.[19]

Not a car, not a person did we meet on this dark stretch; the sensible people were all elsewhere. We reached the Ruan road, safely passing the site of Templemaley House, which was also reputedly haunted. No trace of the walls now remains but the cellars still exist, though filled in. The old mistress of the house decided that the friars from Ennis, who were in the habit of walking this way to pray, should be forbidden to enter her property. A bad mistake, for they cursed her and promised that before the year was out the crows would be flying through the ruins. And so it was. Shortly afterwards, the house was burned and completely destroyed.[20]

Most of the remainder of our journey was well lit so we were troubled by no more thoughts of the other world, and at length arrived at the station tired out but proud of our first day's work.

Disused West Clare rolling stock beside the Athenry line at Ennis, 7.6.61. (Photo: Roy Denison)

Day 2

Ballygriffey Castle to Ruan Station

It was a week before we were able to return to Licknaun and continue our journey, and not because of any weakness of flesh or spirit. School it was that intervened, but since Keith insisted that he be allowed to finish what we had begun together, I thought it better to wait for him, knowing that soon enough he would be facing into those difficult years when avoiding his father would be more important to him than almost anything else in life.

This time there was no one to point out our way, but what guidance did we need? Ballygriffey Castle was plainly visible, even if the line was nowhere to be seen, so we steered towards it. And right away we were at a river, the same one that provided the castle with part of its defences. We could do nothing now except go due north, and at the next stone field-wall we paused, and there before us was the line again, as if nothing in the world had happened to disturb its continuity. To look backward and forward from this little wall is to see in miniature the fate of the West Clare: ruin where there was once order, and cattle grazing again where their ancestors grazed before the laying down of the permanent way.

The ground leading up to the castle is low and swampy, and the line at this point is on a little causeway. We crossed Ballygriffey no. 1 Bridge, a typical metal-parapet structure, pausing briefly to admire the little series of rapids and rough water that might gladden the heart of any fly-fisherman. The castle is no more than 200 yards from here, and the bridge over the public road also appears to good advantage from this point. In fact, one begins to have an inkling of why the castle may have been built here in the first place, for it is surrounded on three sides by water and little roads. A strategic site it certainly was, though now those same roads are of relatively little importance, and even the course of the river itself has been interfered with.

As we passed at the rear of the tower, we noted the high ivied wall, with little showing save the slit windows typical of all such tower houses, the topmost one wider than those lower down, this being the only visible concession to comfort and light. Up there lived the lord and his family in conditions which we today would regard as uncomfortable in the extreme, but which in the turbulent Ireland of the fifteenth and sixteenth centuries must have been envied by the lesser Irish who had to live in mud huts round about the strong stone walls.

Ballygriffey gates and castle, 1953.
(Photo: Irish Railway Record Society, no. 10636)

This tower is in a good state of preservation, which might lead one to ask, Why is it that of the four such buildings within a 3-mile radius – Ballyallia, Shallee, Magowna and this – only Ballygriffey survived practically intact? The hard knocks of history might explain the destruction of Ballyallia but little is known of the demise of the other two. And their ruin is not recent, either; the Ordnance surveyors in 1839 reported their condition as being no better than it is today. If Ballygriffey had shared their fate it would not have been entirely surprising because an unusual feature of its site is that a small hill overlooks it to the rear – something hardly designed to improve its security against assault. Among the scanty details known about its history are that it was owned by the O'Griffies in 1584, that one of Hugh O'Donnell's raiding parties reached its very gates in 1599 (though whether they captured it is not recorded), and that by 1641 it was owned by the O'Briens.[1]

Just past the castle, a palisade of sleepers marks where the line crossed the road. Here were level-crossing gates and the cottage, which has been so reconstructed that none of its railway features remain. Bradleys were the last keepers of these gates, but they, too, are long gone. At this crossing, 4¾ miles from Ennis, we were entering the 7-mile length to Willbrook that was once under the jurisdiction of Corofin Station.

North of the cottage, a ballast siding was established in 1904 and a quarry opened alongside to supply the needs of the railway after the siding at Skagh Point near Kilrush was closed because of a dispute with the Crown over royalties. One would be hard put now to say where the siding was, since not alone has it vanished, but the line, too. Yet if some of the survivors of the backbreaking slavery undergone here are to be believed, its obliteration is little loss to the world. To be consigned to 'duty in Ballygriffey' was akin to penal servitude, it seems, for even the gangers in command were more truculent here than elsewhere, as if the place exuded some baleful influence of its own.

We would shortly discover it for ourselves. We were directed to a vague point in the wood almost a mile away by a passerby who thought he was being helpful. There, he assured us, we would find the line 'no bother at all'. So we set off cheerfully across the huge intervening field. Our map was of little use here as even the river which rushed strongly southward and under the newly built bridge at the road behind us had been man-made within the past five years. After half a mile we were able to cross by a sturdy concrete bridge obviously built for the passage of heavy machinery, and we bore left, as the map indicated that the line followed close by the road that runs northward from Ballygriffey crossroads. In the process we passed two large farm sheds which were later to take on a retrospective significance. At last we reached the wood. From its fringes the castle was barely visible, almost obscured in the distance by the circling sweep of the trees, part of the same wood we were now entering. Very sensibly we picked our way gradually westward along the edge of the wood, where visibility among the deciduous trees was good. Sooner or later, we reasoned, we must come on the line. One thing only we did not reckon on: that from this very point the West Clare veered off sharply to the north-west on the initial stage of that great curve that takes it first to Corofin Station and then westward through the boggy heart of Clare.

Fallen branches and a thick carpet of moss made it difficult to distinguish what might have been the line from mere forest tracks, so of necessity our progress slowed. Finally, a wire fence brought us to a halt. Outside was an overgrown road, of about the right width, so we did what any normal person would have done – followed it. Anything seemed preferable to plunging into more trees on the far side.

To tell in detail what happened over the next few hours would be tedious in the extreme. Suffice it to say that the silent, listening wood echoed to an unaccustomed tirade of foul and abusive language that day as we beat our way through terrain that would make a military exercise course look simple. Time after time we contemplated turning back, but always there were the hopeful signs that lured us on: stones underfoot, long straight stretches, stone boundary walls. But we knew our luck had run out when we came to a gate – a solitary trace of human interference in all this wilderness – and looked beyond, down into a swampy amphitheatre surrounded on all sides by trees. We swung right, holding on to the stone wall as to some fragile lifeline, but that soon petered out in the wood. A compass would have been a valuable asset just then, especially since our options now were only two: either strike out blindly through the trees, or go back the way we had come. We were not going back, we decided. The unknown at least always has its possibilities. But what we failed to take into account is that those possibilities are as likely to be negative as positive. For a full two hours more we wandered, hopelessly lost, gradually recognising with sinking hearts that we had passed this or that way a short time before. Remembering the dozens of accounts I had heard of people who went astray even on their own land, I began to wonder whether the Good People might not have a hand in this, and debated whether I should turn my coat inside out, the traditional sure cure for 'the stray sod'. Certainly there is a large fairy fort in this wood; that much we knew. What we could not be sure of was whether we had by accident strayed into it in our blunderings, thereby bringing the wrath of 'Them' down on our heads. We hoped not. In the meantime, what we did do was sit down and consider calmly what our next move should be.

That short sitting respite did something else: it showed us what a world apart is a wood. Even the plants here looked somehow different, and the startled cries of the birds sounded unusually loud, emphasising the silence and eeriness of the place. We might well have been the first ever to pass that way, so absent were all signs of human meddling. But this, unfortunately, was no nature ramble. We had to get away before darkness should come and confine us completely.

It was Keith, in fact, who got us out of it – whether by intent or by accident I do not know. He still refuses to say. Even better than that, it was he also who rediscovered the line. That, I am convinced, was accidental, for like a curious dog, he wandered off towards a huge mound of boulders and from its heights caught sight of a clearing some way off. He reached the far side of it long before me, and his shouts and gesticulations told me all I needed to know. We were in business again. I hardly knew whether to laugh or cry. How, I asked, could we have been so stupid as to make the same mistake again. Surely we might have learned by our experience near Drumcliff Bridge. Recriminations were not in order at such a time, however; better to explore while we still had time. We began our trek back to the castle with lighter steps than heretofore, curious to know how we had gone so spectacularly wrong.

The going was easy underfoot here, and in the afternoon light the trace of the sleepers could be seen, a lighter shade of green on the grass of the line, even though they were a quarter of a century and more gone. Beside where we were walking, rubble and monstrous boulders had been pushed back from the fields to within feet of the line, but somehow it had escaped obstruction. And so we made our way back, through all the usual blockages, sometimes having to avoid particularly bad patches of jungle by retreating to the bulldozed fields alongside, at other times marvelling at how well preserved was this embankment or that set of crossing piers. As a general rule, in our travels we were always delighted to see hazel; wherever it occurs good progress is possible since under its thick overhanging foliage nothing else can grow. This section had its fair share of the lovely bush and it lightened our work substantially.

But then, some distance ahead, we noted a building across the line, and even as I saw it a horrible feeling took hold of me, the notion that we had met it before. I was not mistaken, for the closer we approached to its high back-wall, the more obvious it became that this was none other than the larger of the two sheds which we had observed earlier while crossing the huge field. Built squarely across the path of the line, it obscures all view from north or south, so that one might almost be forgiven for going astray at this point. That thought was poor consolation to us for all our wasted hours, but at least to state it here may save other poor souls from making the same mistake. Now, in retrospect, it is easy to know what we should have done at Ballygriffey level crossing site: taken the public road left to the crossroads a hundred yards to the west, then turned right and proceeded by this narrow road for half a mile to the entrance to these two sheds. Here, behind them, all will be immediately clear.

It was decision time again. Should we be satisfied with the little
we had achieved and call it a day, or retrace our steps and try to reach
Ruan Station before darkness? A quick discussion followed by an
even quicker ballot, and Keith was outvoted, I having three votes to
his one. At least this time we had the advantage of knowing which
places to avoid, and so in twenty minutes we were back to where we
rediscovered the line and were ready to continue.

On every side, bulldozed land stretches away and the field divi-
sions here are mere heaps of rocks shoved back to the edges of the
levelled areas. Even a native of the place, some years absent, would
find few familiar landmarks to guide his steps. Happily, though, the
line has largely survived. Complete with its tunnel of hazel, it arrows
its way across the hummocky landscape and between the many scattered small lakes. Here and there, of course, we came on places which
had been plundered, but by and large we were blessed with a surface
that allowed us to walk almost unimpeded.

On these straight clear sweeps, one is inclined to forget the
sort of terrain through which the West Clare was pushed. Only in
the deepest cuttings does it come home to one how prodigious an
effort it must have been to cut away this solid limestone back in
1886. Even yet huge horizontal shelves and triangular buttresses of
rock often obtrude almost onto the line in these cuttings, as if the
workers somehow forgot to complete their job. But the very terrain
that made life so difficult for those sweating labourers worked to the
advantage of 'per-way' gangs at a later date since there was no fear
of deterioration through subsidence. The surroundings might appear
inhospitable but it is true nevertheless that this was regarded as one
of the choice sections for a milesman to be posted to, since there was
a minimum of maintenance work to be done on such a solid foundation. And how well the Irish language catches the peculiarities of
that landscape. For the townland into which we were now passing is
named Bealnalicka (Béal na Lice: the outlet at the flagstone). What
better description could one have of a railway cutting? This name,
just as much as Licknaun (Licneán: a small stony field), which we
had earlier passed through, is surely a more informative guide than

any names bestowed in more recent times. These latter tend to be mere decorations and often attempt to make places sound more attractive than they really are.

Starting across an embankment, however – the land having fallen away into a boulder-strewn swamp on both sides – we were reminded that even in such craggy land there are a few unpredictable places that demand extra care and attention. It may well have been here – it was surely in some place like it – that a difficulty was encountered during construction of the railway. It was found that no matter how much fill was dumped into the swamp, it all disappeared, and the problem was at last solved only by using the natural materials to hand – laying down course upon course of hazel rods and then building the bank on top of them. Or so local tradition would have us believe. Further on, as we passed by a pair of crossing gates, piers and stiles, all excellently preserved, we could only admire the workmanship. Whoever made these gates made them to last.

We had crossed into the townland of Drummeer (Drom Thiar: the western hill) by now, but only by referring to our map could we tell; there is no particular feature of the landscape that marks the boundary. From here to Ruan Station, visibility ahead became increasingly more restricted. Only for a cattle track through the encroaching bushes we would have come to a full stop on more than one occasion. Hither and thither it meandered, and then, quite unexpectedly, we were confronted by a wall across the line, which turned out to be the boundary of the station property as it now is. But we had not reckoned on what now greeted us, for there, 50 yards away, was the station-house, resplendently restored and transformed into an elegant dwelling quite unlike the general run of modern country houses. From the boundary wall to the road, where the crossing gates once stood, the line is now a neat garden and lawn, but even more noticeable is the surrounding stonework, for much care has been taken to preserve it, especially the level-crossing piers. It is altogether a credit to its owner. Hard to believe, looking at it now, that this same building was sold by CIÉ in October 1962 for the princely sum of £15.

Properly speaking, this should never have been called Ruan

Station, since it is in the townland of Kilkee East, and the village of Ruan is a good 2½ miles away. It is easy to see, however, why the more correct name was never even considered; it would have been highly confusing, even on the West Clare, to have two destinations of the same name. So Ruan Station it had to be, and Kilkee remained the western terminus of the line.

It was first made a halt in 1888, but only after some rather novel

Ruan gates, 1953. (Photo: Irish Railway Record Society, no. 10428)

persuasive tactics by the parish priest, Fr Garry. It seems that the railway company had no intention of providing even a halt at Ruan, let alone a station, so the priest (who is described as 'a tall, powerful man and a forceful character' who got his own way in most things) took to driving his pony and trap onto the line, forcing the train to stop.[2] The company at last got the message; since it looked as though they would have to be constantly stopping anyway, they decided to make it official in 1888. Ten years later, however, it was closed, only to be reopened in 1904 – whether by Fr Garry's efforts we do not know. That worthy man continued as parish priest in Ruan until 1912, and is buried there.

But in 1921, the halt was closed again, at which time the platform (on the up side) was demolished. But a flagstone is still pointed out on which, it is claimed, Percy French stood 'and said a few words'. Probably the same could be pleaded for flagstones in every other station along the way, too. Ruan got its last brief lease of life when in May 1952 it was once more brought into service, as a railcar halt, but this lasted a mere nine years before it and all the others closed to passengers for the last time in January 1961.

With this melancholy thought we reached the road and began the trudge back to the car. Lucky for us that we did, rather than attempt the much shorter journey back along the line, for we came upon an old man who had plenty of time to stand and talk. When he heard what we were about, he thought we were mad, naturally, yet he was only too glad to contribute some personal memories of the line, such as the stopping of the train by the military during the Troubles after they had received a tip-off that two IRA men were on it, or the discontent among the public when the Ennis–Lahinch fare was increased from a shilling to one-and-threepence. He could remember crowds of from ten to fifteen thousand people in Lahinch on summer Sundays in the 1920s, and not a single motor car in sight. And he laughed to recall walking beside the train as it laboured up Willbrook Hill one Garland Sunday, unable to manage the gradient while fully laden.

But it was getting dark, and time to be moving on. A handshake, thanks, a wave, and we were on our way, leaving the old man to his memories. We, for our part, had good reason to be pleased. We had gotten much farther than we would ever have thought possible two hours before.

Day 3

Ruan Station to Corofin

The journey from Ruan Station to Corofin Station is a little less than 2½ miles, a forty-five minute walk if the way were clear. In the present condition of the line, it is rather more likely to take two hours, and this depends very much on the weather. If it is wet, the very overgrown stretches will have to be avoided, and all this cuts into one's time. But at least on this section there are no impassable jungles or quaking morasses, and most of the pauses are likely to be voluntary, to admire this or that bit of scenery.

Three weeks of miserably wet weather had prevented us from showing our faces on the West Clare, but at last in mid-October came a few dry days and we jumped at the opportunity. Beginning at the palisade of sleepers just across the road from the station, we set forth, accompanied by a large, friendly Labrador who seemed most anxious to introduce us to the delights ahead. The beginning was encouraging, for a long, shallow cutting is succeeded here by a straight run on which the worst obstacle is a solitary whitethorn bush. But if the line here is in good shape, the same can hardly be said of the countryside round about. A wide expanse of flooding on both sides of the embankment made us very appreciative indeed to be standing high and dry above it all. It is no standing mass of mere rain water, either, for a short distance on to the bank, we arrived over a little bridge, no more than 4-feet wide but carrying a strong flow of water which has cut a considerable channel. At this point we were passing from Kilkee East townland to Kilkee West, and out there, a short way to the left, were the remains of Kilkee Castle, but we could pick out no trace of it. Hardly surprising, this, since it is another of those towers that time has dealt harshly with, leaving no more than a few scattered cut stones to tell of days that were.

One might think, looking out on these miserable fields of Kilkee on a blustery winter's day, that it was devoid of all habitation except maybe for fish life – and so it may be. But it does have at least one claim to fame in the history of Ireland. According to Frost, Conor McBrody, who lived hereabouts, was one of the notable scholars to whom the Annals of the Four Masters were submitted for approval after their completion in 1636.[1] A high honour, this, since Michael O'Clery, the main compiler, was himself an antiquarian of much renown. These McBrodys were chroniclers to the kings of Thomond, and their profession was held in such high esteem that they held their lands free of all tribute. All that ended, however, after the defeat of the Confederacy and the arrival of Cromwell.

The very extent of the flooding to the left made it seem plausible that there should be a regular lake there, but our map showed nothing of the sort. A farmhouse in the near distance looked for all the world like the Ark moored to our embankment by a thin linking strand of stone wall, but we marched on, at least 6-feet clear of all such discomfort. The land rises temporarily here – enough to have made a short cutting necessary – and it was at the end of this that we were halted by a small mountain of rubble that sat directly on our path, and even to climb it was impossible since bushes and briars had taken a firm grip on its sides. We explored no further, only went around it and continued. In the shallow cutting beyond, a cattle crush and a scatter of silage were demonstration enough of how farmers have tended to use the line, wherever convenient, as an ideal congregating place for their cattle. Sensible, too, because often in poor land it is the only surface for miles firm enough to support a laden tractor, and cuttings such as this provide some shelter for the poor beasts. This is all the more necessary today when the infectious lunacy of removing hedge-rows on the grand scale has become an epidemic over large areas.

The dry land here is only an aberration, for soon we were traversing another causeway, this time with the water on both sides reaching to the very foot of the bank. A more dismal scene it would be hard to describe – shades of grey and brown receding into a grey-green distance, and water everywhere. Again we could find no trace of a lake on our map, only a stream, so presumably there is a blockage somewhere. Probably in summertime all this would look very, very different.

There was a coldness in the air, a touch of sleet, as we pulled away from this sombre scene, but we were cheered somewhat by sight of a house ahead. It could only be Laurel Vale crossing cottage, we decided, and we were right, for when we climbed the 6 feet necessary to get over the concrete wall that barred our way, we were standing in the yard of a newly decorated dwelling, conveniently named 'Laurel Vale Cottage'.

Our enquires and our apologies for arriving by such an unortho-dox route were met with good humour, and it was confirmed that this indeed is Laurel Vale crossing, '7 miles and a bit' from Ennis. The woman who lives here attended the crossing gates for seventeen years and in all of that time there was only one accident. A night special was expected from Kilkee but failed to arrive at the scheduled time, so the gates were closed. But shortly thereafter a loud crash was heard. The train had arrived and carried the gates 500 yards down the track towards Ruan. The name Laurel Vale itself reminded me of a serious but amusing incident which occurred a century ago in this area, and I had a mind to ask whether it was still remembered here. But I thought better of the idea and held my peace. Let me quote the newspaper report of the happening, though: 'About 4 o'clock yesterday afternoon an outrage of a singular and extraordinary char-acter took place at Laurelvale, the former residence of Rev. Robert Fitzgerald. A small farmer named John Hayes, who lives at Kilkee, the adjoining townland, was engaged in ploughing some land for the Rev. gentleman when he was startled by a shot fired from behind a ditch close by. He turned around, and forthwith five shots more were discharged at him, and within a very short distance. Fortunately the shots proved to be harmless, but the strangest part of the whole affair is that the man who fired the shots, and who was plainly seen by Hayes, was stark naked, and only wore a red handkerchief over his face, with holes for the eyes. Hayes ran for his life, leaving plough and horses behind him in the field'.[2] Apart from these bare facts nothing else came of the case. Presumably such a person would be difficult to identify.

Two hundred yards to the south-west is Macken Bridge, which crosses the river that had accompanied us on our left for some distance back. Tradition has it that part of the fighting in the decisive battle of Dysert O'Dea took place in this river valley, and that many of the slain are buried here. If so, damp is the bed they sleep in. Such an account may very well be true for it seems that Tullyodea, 2½ miles to the north-east, and the Hill of Scool, 2½ miles to the west, were staging points for detachments of the opposing armies, and the valley had to be crossed at some point or other by Richard de Clare's men on their way to attack the Irish forces. It is even said that de Clare himself was killed at the site of Macken Bridge before the battle proper started. Many historians have mulled over the old documents and searched the country around here in hopes of finding some physical relics of the battle, but precious little has ever been turned up, even in this age of metal detectors and other technology. But there can be no doubt that the events of that May morning in 1318 had tremendous implications and far-reaching consequences, for they rid Thomond of Norman influence and the power of the English Crown for almost three centuries, allowing the Irish chieftains to get on with the petty squabbling that was to bring the whole Gaelic system to final destruction in the seventeenth century.[3]

Hardly 2 miles south-west of here is the famed Dysert itself (originally Dísirt Tola: the wilderness of St Tola) – monastic centre, stronghold of the O'Deas, focus of much agitation in landlord days, and in more recent times a cultural and educational centre. Here, in close proximity to each other, may be seen St Tola's Church, a round tower, a high cross and a holy well. A short walk away, the newly restored O'Dea tower house once more lords it over the surrounding countryside.

St Tola's Church, a mainly twelfth-century structure built on the site of an earlier monastic foundation, is best known for its fine Romanesque doorway which has been much featured in tourist-orientated photography A colourful legend attaches to the nearby round tower, to the effect that it was uprooted from its original position at Rath by Mannawla, 'a poor weak woman, but a saint'. She made off with it one night, but was pursued by St Blathmac, who had almost overtaken her when she flung it as far as Dysert.[4] Other versions of the story say it was thrown here by some fleeing giant.[5] It may have survived such an impact but it was no match for the Cromwellians, who badly damaged it in 1651.[6] Their vandalism was not confined to this, however; they also demolished the beautiful twelfth-century high cross in the adjoining field and part of the castle.

St Tola's Cross, originally Cros Bán Tola according to John O'Donovan, was re-erected in 1683 by Michael O'Dea, and a stone plaque still proclaims this deed. Up to recently its curative powers were highly valued by sufferers from migraine. The afflicted person had only to lay his head in an angle formed by a loose piece of stone detached from the side of the shaft. But this piece has recently been cemented into place by some person with more regard for symmetry than the well-being of heads, and so the cure is no more.

Outside the wall of the graveyard is the Synge burial place. The family, landlords of the area, are not kindly remembered and all due to the deeds of a few members of the clan. To them has been attached the epithet 'souper'. This single word speaks volumes for their activities as proselytisers during the 1830s and later, during the Famine. Edward Synge was especially active in this regard and almost paid for it with his life when in February 1831 he was fired on at Ballycullinan, half a mile east of the castle. He escaped only because the shot lodged in a Bible which he carried in his pocket.[7] This same book is now preserved in the heritage centre in Corofin. The boulder behind which his assailant waited is still there and likely to remain so even though road widening is taking place all around it. They are acutely aware of history and heritage in Dysert O'Dea nowadays, so much so that the castle has been restored and transformed into a museum and archaeological centre, which opens to visitors from May to September.

Outside the front gate of Laurel Vale cottage, turn right and take the road to the north-west for half a mile if you wish to visit Drumcavan hillfort, the large earthen banks of which are overgrown but still impressive. Two miles farther along the same road is the previously mentioned Tullyodea, but there is little of interest to be found there except the remains of a large ring fort which contains a blocked-up souterrain.

Thanking our informative hostess for her help, we continued on our way into the townland of Drumcavan. Progress over the next quarter of a mile is easy, for the line is in good condition. Outside the dilapidated boundary walls, the land is the same as before – alternating crag and swamp. This latter must not be quite as cold as we humans might imagine for more than once we caught sight of straggling herds of cattle standing to their knees in the stuff, chewing away contentedly, looking warm and comfortable despite all the dictates of common sense.

Once or twice we had to leave the line to avoid fences, but the delay was never more than a few minutes. Our good humour at this point extended even to extravagant admiration for those who had excavated the two sizeable cuttings we had to pass through – no mean feat since they are both over 10-feet deep and cut into solid rock. But as was becoming all too usual, our rejoicings were somewhat premature, for before us once again lay all the signs of recent reclamation. Our whole attention was for the line: had it been destroyed or spared? It is gone. We were standing now on a little plateau, higher by a couple of feet than the land before us. This latter had been lowered by the bulldozers, just as at Ballygriffey. Only the right-hand fence remained to give us guidance, and we used it. A few minutes farther on and we came on an odd-looking mound which turned out to be an intact cattle pass, itself a surprising survivor in the all-embracing destruction – surprising because the cut-stone abutments of these little bridges are much sought-after for building purposes. In walls and other constructions up and down the country can be seen the cannibalised remains of such older stone structures. The same virtue, alas, is very unlikely to attach to that more recent interloper, the concrete block.

No remnant of the line is to be found in the next quarter of a mile, to Drumcavan level crossing (Murphy's crossing, as train crews called it) and all we could do was hope we were going in the right general direction. But then, so suddenly as to surprise us, we were at our destination, recognising immediately that this was the right place because of the piers, complete with stiles, on either side of the Ennis–Corofin road. These are all that remain.

Drumcavan was always regarded by railwaymen as a dangerous crossing since there is a turn in the road here and the engine drivers were to some extent unsighted on down journeys owing to the approaches being lower than the level of the road. That accidents here were so rare owes much to the extra care that was necessary on passing it.

Across the road, a hundred yards off, is the cottage, but unoc-cupied. There is no difficulty in finding the line behind it, so again we were able to move on speedily. But we were soon up to our knees in briars, and worse again, wet briars, for it had begun to drizzle steadily. Even in dry weather it would be a vain fight to get through these, and we needed our energy for whatever might be in store for us farther up the line, so we retraced our steps to the cottage and walked by the road instead. The line here runs directly by the roadside and quickly attains a height of over 8 feet, so when we were able to rejoin it, a hundred yards on, we found ourselves looking down on the roofs of cars passing by us to and from Corofin.

The going was still very rough along here, but at least we had a good view of Ballycullinan Lake directly beneath us and stretching off to the west. Long, narrow and surrounded on all sides by reeds, it looked on this showery day every bit as lonesome as the swamplands of Kilkee. Even more lonely is the pair of piers, with gate carefully

Drumcavan gates, 1953. (Photo: Irish Railway Record Society, no. 10637)

closed but with no fences or ditches attached – standing there, half-way to the lake in mysterious isolation.

At the north-eastern tip of the lake, where the railway passed nearest to the water, there is now a car-park and an access passage to the shore built directly on the site of the line. It is a place much frequented by fishermen during the summer months, but on this grey day not a sinner was in sight. Right at this extremity of the lake, and on the road, is another railway cottage, in good condition but also unoccupied. This is Cragmoher no. 1 crossing, 7½ miles from Ennis, and here Dysert parish gives way to the parish of Rath. For the next 8 miles (until Monreal) the West Clare travels almost without interruption within this very strung-out parish, in the course of which journey are to be seen some of the sharpest contrasts of scenery on either the West or the South Clare Railways, from the delightful Fergus Valley under Clifden Hill to the open bogland of Drinagh and Clooney in the west.

The gates at Cragmoher no. 1 guarded a little road which leads off towards Beggar's Bridge a mile away, forming the bounds between Cragmoher and Killeen townlands as it goes. The road, if not the cottage, has fallen into disrepair. As we huddled on, into the gloom, we caught sight of several bungalows some way up the line, their front lawns where the track once ran. Anything was better than being out in the 'softness' of this Irish day, so we did the only sensible thing left: threw ourselves on the mercy of the nearest doorbell. We were lucky. Quite by happy accident we had come to the house of one of the most knowledgeable men in the district. With an expert eye to the weather, he assured us that the rain wasn't 'down for the day' and that we would soon be able to go our way. In the meantime, we were made welcome to dry ourselves off and were treated to a veritable compendium of information about the locality. It is extraordinary just how much knowledge one old person may possess – material that is unavailable in books because it is too local. Yet this is a main part of its value, though a value unappreciated of late in Ireland, where a whole generation, fed on nothing more substantial than loud music and the usual milk-and-water television fare, has let slip almost all knowledge of, or interest in, parish or townland. It is the children of this generation who will be the real losers, for at least now there are still people alive like this old man, ready and willing to tell, only waiting to be done the courtesy of being asked. In twenty years' time there will be none. So the modern wave washes over Ireland, washing Irishness away in the process, all for lack of roots to hold together the soil of what we are.

This is Killeen, he says, and it was from here in 1922 that Free State forces intended to shell Corofin workhouse, which had been occupied by 'Irregulars', with guns brought by rail for the purpose. The proposed bombardment never took place, however. The occupiers of the workhouse received a warning of what was afoot and retired on 24 July, leaving the building a burning wreck behind them. And so ended the career of one of Clare's shortest-lived workhouses (that at Killadysert being burned at about the same time). Completed in 1850 when the worst of the Famine was over, it received its first inmates only in 1851, serving to relieve some of the pressure on space in the neighbouring workhouses at Ennis and Ennistymon.[8]

What Irish person has not heard horror stories of the tyranny and degradation endured within the fine cut-stone walls of these

Victorian edifices? And yet, during the Famine years, they were resorted to by the homeless and destitute in their thousands, for terrible and inadequate as they were, and mean-spirited and unchristian as was the system under which they were set up, there was nothing else between the poor and starvation. Corofin workhouse, thankfully, had none of those terrifying and seemingly endless rolls of deaths that were the lot of its sister-institutions in Clare, but life here was still never designed to be comfortable, despite the fine view of Lough Atedaun, and no opportunity was lost to remind the inmates that they were a burden on society, moreover a burden that the gentlemen of the neighbouring Big Houses were being forced to shoulder on their spotless frock coats. Each poorhouse was built at least 9 miles from the next so that beggars and able-bodied tramps would have to, at the very minimum, do a day's walking in order to get to the next night's shelter. One of these tramping men, a fellow with a flair for rhyming, composed the following couplet after a restless night beset by fleas in the Corofin Union. On his way out in the morning, still scratching, he looked up at the fine stone façade and said:

> *Fair without but foul within,*
> *My curse upon you, Corofin.*

Today, a housing estate covers most of the site. Only fragments of the main house survive, and a few out-offices – one of which was the boardroom of the workhouse guardians – is used as a depot by the Board of Works, from which maintenance work is done on national monuments in the Burren area.

Less than half a mile away from us, he says, is situated the shell of Cragmoher House, only recently accidentally burned. Once owned by the ubiquitous Studderts, it was the centre of an estate of almost 900 acres.[9] An interesting tale is told locally of it: a former owner scoffed at a workman of his who requested time off to visit a holy well in the vicinity in order to seek a cure for an eye complaint.

'Take the oul' mare there with you, while you're at it,' he laughed.

But at a hunting party less than a week later, an accident occurred;

a shot was fired, the master's eye was damaged and in no long time afterwards he went blind.

There was nothing the matter with our host's sight, though. Even as he told his tale he was sizing up the state of the sky, nodding approvingly. 'Ye could do worse now than be movin'.'

We were on the point of voicing our thanks when he reached for his coat and stick. He had a few things to show us, he said.

Where the string of new houses flanks the road the line has been cleared away to make room for gardens, and even beyond them is a bare field – recently levelled, he said, and soon to be built on. But not to worry; a hundred yards off the line continued its interrupted way to Corofin. In a little cutting here, directly inside the road wall, is what he wanted to show us. Pointing to the solid rock of the cutting, he brought our attention to long vertical cylindrical scars. These, he explained, were the marks of the jumpers – metal bars like crowbars – that were used in the excavation of this cutting. One man would hold the bar, turning it while two others hammered it alternately with sledges into the rock. The broken stone was then taken from the cutting in barrows – four men to each barrow – to the site of the next embankment, where it was used for fill, and so nothing was wasted.

As he stood among the scant remnants of the line he knew so well all his life, he dredged up stories he heard from fifty years ago about the men who built this railway, how they walked 13 miles each day to and fro between Ruan and Ennistymon, glad to get the work offered. Did he know what class of people they were, I asked.

'Oh, they were all local men. Farmers' sons and labourers.'

No doubt he was substantially correct, for in all the stories that have come down to us about this construction period, there is no mention of villages of huts, which were such a feature of British railway building and which, indeed, were also part and parcel of two of Clare's largest engineering projects, the Fergus reclamation works at Islandavanna in 1881 and the Shannon hydro-electric scheme at Ardnacrusha in 1929.[10]

But not all labourers were countrymen, nor did they all speak English, it seems, as the following story suggests:

'There was tramping fellows out from Limerick that time, doing jobs here an' there, an' they'd be working on the railway on an' off. An' one of 'em was below at the bottom of a hill when they were building near Corofin. Now, there was a local fellow above on top an' he rooting like hell – they were in dread o' their life o' the ganger that time – an' didn't he loosen this big rock, an' it came rolling down the hill towards the tramp below. The lad above started shouting, "Seachain! Seachain!" (Look out!) By God, it passed down an' just grazed his leg. An' he turned up – "Don't mind your cursed shuckin-shockin," he said. "Wouldn't you tell a bloody man to look up."'[11]

Common sense, apparently, was often the main difference between the seasoned navvy and the enthusiastic but unskilled countryman.

In more recent times, milesmen in this area showed their resourcefulness by frying their dinners in shovels over an open fire, having first scoured the metal with sand and grass, then rubbed lard to the shining surface.

But apart from the marks of the jumpers, the only evidence of the presence of workmen in this cutting today is a large concrete slab. Bord Telecom had taken advantage of the proximity of the line to the road and used it to lay their cables, thereby helping to spare the harassed motorists of Clare even more flittered tyres and shattered suspensions.

Such details as our friend had given us had even now lent this otherwise unremarkable place a wholly unsuspected life, but he was not finished yet. If these snatches of scenes from the construction of the line remain with him, his knowledge of its demise is far more graphic. He was one of the last passengers to travel along here, and he still remembers vividly the taking up of the line in 1961 and the man in charge, who worked his men hard. They had a wagon at Corofin Station in which they cooked and slept, and at first light each day would set off for their work of destruction. But his final comment is significant: 'If they worked half as hard to keep the track as they did to take it up, it wouldn't be taken up at all.'

With that piece of wisdom he left us. The old bones, he said, weren't as good as they used to be, and he had walked enough for one day.

It is more practical to walk on the road beside the line as far as Cragmoher crossroads for there is little to see along here, and there is every chance of turning an ankle in the long grass which blankets the way. Near the cross, the line swings away from the road towards Cragmoher no. 2 crossing, but it is always in sight so no map consultation is needed. A few minutes' walk brought us to the crossing cottage. It is unoccupied, its little plot of land neglected. Mrs Collins, the last owner, has been dead some years and so far no one has replaced her. There are a number of similar-looking cottages close together here, but the familiar palisade of sleepers clearly marks out the correct one, so that enquiries are quite unnecessary.

We sat a moment on the piers to consult. Ahead and to the right is a wide vista of the surrounding country. A comparison with what the map shows is instructive, for on paper Lough Atedaun should be off to the north-east at a distance of almost a mile. The truth is that at this time of year the low-lying valley of the Fergus, between us and the high ground upon which Corofin is mainly built, is almost completely flooded, practically doubling the size of Atedaun. The floodwater even touches the West Clare line in places. In summer-time, however, this is a fisherman's paradise, with anglers from the Continent especially delighting in the rich returns to be had from the chain of lakes which runs onward from Atedaun to the north-east – Knockaundoo, Cullaun, Ballyeighter and George. Equipped with ice-packs in which to send home fillets of pike, they marvel that most Irish people regard as mere vermin a fish that is sought as a delicacy in Europe.

Lough Inchiquin, the first and perhaps the most famous of all the lakes on the Fergus waterway, is not visible from any part of the West Clare line. It lies under the steep eastern end of Clifden Hill, which towers 625 feet over it and whose elongated outline looks a fair imitation of the more angular Benbulben. A number of interesting tales are still told locally to explain how the lake came into being and got its name. All this area once belonged to the O'Quins, one of whom married a fairy woman who came out of a well which was situated where the lake now is. Her one proviso on marrying him was that he should never invite an O'Brien to his home. Later, under the influence of drink, he broke this taboo, whereupon she fled with their children back into the well. It immediately flowed out, flooded the countryside, and Lough Inchiquin has ever since been here.[12]

Up to the last generation, stories of Fionn and the Fianna were still told in the area, for many of the great adventures of that warrior band had the country round about as their setting.[13] In recent years, an attempt has been made to keep an echo of that tradition alive in the annual Festival of Finn held in June.

Only when one closely examines a map does one realise how extraordinarily varied this region is, with its many attractions for the sportsman or the naturalist, the archaeologist, historian or genealogist. The latter is catered for by the Clare Heritage Centre, the first of its kind in Ireland. Established in 1979 and the brainchild of the late Naoise Cleary, it is housed in the early eighteenth-century St Catherine's Protestant church and provides a genealogical service for all five continents – wherever, in fact, people of Clare extraction are to be found. So successful has it been in its first decade in operation that a new premises has recently had to be acquired.

A few hundred yards from the centre, on the same street, stands St Brigid's Catholic church. Unremarkable in itself, it was built in the early 1820s by a most remarkable man, Fr John Murphy, who achieved national fame in his short lifetime for his support of Daniel O'Connell during the election of 1828.[14] He it was, too, who so strenuously opposed the 'educational' efforts of Edward Synge of Dysert, paying out of his own pocket part of the salaries of the teachers in the alternative schools he founded. Much loved, much hated, he died in 1831 and is buried in the church he built.

But apart from any uniqueness which it may itself possess, Corofin can also be said to be the southern gateway to the Burren, and 3 miles north of the village, by the time one is in Kilnaboy, the surroundings are typical Burren landscape. Anyone wishing to lose himself for a time in the delights of those limestone uplands may happily do so. Luckily, there is no shortage of excellent publications to make such an experience even more worthwhile.[15]

Reluctantly, we jumped from our respective perches, squeezed through the sleeper-fence and trudged on. Fortunately, there are no obstacles here, only the water lapping close by on the right and poor lonesome fields to the left. Surprising how well preserved the surface is here. Probably it is too useful as a roadway in the midst of all this swampland to have been quarried. So complete is it that even the imprints of the sleepers are still clearly visible as mossy bumps and hollows.

The only real hindrance we met between Cragmoher no. 2 and Corofin Station should have been no obstacle at all, and would not have been had destructive hands not intervened. What had happened was obvious: the covering of a culvert had been removed, or so we thought, leaving a fast, deep channel of water dividing us from our destination. If the abutments had been left undisturbed, crossing would have posed no problems, but all the stonework had gone, leaving ill-defined and weedy verges. We cast about, but no more solid crossing place offered. So we took our lives in our legs and jumped. For Keith, it was a close shave, but he balanced somehow and dragged himself up with nothing worse to show than a bootful of water. Yards away, in long grass, we stumbled over a large metal object. It was a sizeable and rusting bridge, the very one we should have been crossing over. It had been lifted entire from its foundations and dumped here to rot. We knew, however, that the breaking of bridges was no new occupation in this district. Had it not been practised on the grand scale during the Troubles? As a result of such handiwork, the village of Corofin became almost isolated in July of 1922 and business came to a standstill.[16] At this very place also, on the night of 25 August 1900, engine no. 9, *Fergus*, bringing empty carriages to Ennis for the regular Sunday excursion on the following day, ran into a rock which had been maliciously placed on the line. Fortunately, there were no injuries, except to the rock, which was shattered.[17]

A flourishing whitethorn in the centre of the line at this point demonstrates vividly just how long the track has been gone, but through its spreading branches we could see buildings beyond and a grey stone gable facing us. But the most distinctive feature to catch our attention was the straight stone edging at ground level in front

Corofin Station, 1953.(Photo: Irish Railway Record Society, no. 10430)

of the house. There was no further room for doubt. This was Corofin Station. Other typical features we quickly noted – the layout of the buildings, timber-work as at Ruan, the stonework, etc. With satisfaction we concluded that it had not changed very much in all the years since the line's closure. But our immediate task was to explain ourselves and apologise for trespassing. Nothing could have been easier, for the woman who now owns the property is most pleasant, hospitable and willing to share whatever she knows of the station in its working days. The building itself has been altered little and the yard is unmistakably a railway yard yet. The stone edging of the platform, already noted, is well preserved, but where the line ran has now been filled in to make a lawn and flower garden.

Next door to the station is Minihan's public house, a hostelry that was a necessary amenity for rail travellers. Not surprisingly, it features in many stories about the line, as for example the following: a priest, rushing for his train at Ennis Station, found himself without cigarettes. A black smoker, he was gasping by the time the train pulled in at Corofin. Rushing into Minihan's, he slapped his money on the counter and demanded his smokes, quick, before the train pulled out.

No sign of hurry on the bar-woman. She slowly counted out his change penny by penny, while he stood in a fritter of impatience. 'Hurry! I'll be late!' A hand was laid on his shoulder, a voice growled in his ear: 'Yerra, take it easy, Father. They can't go without us.' It was the engine driver and fireman, in for their customary refreshment, pints of porter.[18]

Anxious to preserve this old tradition to the bitter end, the travellers on the last train on that rainy Tuesday in January 1961 'ran out, jumped a wall and hotfooted it' to this same premises 'and drank for twenty minutes while the train waited at the station.'[19]

Minihan's bar is still to the good, as is the freight shed. A siding led to this shed, which explains why the line is so wide for some way back. We had noticed this but could see no reason for it at the time.

The front room of the station-house is still recognisable as the waiting room, and what was the stationmaster's sitting-room is now a comfortable living-room which to us seemed very desirable indeed on this cold winter's day. Outside again, we were shown the wall to which the station sign was fixed and, sure enough, the marks of the bolts are still to be seen. But these reminders, plus a metal gate-post in the yard still painted its original railway green, are all that remain

Corofin Station after closure, 7.6.61. (Photo: Roy Denison)

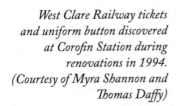

*West Clare Railway tickets
and uniform button discovered
at Corofin Station during
renovations in 1994.
(Courtesy of Myra Shannon and
Thomas Daffy)*

of what was Corofin Station, which, at 8¾ miles from Ennis, was the first block-post on the West Clare system.[20] As well as the platform, goods' store and a short siding, it also had a passing-loop, all on the up side, and the water tank (145 gallons) near the platform on the Willbrook end would have been a familiar sight to travellers in the earlier years; no doubt to Percy French, too, who, we are told, composed 'Are Ye Right There, Michael?' in this very station.

With this final piece of information to mull over and believe if we chose, we started back. What was left of the short evening might, just might, allow us to get to Ruan Station and our car before dark.

Day 4

Corofin Station to Willbrook Halt

Two months were to pass before we could once more continue our journey, two months of rain, hail and cold. It would have been pointless to venture out during that time; no maps or clothing could have stood up to the conditions. But as one week's rain followed another into early 1988, we began to get restless. At last, we set out for Corofin Station on a clear Saturday morning in January against our own better judgement. For though there had been no rain for three days we knew that the land would be flooded. We should also have expected that the same might be true of parts of the railway. It would have saved us much misery that day, for it must be said, and forcefully, that conditions on the 1¼-mile journey from the station gates to Roxton crossing were atrocious. Parts of the Newtown–Willbrook section were almost as bad, but not quite. Nothing could compare to that first mile and a quarter, where the mud and flooding formed quagmires that forced us time and again to take detours through fields that were themselves quaking bogs. In places we were jumping from one clump of rushes to the next, not daring to stop for more than a few seconds for fear of sinking; at other times we swung from branch to branch of the bushes flanking the line while we judged where next to put our feet. Tarzan would have felt himself challenged had he seen us.

And for all of this we had no one but ourselves to blame, for we made one simple but unforgivable error that morning: we came equipped only with boots, not wellingtons. It was to cost us dear in time wasted, for while we were pussyfooting here and there, testing the depth of the muck, we could, with the correct footwear, have gone straight through it, for over the whole sorry journey we never once came on a place where the line did not form a solid base, even if it was buried by a foot of mire or water. So, little did we know what was facing us as we crossed the road at Corofin Station, carefully examining the two parallel ridges on the road surface which suggest that the rails were merely tarred over.

In quick succession we passed through two cuttings where the solid rock comes near to where the track must have lain, though the boundary walls are several feet farther back. It gives a very claustro-phobic feeling, and must have seemed even more so to train travellers. Considering these surroundings, it would be no surprise if evilly dis-posed persons had decided to turn them to their advantage. Yet this does not seem to have happened here but in the more open section at the Ennis side of the station, as in the attempt in 1900 already alluded to.

Directly beyond the second cutting problems begin, for land reclamation has played its usual havoc. First, a huge spoil-heap has to be climbed. Then, for what seems longer than it actually is, there is nothing to guide one except a solitary stone wall surrounded by Flanders-like mud. Here began our purgatory, and though I cannot recall how long it took to pass this terrible place, it seemed ages. Mud, reclamation work and then more mud. That is my recollection of the townlands of Ballykinnacorra South and Liscullaun. Perhaps, to do them justice, I should look at them again in summertime, but I do not think I will do so. Ever.

We were quite lost when eventually a group of people hailed us from a nearby hill. Hugely relieved, we headed in their direction, only to be told that we must have been out of our minds if we expected to find any sign of the railway here. It had been removed several years ago, they informed us. However, if we were determined to persist we would find it the best part of half a mile away. They led us through a clutter of farm buildings, across several concreted yards, to the open fields outside, where, they assured us, we might eventually discover what we sought 'if we kept a sharp eye out'. But there lay the problem. How can you keep a sharp eye out when the ground under your feet is a quaking moonscape, broken into pieces by a million cattle-prints? We never learned the trick, and so were soon wandering again, up little hillocks in expectation, down their far sides crestfallen.

Only when we came within sight of the next house, at the butt of a long gentle slope of hillside, did we stop a moment to catch our breath. And for the first time that day we noticed something that should have been the highlight of our day's trek: the broad river valley north of us, and the junction of the Craggaunboy River with the Fergus. Over them towers Clifden Hill, extensively wooded, and with a lone stand of firs almost at the top, giving it added distinctiveness. What surer measure could there be of the beauty of this strip of land on the southern and western shores of Lough Inchiquin than that so many of the gentry built their houses here? For they, like the monks of a previous age, had an eye for a good site. Within a distance of little more than a mile, one comes on Baunkyle House, Clifden House, Riverstown House and Adelphi.

Mention of Baunkyle brings to mind a remarkable fact: some of the most dedicated Irish antiquarians and folklorists of this century have either lived within sight of Lough Inchiquin or been drawn here to conduct their studies. Dr George MacNamara (after whom the MacNamara Gallery in the Heritage Centre, Corofin, has been named) owned Baunkyle House at the beginning of the twentieth century, and the indefatigable T.J. Westropp often stayed here while engaged in his explorations of the Burren.[1] More recently, Dr Máire MacNéill lived in the area until her death in 1987. And what a strange world we live in that she, a scholar of international repute, who donated a magnificent art collection to the nation and wrote about her adopted Clare so feelingly, should get only a few inches of newspaper space on her death, when yards of newsprint can be devoted to the most trivial antics of this or that obscure county councillor.

Riverstown House, just south of the bridge over the Fergus, is

now a ruin, but has had an impressive list of owners in its two centuries' existence. Originally a property of the Burtons, one of the most
highly regarded of local landed families, it was also for a time in the
hands of the Studderts as well as being used as an RIC barracks.
The nearby Clifden House also counts these two families among its
former owners, but time has dealt more gently with it, for it is still
inhabited and in fine condition. Near the house are the ruins of a mill
which Edward Burton helped establish and which provided much
relief during the Famine, a circumstance remembered to the Burtons'
credit even to this day.[2]

The property known now as Adelphi was, prior to 1800, known
as Tiermacbran. Why the Fitzgeralds, the lessees at the time, should
have changed the name is obvious; one look at the scenery on all sides
will explain that. But in ignoring the older name they also helped to
obscure much of the antiquity of the place, for this rugged country
was the hunting ground of Fionn Mac Cumhaill and the setting for
'Feis Tighe Chonáin'. Tiermacbran Lake, just south of the present
house, is reputedly where Fionn's hound, Bran, jumped from a cliff
in pursuit of a white deer. Both vanished beneath the waters of the
lake and even yet story and rumour make it a place of mystery.[3] It
is now known as Molly's Lough (after a Molly Blood who is said
to have drowned in it) and is reputedly 'bottomless'. The ruins of
Tiermacbran Castle, a short distance away, are, it is claimed, haunted
by the lady's ghost, though this is probably no more than an embel-
lishment of the original tale. To the rear of Adelphi, a miniature
funicular railway was constructed by the landlord E.W. Burton in
the nineteenth century, and used to bring turf to the house from
high up on Clifden Hill.[4] It has shared the same fate as the West
Clare.

A dog barking furiously as he pelted up the hill towards us interrupted our sightseeing. Even to a dog we must have seemed suspi-
cious, standing motionless for so long on a bare hillside, so we started
towards him, but warily. He was harmless, however, more bark than
bite, like most sheepdogs, though you should never let them out of

sight as they circle you. A lump out of the back of a leg may be the price of such inattention!

The woman of the house seemed in no way surprised to see us. Others have been passing this way for years on the same quest, she assured us, a straggling few every year. The state of the land here is no great help to such people, she conceded, but she had some good news for us: a mere 30 yards away, though blocked from view, the line continues, intact and entire, towards Roxton. We were so relieved to have rediscovered it that we had no hesitation in delaying a while to talk.

This is the townland of Curraghkeel, and the surrounding land was cleared about six years ago. At least one cattle-pass was demolished in the section we had just walked but there was another intact, she said, a short distance before Roxton crossing. A half-mile to the south-west, we could see a church bell-tower peeping over a hill. This is St Mary's, the modern parish church of Rath. Completed in 1869, it was just now being re-roofed and might be worth a quick visit, she suggested. We agreed, for it was unlikely that we would come this way again specially to see a building so modern. As we took our leave, she told us to be sure to call to Applevale House if we had time, that it was just beyond the crossing and would not be far out of our way. In the case of that particular house, I needed no encouragement beyond mention of its very name. For I had heard terrible tales about it and the ferocious murder committed there in 1831, and had long intended to visit it, anyway. But only in bright daylight. I would hesitate to visit such a place at night, irrational as that might seem.

On the line itself there was only one large obstruction on the way to Roxton crossing, and a most peculiar one, too. We had just crossed an embankment from which there is a fine view of the Craggaunboy River where it meets the Fergus; already ahead, clearly noticeable, the line had begun to rise, but only when we reached what appeared to be a little plateau at the summit of the hill did we appreciate fully how sharp this incline is. For before us we were amazed to see a kind of ravine and a giant step chopped out of the far side of the hill. Perhaps this is the result of more land improvement, but if so it is hard to know what its purpose was, since there is little to be gained by reclaiming a cutting – and that is what we were in by the time we had clambered down the 12 feet to the lower ground level. The odd thing, though, is that above and below this cliff the line appears to be intact. But how could this possibly be so, unless there has been an earthquake and land subsidence here? All we could do was scratch our heads and walk on, past the solid rock walls. But despite our perplexity, we did not forget to search for the marks of jumpers. In quick succession we found several.

As we emerged from the cutting, Rath Chapel was clearly in view on its eminence, but of the promised cattle-pass there was no sign. With no more than 300 yards to go to the crossing, we passed over an embankment at least 25-feet high, and not for the first time were forced to marvel at what difficult terrain the builders had to contend with. Then suddenly we were on it, the overpass we had been expecting. It is all of 20 feet to the ground below, and since there are no parapets we had to manoeuvre cautiously as we tried to get a clear view of the fine stonework, still as impressive as it must have looked when newly laid a century ago.

We were in the townland of Roxton now, and with no further delay we reached the road. For a moment we stood to examine this lonesome place, but there is little to interest the passer-by. The crossing cottage stands inhabited and relatively unchanged from railway days, but a shed has been built on the line by the side of it. There is no passing that way, so one must go either up or down the hill to go on. Of the gates, at which a former occupant of the cottage was killed, there is no trace; no vestige, either, of the little platform on the up side which was used in the early years of the railway.

But if there is little here today, Roxton crossing was once a place of more than passing interest, especially to train crews in steam days, because it marked the beginning of a 2-mile section of almost continuously rising ground. The gradient here is 1/61 and is even worse further on towards Willbrook, so it was a severe test for down trains fully laden. At least 100 pounds of steam was needed to get up here, and that this was not always forthcoming is well attested to by many stories of unscheduled stops. Edward McLysaght recalls one such:

'What I remember so clearly is the sound of the little engine labour-
ing up the steep gradient near Corofin and the way the train finally
stopped, apparently miles from anywhere. That was nothing in itself:
what fixed it in my mind was my father telling me afterwards that
Percy French was on that same train and the breakdown prompted
him to write one of his best-known songs, "Are You Right There,
Michael?"'[5]

Whatever about the song, the delays were real enough and provoked much resentment among passengers, but until the coming of
diesel engines there was little that could be done. The corollary of
all this was that up trains often found it difficult to halt between
Willbrook and here, so the gatekeepers at these crossings always had
to be extra vigilant and have the gates open in good time. Incidents
occurred which might easily have had serious consequences. After
the amalgamation of 1925, for example, some drivers were transferred
from the Great Southern, but not being accustomed to the narrow
gauge, they were inclined to travel faster than was safe. Legend has it
that one of them actually outran his wagons on this section and had
to slow down and wait until they caught up.

What the condition of the line was like behind the shed we could
not tell. A detour here was unavoidable in any case, so we used the
opportunity to have a look at the church. It is a pretty little limestone building, and when we arrived some work was in progress.
But the workmen seemed glad at our coming. It was an opportunity
for a break, a chat. Most of them were more interested in asking us
questions than in being questioned themselves, but one was both
knowledgeable and open, and from him we found out much about
the locality. Directly opposite the church he pointed out the cut-
stone piers of Roxton House, once the home of 'Old Bill' Blood, high
sheriff of Clare in 1750.[6] The house itself still stands but in a sad state
of decay, a faint shadow of the impressive residence it once was.

A mile and a half further south is the Hill of Scool, already mentioned in relation to the battle of Dysert, and in its shadow lies Rath
Lake, home and prison of the infamous Broc Sidhe, the fairy badger.

This creature first appeared in the early sixth century and began to terrorise the people of the vicinity. The clergy were sent for, but even St Blathmac (now patron of the parish), a man of some power, could do nothing, though armed with bell, crozier and reliquary; on the contrary, this attempted interference only angered the creature all the more. Assistance had to be sought further afield, and at last a champion was found in St Mac Creiche of Ennistymon. He had already successfully routed several monsters in the Liscannor area, and he it was who vanquished the Broc Sidhe and chained it to the bottom of the lake. But the saint was a man not without feelings; he allowed it its freedom for a single day every seven years, and it has reputedly been seen as recently as 1931, none the worse for its long confinement.[7]

To the south-east of the lake lie the ruins of St Blathmac's Church, but it contains little of interest except a few carvings and a sheela-na-gig. St Blathmac's crozier and two bells originally from this church survive and are kept in the National Museum.[8]

Of Applevale House our friend knew surprisingly little besides the fact that a murder had taken place there, but he suggested that we speak to the owner of the land, a man with a keen interest in local history. Before we could go he had to show us something. From the chapel yard we could see for a couple of miles around, and large blotches of reclaimed land stood out clearly, even at this season of dull colours. Farmers who are so impatiently pushing walls, hedges and ditches as far as possible into the background will be the first to need artificial shelter later on for those same friesians for which they are now so busily clearing the land, he said. Only in a sheltered environment do these cattle thrive best, so why is it …? The futility of his question seemed to occur to him, for without finishing it he shrugged and with a little wave returned to his work, leaving us to ours. It took us some time to do so owing to a thick barrier of blackthorn beside the line, but once on it we made good progress, through yet another cutting, over an impressive cattle-pass, finally reaching our destination, Applevale, in no more than ten minutes.

Perched on its hill crest a mere 200 yards to the left of the line, it certainly fitted the mental picture I had formed of it – gloomy, spirit-ridden, watching. The much more pleasant view to the north of the line, of smooth fields sweeping down to the valley bottom and on up the majestic flank of Clifden Hill, is all but neutralised by this dark, ivy-clad shape on its outcrop, compelling yet forbidding, scowling down on the onlooker. We held a brief conference while we surveyed the ivy-laden gable and extensive stone out-buildings and walls stretching hither and thither, concealing we knew not what mysteries. Sinister or not, we had not come so close to it only to pass it by. We set off to investigate.

At the gable, an entrance of some kind faced us, but led only to a blank wall. Nor had we better luck at other entrances on this side of the house. Eventually, we made our way round a corner to the front, where we had a better view of the whole. The door and window frames are still in place, as well as fragments of glass, so it would appear to have been occupied up to relatively recently. The roof, though, has collapsed or been demolished. Adjoining the southern gable is a medium-sized walled yard, and it was here, on the night of 21 January 1831, that William Blood, the owner, was murdered in a most brutal way by a band of Terry Alts, the Clare version of the Whiteboys. According to one of those who gave evidence at the inquest: 'I never witnessed such a sight; the head was beaten perfectly flat and his brains and blood spattered on walls and door about him. A large piece of a rock and broken pieces of a gun scattered about him showed with what he had been killed.'

The county at the time was in a very disturbed and lawless state, but the savagery of this killing threw the landed class into such alarm that many of them began to pack up in preparation for a hasty departure for the safety of the towns. It also, naturally, provoked much frenzied police activity, and at last two men were convicted at the end of June and hanged publicly within sight of Applevale. This was by no means the finish of the land agitation, however, and the 'outrages' and hangings continued well into 1832, when, combined with other factors, the intervention of Daniel O'Connell at last brought relative calm.

Since the doorway to the yard was fenced off, we were about to go round to the main gateway when the owner, Mr Houlihan, joined us and kindly offered to show us round. We were fortunate that he did, for his knowledge of the history of the locality is extensive. How else could we have discovered that the roof timbers and slates have gone to renovate Ballyportry Castle, visible 3 miles away, north-east of Corofin; that there have been five different owners since Blood's time; that the property was originally called Bóthar Salach (the Muddy Road) but that the name was changed to Applevale by Neptune Blood in 1729; that Captain Thomas Blood attempted to steal the Crown Jewels in 1671?[10] In the yard he showed us the well, near which William Blood met his death. Legend tells that in his attempts to defend himself, he tried to wrench an iron handle from a pump just here but had only succeeded in bending it when he was set upon and bludgeoned to death.

The interior of the house contains nothing of interest now, but the stables and other out-offices are solidly built and will stand for many years yet. Radiating out from the rear of the house is a maze of walls, both high and low, and what impresses most of all is the sheer quantity of stone it took to build this complex – that, and the quality of the masonry. A true saying it is that the only craft that has never been improved with the passing of time is that of the stonemason.

Though long past its prime, Applevale is still impressive, and is far less forbidding when one has examined it at close quarters. But I still doubt whether I would spend an easy night in that grim yard.

It is hardly three-quarters-of-a-mile's journey from Applevale to Newtown crossing, and though the line has disappeared in several places there is no difficulty in finding one's way since where it has been removed it is only for short snatches; also, the single cattle-pass and culvert on this section are still intact. One's attention is much more likely to be on the surrounding scenery than on the line, for this is a landscape of secret little hollows and picturesque streams alternating with long drab-looking belts of rushes streeling out, it seems, for miles. More than once the notion occurred to us that here is the basis of a huge St Brigid's Cross-making industry, with no possible end to the raw material available.

For some reason, the country north of the railway seems to have inherited all the beauty spots, that to the south all the rushes. A large contributor to the former is the little Craggaunboy River, which accompanies the line for practically the whole way to Willbrook. It is the kind of stream that makes one want to reach for a fishing rod and give all other concerns the cold shoulder. This is definitely a place to be savoured again at a more opportune time.

During the Troubles, it happened that a group of Volunteers gathered here one night, intending to remove a rail in order to halt the train the following morning. With them was a part-time railway labourer who should have known how to loosen the fish-bolt; but the more they hammered it the tighter it grew, so eventually they had to call off the operation in disgust. Some time afterwards, the same labourer was working in a per-way gang near Monreal, where efforts were being made to remove a similar bolt so that essential repairs could be carried out. An inspector was present, so the ganger was impatient to get the job done quickly, and when a wrench failed to shift the bolt, he ordered the labourer to 'take the hammer there an' knock out that'. Expertly or luckily, he did so at the first blow, but the bolt flew, hitting the poor inspector in the shin. As he danced about in pain, the ganger, highly amused, whispered to the labourer, 'God, 'tis a pity you weren't down the night near Applevale. You'd whip the bolt for 'em.'

'Jeeny,' says he, 'I *was* there!'

At the eastern end of Applevale townland, in the final 300 yards before Newtown crossing, a lordly embankment stalks across low, soft ground and gradually levels out as the land on both sides rises to the road. It is one of those immediately recognisable relics of the railway and much photographed, since it is so visible to passing motorists. The crossing cottage is here, too, still unmistakable as such, though it has been renovated. We were not only greeted civilly by the woman of the house, but even invited in for tea, an offer we gladly accepted since our fingers were beginning to fall off from the cold. While we were moving we had hardly noticed it, but now that we were indoors it became painfully obvious.

Applevale Cottage she called the house, and over tea she told us of the mass of material relating to the railway that she burned while clearing out when first she came to live here. All that she had kept was a timetable of 1961, the last gasp of the line. But because she was born locally, her memories of the railway remained vivid. She remembered that during the Second World War, when the available coal was of poor quality, the train failed on many occasions to climb from Roxton to here, and that the passengers were indeed sent gathering sticks, as Percy French claimed in his song. With a laugh she confirmed the stories we had already heard about trains coming in the opposite direction, from Kilkee, and the difficulty they had in stopping on this downhill run: 'You had to have the gates open well in time, that's all.'

On one particular occasion at the turn of the century, these gates were not opened, with amusing consequences: 'There was an oul' driver that time, Rosy Loughlin was his name, an' he was driving down a goods' train late in the evening from the west. An' the people in Newtown cottage, there was a sister o' theirs home from America, an' sure, they had a great session going for her inside. There was a lad playing the concertina an' they all dancing like mad in the kitchen, an' they rising this Yankee lady for a height going round. But the next thing, the train was blowing like hell for the gates – no one there to open 'em! It carried the four gates – there used to be four iron gates that time; they made 'em o' timber an' crossed 'em later.

'Loughlin got the train stopped below at the bottom o' the hill an' he came up along with a hammer in his hand an' he fecking an' lighting. He'd have to report it, you see, how he broke the gates. He'd be writing for a month, you know. He came up, anyway, an' he like a lion, with the hammer. An' the Yankee lady went down. "You'll come in, Mr O'Loughlin," she says, "an' you'll have a drop o' tea with us."

'"Ah, f..k you an' your tea. Why didn't ye open the gates?"

'She was lucky he didn't split her with the hammer.'

But though it might be a source of annoyance to drivers to

demolish crossing gates, most railway employees were rather cynical in this matter: 'Look, don't you worry. Every one of them gates got broken at some time or another. There was a gang inside in Limerick full time making gates, an' they had to be kept going.'[11]

We would have been welcome to sit and talk for much longer but Willbrook still beckoned in the distance and we thought it better to be on our way while we were yet inclined.

The townland of Carrowduff may present one with a fine view of the Craggaunboy Valley, but it was also the first place on the line where we saw rushes spread from the fields alongside right across the track itself – even on relatively level ground. At the first cutting – a shallow affair – there was no passing, since it was quite flooded. Seepage must always have been a problem here, though controllable while the per-way gangs were on hand to keep the wayside drains clear. Now, however, with grass choking everything, long neglect has done its worst. For considerable stretches there is little to distinguish fields from line; all are equally under water. Only an embankment here and there brings momentary relief.

But one thing slowly made itself obvious: the landscape had changed from the limestone crag that had been so common up to Applevale. Now the fields were open and boggy, the hills no longer steep but undulating. The next cutting was different to any we had seen so far, in that it was driven not through rock, as heretofore, but through gravelly soil – moraine of some sort. It was the beginning of quite another set of landforms, as we were later to acknowledge. But even if we had few opportunities for viewing the Craggaunboy River in Carrowduff, at least its rattle and babble was audible most of the time as it poured itself over a series of little rapids near the line.

The first of the bridges here begins as a culvert, carrying a little *glaise* through a kind of stone pipe and off to its junction with the river.[12] A mere 10 yards farther on is a substantial bridge, under which flows only a trickle of water on a broad smooth sheet of solid rock. The culvert must at one time have been an overspill escape for this stream, but for some reason their roles have become reversed. A short distance upstream, the two channels diverge, and it would take a considerable flow of water now to raise this rivulet by any significant amount. All this scenic riverside section of line is well worthy of preservation for a future generation's enjoyment.

A very notable cutting just south of Maghera crossroads gave us some reason for pause, for here a stand of fir trees grows over the left sidewall to a great height and a farmhouse backs almost on to its edge. But the floor of the cutting is littered with old cars, quietly decaying, like the West Clare line itself.

Even if we had wished to turn south here and walk to the site of Carrowduff Castle, half a mile away, time was against us. The journey would have been rather pointless anyway since hardly a trace of the building remains. One of the five castles in the parish of Rath, all owned by the O'Briens, it was still in their hands in 1656. What happened it after that no one is quite sure. But it is gone, in any case. Nearer to hand there were more interesting things to see, notably the handsome bridge over the Craggaunboy River, which here forms the boundary between Carrowduff and Craggaunboy townlands.

A stone's throw north of the Ennistymon road, though not visible from the line, is the site of Willbrook House and close by it the 'Maghera Castle' shown on our map. This, in fact, is not a castle but the ancient ruin of Kilnoe Church, of whose history practically nothing is known.[13] What is not in doubt, however, is that its site, as well as extensive lands round about, were owned during his lifetime by Conor O'Brien of Leamaneagh, husband of the famous Máire Rua. The original Willbrook was an eighteenth-century Georgian house, picturesquely sited overlooking two scenic river valleys, but it has been long demolished. The present house is owned by the artist Louis le Brocquy.

Apart from the shape of the line itself – a notch cut out of the hillside which rises towards the north – there is little to be seen until one comes almost to Willbrook school. But the steadily rising ground is quite noticeable, for the gradient here is as sharp as 1/50. Steam engines could do no more than crawl up this incline, and an excellent account of one such journey, just before a Christmas during the Emergency, is to be found in the files of the *Clare Champion*. There was no coal that night, only turf, which was a poor substitute on hills like this. The driver was uneasy: 'I'm worried about that hill tonight. 'Tis a hell of a long run up there pulling all that weight. If only I could get the engine and two carriages over (Toloughlahan) bridge I'd be home and dry. That turf isn't worth a shit to keep steam up,' he added resignedly.

'How would a bag of coal help if you had one?' said grandfather.

'How would it help? I'd knock sparks off the tracks and dust off my arse, so I would'. [14]

And so he did, with the help of the precious sack of coal that the old man had been saving for Christmas. But no doubt he returned the compliment later, for the West Clare crews were, in the main, men who regarded themselves and the people they served all along the line as one large family. Many a poor widow or cottager was kept in winter fuel by these kindly men, who would sling out lumps or shovels of coal at points convenient for collection.

So rapid was our progress here, where the Ennistymon road runs parallel with the line for almost half a mile, that we quite missed the holy well alongside. Thinking it a pity not to pay our respects, we went back and without any great difficulty found Tobarparthanane, for a large tree marks the place. A pattern was formerly held here, and stations performed on 24 August, but even in 1839, when John O'Donovan visited it, organised devotions had ceased, and since then, together with the majority of other holy wells, it has almost entirely lost its attraction to other forms of public devotion.

Willbrook school, a few hundred yards farther on, has also been a victim of social and demographic change, for in the summer of 1988 it finally closed its door to pupils, having served the community for exactly 103 years. A glance at its enrolment figures down the decades gives a fair idea of how rural parishes like this have suffered during the past century. From a high of 81 children in 1919, there was an almost uninterrupted decline until its closure, when there were fewer than ten pupils on the rolls. A similar fate has been the lot of most of the other small country schools in the area, among them Ballykinnacorra, Cahersherkin, Kells, Gortbofarna and Inchovea (in which Pat Lenihan, grandfather of Tánaiste Brian Lenihan, taught).

The line passes 10 feet beneath the level of the road here, and luckily we remained on it. If we had taken to the highway we would have missed one of the most beautiful little cascades I have ever seen. High and narrow, a miniature version of the Angel Falls, it pours into a mossy pool and from there rushes off through a narrow cleft to some secret destination – a startling contrast to what follows. For, a few steps away, a large modern development has clawed out a whole chunk of the hill and levelled it onto the line to make a flat enclosure. To one side is the house that was once Willbrook Station, but nothing could be further from a railway-style dwelling than this.

Horses were being exercised as we pulled ourselves between the strands of the boundary fence, but we were made welcome and given permission to look around. We did look, even searched, but the old Willbrook is no more. We crossed the road, hoping to recognise it from a different perspective, but though we had seen old photographs

Willbrook, 1953. (Photo: Irish Railway Record Society, no. 10639)

of the station in its working days, we could not reconcile this newly renovated two-storey building with any of them.

Only the facts and statistics remain: Willbrook Halt. 11¾ miles from Ennis. Opened for traffic in 1888 with an up platform. Like Ruan, closed ten years later. Reopened 1904. Closed once more 1921. Finally reopened 1929. Served as a halt thereafter until the demise of the whole system. Built on a gradient of 1/59, it, like Newtown, was a severe test of steam locomotives hauling down trains fully laden, but the later diesel engines took it in their stride.

With such details must a visitor console himself today.

There was little more that we could do but seek out our car at Corofin, and that we did sombrely, accompanied from the direction of Boola Bridge by the rasping of a chainsaw, that most familiar music of the Irish countryside now that the corncrake has been seen off.

Day 5

Willbrook to Ennistymon Station

From Willbrook Halt to Ennistymon Station is roughly 7 miles, and for the first 2½ miles, to the site of Clouna Halt, good progress can be made even though it is a boggy valley all along here. But then, until Monreal crossing is reached over 2 miles farther on, the going is much tougher. This is the very centre of Clare, the forgotten heartland of the county. Few tourists ever see this place, and since the passing of the West Clare few Clare people, either. It is in the main a featureless land; drab, lonely and windswept. Well might the ancient manuscripts refer to it as the 'Breintir' (Bréan Ithir: foul land). All this being said, it seems ironic that the best-preserved portion of the line to be found anywhere along its 54-mile length should occur here, extending westward for over a mile from Toloughlahan Bridge. One soon enough comes to see why: the Department of Forestry is using it as a roadway to serve a large, newly established plantation. And so it is that where crowds of people once gathered to be collected for trips to Ennis, Lahinch or wherever, only a scatter of houses now remains occupied and trees grow where people reared families, however poorly. From Monreal, there is quite a dramatic change in scenery. In the space of 2 miles, the bogland is left behind and the configuration of the landscape becomes typical of west Clare – open, stone-walled, relatively treeless. Weather allowing, it is a journey that can be accomplished comfortably in a brisk day's walking, provided one makes none of the mistakes I made!

The Craggaunboy River is difficult to shake off. From Boola Bridge it stays close to the line for over half a mile and makes two further bridges necessary before it tails off to the south-east towards Knockarradaun and the site of Moyhill Castle. From Willbrook cross, two roads snake westward like the prongs of a tuning fork, one towards Drinagh in the south, the other to Russa in the north. The West Clare wends its course in the valley between them. A few hundred yards from the bridge, one is surrounded by water, though on the left it is audible only, in the form of an impressive-sounding cascade. Too much scrub intervenes to allow a view of it, but even today it is vividly remembered by those who crewed the trains all those years ago, for as well as its distinctive sound it marked the site of the twelfth milepost.

In August and September of 1892 there were a number of close calls at this point when trains were derailed owing to faulty sleepers. No one was injured, but the passengers, once they had made sure that they were unscathed, found time and energy to be annoyed, even disgusted, at the loss of connecting trains to their various destinations. But at least the company learned something from the experience. Shortly after, over 7,000 new sleepers were laid.[1]

Just beyond this, we came to another crossing, but whether a bridge or a cattle-pass we could not tell, since with still, deep water on both sides we were unable to get down to have a closer look. On this, our fifth outing, we had brought all the necessary equipment – wellingtons, balaclavas, anoraks – yet not even these can save one from drowning. So we took no undue risks. The line now runs right through a little hill, and in this cutting we noted the gravelly soil. The builders, in chopping out a way here, met with no solid obstacle. How much more happy they must have been to labour on this section than on the works below Corofin, especially since the pay they received for shovelling was the same as for hacking. Here, though the land is monotonous, they would at least have the satisfaction of seeing progress at the end of a day's drudgery.

A long river-bridge is the next object of note, and the map showed us that the rapid stream flowing diagonally underneath was the upper reaches of the Craggaunboy. We were about to pass into the townland of Knocknagraigue East. In the short distance between the cutting and this bridge, we had felt a sharp fall in ground level, so we presumed we must now be over the heights and beginning the descent to Ennistymon. We were, as it happened, but it was to be nothing as sustained as the climb from Roxton had been. A sharp dip would be succeeded by a long relatively level sweep, and that then again by another dip, as at Russa Bridge. Little wonder that Ennis-bound steam trains could never get up sufficient speed to make a businesslike approach possible.

But then something odd intruded itself: a wall across the line, and a straggle of boulders and stones lying at intervals on the line beyond. But their texture was somehow out of place. They were of red and brown sandstone, and rounded, like river stones. They intrigued us, and made for variety in a place where there was otherwise none, for the low hills and the rushes which were to be our constant companions to Cullenagh Bridge had begun. On one of these hills just south of the line is a name, a beautiful name, too: Lisfarbegnagommaun – the fort of the small man of the hurleys. Presumably the reference is to one of the Good People, for they were very given to hurling matches, the fairies of Clare. A pity it is, though, that the fort is no longer there; Clare hurling could badly do with players of the calibre of the fierce little inhabitants of places like this!

The marks of other fierce inhabitants are also to be seen in this uninviting boundary land between Knocknagraigue and Tullagroe, but there is nothing otherworldly about these, the faint outlines of potato ridges etched on the inhospitable slopes. Hard and hungry times they were, surely, that forced people to avail themselves of land such as this for their staple diet, and a true saying it is that the two traces hardest to remove from the ground are a *claíochán* and the print of potato ridges.[2]

The line itself presents only the normal difficulties here, and none are formidable enough to distress the lively walker. Another cattle-pass, facing into the stream on the right, provides a welcome distraction, but since there are no parapets, precautions have been taken and both ends are wired off. But there is no problem in passing.

A map consultation showed that here we were exactly midway between Willbrook and Lough Nagowan.

Many of the embankments on the West Clare are impressive, but only occasionally does one call for special mention, either because of its height or for some other unusual feature. I would not omit the final raised section in Knocknagraigue from this latter category. The top may be worn down into a rounded, humped outline by generations of cattle, but the cut-stone facing on its northern side – a protection against the action of the stream – is enough to set it apart from many others of much more majestic aspect. Not until the causeway leading to Moyasta river-bridge does one again see a similar design, in fact.

We had yet to meet, or even see, anyone on our travels that morning, so it was with some relief that we picked out the humped figure of an old woman herding cattle in a field to our left. I had to ask all our questions at the top of my voice across the breadth of the field. In like manner she confirmed where we now were: Knocknagraigue, though she gave the word its Irish pronunciation, Cnoc na Gráige. 'An' when ye cross that bridge beyond, ye'll be in Torlahan.' Monreal was 4 or 5 miles away, she yelled, and though we were comforted to know so much, we decided to forget completely about it for the moment. From harsh experience, we thought it better to make no firm plans until we could see for ourselves what conditions were like. With a wave in lieu of thanks, we soldiered on.

'The bridge beyond' was a mere two fields away and beautifully approached by an elegant embankment. Both ends are securely fenced and the reason is obvious, for even though the metal parapets are intact, they are low, and any creature, human or animal, which fell from either side would have little chance of picking itself up intact from the river bed below. This, the final bridge over the Craggaunboy River, is, given the surroundings, a bold structure, and has attracted the attention of more than one artist.[3] But it was not for its aesthetic qualities that it held a special place in the affections of railwaymen, especially in steam days. Rather was it a landmark, the point at which crews of both up and down trains could breathe easy, knowing that the worst of their climb was over. During the Emergency, particularly when turf fuelled the engines, firemen looked forward to Torlahan since from here on their job became considerably easier on the down-hill run. In those years, a full wagon of turf was carried behind the bunker and there was a 'turf boy' (though he might be sixty years of age!) to help the fireman; otherwise he would have been worked half to death, so great was the quantity of turf burned (a laden train would require up to six bunkers of turf from this bridge to Ennis, a distance of only 12½ miles). Strictly speaking, the regulations forbade anyone to ride in this turf wagon, but a blind eye was, of course, turned in order that the trains might continue to function. That they did so cannot be denied, even if sometimes the proclamations of excellence sounded just a bit forced. Take this report of 1942: 'There is one pas-senger train each day from Kilkee to Ennis and another from Ennis to Kilkee. Both are largely availed of and everyone speaks highly of the comfort they experience and the assurances they receive from the various officials along the line that they will reach their destination in good time.'[4] The officials, no doubt, meant well, but the inescapable fact was that the engines were designed to function best on coal, and so delays were inevitable since even good-quality turf could not be guaranteed. One crewman well remembers that when the train stopped here, both himself and the fireman had to hike off into the bog in search of bog deal and other combustibles.[5] Percy French, it seems, told no more than the truth, after all!

There is scarcely an embankment off the bridge, so quickly does the land rise. But there is something else to catch the attention: a bare, grassless way ahead for as far as the eye can see – a walker's paradise. It took us some time to pick out the reason for this: little newly planted trees, only inches high. More visible were the flooded drainage channels glinting into the distance. They will not be long visible, for in a very few years this will be a forest road. One's view along here is as unimpeded as the way, and at the top of a gradual rise at least a quarter-mile long, invested with all the oddness of some

eighteenth-century folly, sits the most curious bridge I have ever
seen. Square-opened, it seems to be a mixture of architectural styles
from different periods, for the abutments are of cut stone whereas the
deck is of steel and mass concrete. It was probably once completely
stone-built and arched, but altered when the railway closed, in order
to facilitate traffic on the road above. It is certainly of no special
merit in itself, but on its little hilltop, to one approaching from either
side, it looks peculiarly impressive and much higher than it actually
is. Directly south of the short cutting which this span straddles is
Lough Nagowan. It lies in a boggy hollow between two hills, but is
quite featureless. Whether its name refers to blacksmiths, kingfishers
or calves is a moot point – and one better left to the comfort of a
well-stocked study.

The condition of the line for over a mile straight ahead, all through
the townland of Loughnagowan, leaves nothing to be desired, except
that there might be rails on it, and walking here with nothing to
distract us from the task in hand, we were at leisure to complain
– mainly about how disastrously shortsighted a policy it was to dis-
pose of the line piecemeal, as was done in 1962 and after. What an
excellent amenity it would now be as a walkway or cycle-route, at a
time when the last thing many tourists want, especially those from
crowded Europe, is the annoyance of travelling on roads that are both
overburdened and badly surfaced. *They* would have few complaints
about the monotony of the silent rushy valleys of mid-Clare. Nor
had we, to tell the truth. This was a bonus, and we knew it. In fact,
some form of transport would have been very welcome here; one of
the bogies used by the per-way gangs, for instance. Every gang was
supplied with one – for transporting gravel, ballast, ash and so on, up
to a weight of 5 tons – but the standard model, made at headquarters
in Limerick in CIÉ days, was regarded as too heavy and was usually modified by the various gangs to suit their own conditions. The
Corofin gangs were envied all along the line; they possessed almost
racing models, and so light was the bodywork that they rarely had
to get off to push uphill. A well co-ordinated gang, their boots hitting the sleepers all together, could reach speeds in excess of those

permitted to the trains. 'Footing it', as this was known, was a means of propulsion even more efficient than the bicycle. But great care had to be taken, especially at curves and when a heavy load was on board. There were some narrow escapes, inevitably, such as the one near Russa Bridge when three men were caught by an unexpected goods' train and were unable to manhandle the load off the chassis in time. The engine, no. 6T, one of the Tralee–Dingle models, was damaged in the resulting accident, but who back at headquarters was to say that a rock had not fallen from a cutting-face and done the deed!

That there were so few derailments during the War of Independence and civil war was due in no small way to these little vehicles, which allowed the gangs to do a quick survey of their individual sections each morning before trains passed; thus, even though the Volunteers or 'Irregulars' might take out sleepers or bolts at night, the loss was likely to be discovered first thing in the morning and remedial action taken. Why did those whose nocturnal efforts were being thwarted by conscientious workers not resort to intimidation? It seems remarkable, but few accounts of such behaviour have ever been reported.

A mile to the south, in the parish of Inagh, is the much ruined Bohneill Castle, and a little way off Cloch an Airgid, under which treasure is reputed to be buried; hence the name. On the stone are scratched letters and numbers, including the date 1614, but far from being any kind of directions to the 'treasure', T.J. Westropp, eminent investigator of such matters, declared them to be no more than the scribblings of a member of the O'Neill family in the reign of James I.[6]

When at last the clear forestry road ended, we knew we were in for tougher times, but for a short distance farther we were still able to make good headway, though with a spongy growth underfoot now. The deterioration was rapid thereafter, culminating in a section where the line has disappeared entirely and only a huge mound of bog deal sat in our way. How remarkable that trees of their girth should have grown here once, where only stunted conifers now cling precariously to life.

Two fences in quick succession saw us to an area of some human activity. The line had surfaced again, too, and moreover was wide

– about 30 feet. This, together with a farmhouse, a pair of crossing gates, a little grove of trees, a manure heap and an old Pierce hay rake showing its spikes like a skeletal ribcage, assured us that this was a place of no little importance! In fact, it was Clooney Halt (or Clouna, as it was more commonly known), 14 miles from Ennis, and opened as a stopping point in May 1954. Today, it may seem that this whole side of country is devoid of all but a scanty population, but the memories of better days here still remain fresh in the minds of people by no means old. They can recall the crowds that would gather here, especially on Sundays, to travel to hurling matches or to the seaside – 5/9d would bring one to Limerick and home, while the return fare to Ennistymon was 1/6d.

There probably was never very much to see at Clouna, even when trains stopped here; consequently, we made no delay, only launched ahead into rough ground, where the surface had been removed in chunks, no doubt for road surfacing somewhere. A grove of conifers blocks off the way at this point, and their considerable size suggests that they must have been planted very soon after the railway's closure. And if the sight did nothing much to cheer us, the herd of very contented-looking cattle sheltering there seemed quite happy with their lot.

Turf banks approach to within arm's length of the line here; a great temptation during the lean war years, doubtless, though they were probably diligently guarded. In fact, one is never for a moment allowed to forget turf and bog in this district, for gradually the line takes on the characteristics of the surrounding land, and in places one would have difficulty imagining that trains could ever have ventured this way. As if overflowing from its own place, the bogland has begun to claim even this solidly compacted foundation for itself once more, and the springy moss at least 6-inches thick beneath our feet was proof conclusive that bog does grow, and quickly when the conditions are right. But this is not the only kind of obliteration the line has suffered in the mile between Clouna and the site of the fifteenth milepost, near Russa Bridge. Trenches have been dug across it, and more reclamation has taken its toll for substantial distances. Without difficulty, we wandered as at Ballykinnacorra and Liscullaun. This time, however, fortune saw fit to favour us: at one of the large drains blocking our way we noticed traces of stonework at water level – the remnants of a culvert's foundations. Only by such little clues is it possible to counteract the disorientating effects of large, open ranges of featureless land.

More by chance than design, we found the next culvert a quarter of a mile off. This was one of the few arched culverts we had come upon, but the top of the arch was gone, leaving no more than the spandrels. What a pity that people nowadays are exposed to so little of the stonemason's art; no one who had seen the craft involved in shaping these stones to fit together so precisely could lightly destroy such perfection of design, even if it were no longer serving a practical use. As we struggled up on to the high ground on the far side of the stream, something else caught our eye: a broken, rusting wheel and axle lying in the stream bed nearby. We could hardly ignore it. So little metal debris had we found so far that every piece we treated like so much treasure. This one, in a way, was a treasure. From descriptions we had heard of the bogies, we were sure this must be part of one. It was tempting to think of this as a remnant of the bogie that had collided with no. 6T engine all that time ago. In any case, it was to us an affirmation of the value of all the stories we had listened to and an encouragement to go on at all costs.

We needed that encouragement just then because we were to see no more of the line until we stood on Russa Bridge. It has vanished into a chaos of swamp, bushes and trenches. At a low wind-swept farmhouse we sought help, but the only sound was the wind mut-tering through the branches of a grove overhead – that, and our own footsteps. In a second yard round a turn of the boreen we were brought to a halt with a start; watching us from a gateway, an old woman stood, still as a statue. She was even more shocked than we, and frightened, too, though she did her best to hide it. Our apologies seemed to put her somewhat more at ease, and we learned that we were in the townland of Monreal – had been, in fact, since the place at which we found the wheel. She could tell us that Ennistymon was still 4 miles away, but little else, and nothing about Clouna or Monreal Halts.

We did not attempt the valley floor again but kept to the boreen leading to the nearest road. As we moved parallel to where we knew the line must be we stopped several times in hopes of catching even the least glimpse, but there was nothing. But in guiding us at least to Russa Bridge, our map served us well. From this miserable vantage-point we gazed back in the direction we had come, and picked out the faint imprint of the line through the rushy lowlands. We were glad that we had abandoned it when we did. Had we persisted we would now be standing in saturated wellingtons, with a long journey still to go to Ennistymon. The feeling that we might yet come in bodily contact with water was not allayed by what we saw in the cutting beneath the bridge: a veritable river, and long water-grass beckoning to us most alluringly. We did not take kindly to the invitation, but what else were we to do? As if to help us make up our minds, a cold, sleety rain began to fall and, truly, all that decided us to go on then was the notion that as we were about to get wet and frozen in any case we might as well be seeing a bit of the countryside rather than cringing somewhere under a bush. Balaclavas down, we made our way to the level of the line, well away from the cutting, but even this simple operation nearly cost us our lives, for we were halfway into a quaking morass, surrounded by exotic, chest-high rushes before we realised the danger. Every step through this shivering, sucking ooze was heart-stopping for me. I can only guess what it felt like for a twelve-year-old, but his face told me all I didn't want to know. We survived, though, and his pride knew no bounds as he sat and cleaned his wellies with fists of grass by the side of the line.

If we had calmly unpacked fishing rods then and begun to fish, no one would have thought us mad. The stream of water that rushed down here and towards the west would have comfortably accommodated a shoal of salmon. Unfortunately, we were also heading westward but without the advantage of being in a position to swim. But first we rested, to allow our swamp fright to subside and to consider Russa Bridge. Like the bridge at Loughnagowan, it has been tampered with, and drastically. But this was most necessary, it seems, for so humpbacked was it that even a Morris Minor could not negotiate it without getting caught amidships. The Volunteers tried to alter its profile in 1920, but they made the elementary mistake of trying to blow it down instead of up. The County Council made no such mistake; at its demolition, all the JCB driver had to do was raise his bucket underneath the arch and the whole thing collapsed. As usual, the rebuilt article is not pretty, but it is at least functional. A story is still told that the bridge was built down on bog, and since no solid foundation could be found, piles had to be driven and the stonework raised on them. It is said that the north-eastern corner of the bridge is still out of line with the others today because of this.

We did not verify this, only gathered ourselves for the down-stream trek. The very swiftness of the flow was a sure indicator of a substantial hill here – as it should, with gradients ranging from 1/50 to 1/70. It was this hill that gave so much trouble to the 0–6–0T locomotives when hauling laden trains up from Kilrush. As well as the engine in front, a second engine often pushed from behind until 'the top of Russa' was reached, at which point the driver of the lead-ing loco would whistle – a signal to the man behind that the worst was over and that he could proceed from there under his own steam. This procedure was necessary since no 'double-heading' (coupling of two locos in front) was permitted on the West Clare owing to the nature of the buffers with which the trains were equipped.[7]

The one advantage of the strong current was that it kept clear a channel in the all-smothering weeds, so we could at least be sure of what we were stepping into. But though the underfoot was solid we had to keep alert for holes. A single stumble would have meant a quick end to our excursion, and the waste of much of a day. With a water depth of over a foot and on such a hill it is little wonder that we found the current pressing strongly behind us. It brought vividly to my thoughts what I had heard of the driver of a cattle-train who, seeing that his water supply was low and that he could not possibly hope to get over Russa, decided to uncouple the laden wagons and leave them braked while he took the engine on to Corofin for water.

While he was gone, the brakes on the van failed and the wagons rolled back towards Ennistymon, gathering speed as they went. The guard, in a panic, was about to jump but was persuaded by a companion that to do so would be suicide. At last, they came to a halt within sight of Ennistymon, and in the station they could see the passenger train on the point of pulling out, it being presumed that they had cleared the section. Their engine soon returned from Corofin and they continued on their way, but it had been a close thing.

At the foot of the steep hill south-west of Russa Bridge we found ourselves in a swamp which defied all our efforts to get through it. We took to the low hill alongside, but even this was half mire.

We slithered on, now on the edge of a cutting, now wading through mud again, but all movement was finally stopped by a vicious-looking hedge. It was almost to be my Waterloo. We searched for a weak spot and found it at last: an ash tree whose branches were climbable. Getting up was easy, but getting down! While testing a branch which I might use to launch myself into the next field, my foot slipped, and in a mad flurry of curses and cracking timber, I was dumped into 2 feet of water at the bottom of a concealed drain. So icy was it that I was up and out before damage had even registered, but damage there was: coat and trousers saturated, maps and other papers muddied and wet. But no cuts or sprains, at least. It could have been worse. And in any case the journey back was not an option. The way ahead could hardly be worse. So we pressed on, letting the wind dry what it might. Only our innocence was greater than our ignorance, and just as well. Had we known then that it would take us the best part of an hour to travel the few hundred remaining yards to Monreal Halt, we would willingly have swam back up Russa hill, the current notwithstanding.

Rarely have I seen land so bare and woebegone as that which greeted us farther down the valley. Rarely have I experienced jungle so impenetrable as that which succeeded it. How such a dense knot of foliage could come to thrive in terrain so bleak is still beyond my understanding. We could not get through it, try as we might, and even to work our way round it almost failed us. Somewhere along here, on 3 February 1888, an attempt was made to derail the evening train to Miltown Malbay. A large rock, favourite weapon of the would-be derailer, was left on the line, and though it did some damage to the engine, no one was hurt. The newspaper report on the incident implied that jealousy of the crossing-keeper and a desire to get his job were at the root of the matter, but nothing was proved.[8]

At the valley bottom things at last began to look up, for at the far side of a stream a house and a road of some kind were now visible. Fortunately, before climbing onto it we took the precaution of removing our balaclavas. Just as well, for at the cottage door an old woman stood considering us. She had been following our movements across the valley for some time, she said, and had been about to lock the door, thinking we were 'The Boys'. If truth be told, I was feeling very foolish indeed as I stood there, still wet from my recent crash-landing. Sharp lady that she was, she noticed my predicament and invited us in, answering questions and asking others as she went. Nothing would do her but that I should dry my coat, at the very least, to the fire while she made the tea, and I had no argument with that. She was amazed to learn what direction we had come from. She well knew what the way was like at this time of year. 'Well, how did ye come down that way? 'Tis a wonder but ye were swallowed,' was her succinct analysis of our folly. But she was a mine of knowledge about the railway and the surrounding countryside, having lived here for forty-five years. This is Monreal crossing, she confirmed, 15¾ miles from Ennis, and she remembered well when it was opened as a halt: in November 1952, shortly after the coming of the diesel railcars. It is a place of many boundaries, she said: the townlands of Monreal and Cullenagh meet here, as do the parishes of Rath and Clooney. But more importantly, the rivulet which we had so lately crossed separates the dioceses of Killaloe and Kilfenora. She could show us the remains of various old roads, too, if we had a mind to delay, but first things first: tea and thick doorsteps of bread and jam, 'to put a bit of life in ye'.

While we ate we observed. Nothing had changed in this little kitchen in probably forty years. The flagged floor, the old-fashioned high hob, the smoked paintwork of the dresser, the flitch of home-cure bacon, all bore testimony to a style of living that has all but passed away. The woman herself, talking to us as though we were long acquainted, represented, it seems to me, a kind of trust and hospitality alien to most city and town dwellers and, alas, to a growing number of those now living in rural areas. 'There's no *cuaird* in the times that are there now,' was her wistful verdict on modernity, and it is difficult not to see the ebbing of old customs in tandem with the ruin of the West Clare as two symptoms of a change in Ireland that has been all-embracing though not all-beneficial.[9]

This cottage, she informed us, is not as old as the railway itself. There was only a hut at first, a sort of sentry box for a part-time watchman, but close to the turn of the century a man returning home from Ennistymon at night was killed here by a train, so this dwelling was then built to accommodate a permanent gatekeeper. Her information was quite correct, as I later found when I consulted newspapers of the time. The man in question was killed here on the night of 17 November 1901, and discovered the following morning by the driver of the early train, none other than the Michael O'Loughlin of Newtown-crossing fame (see p. 95).[10]

Talk wandered back again to the terrible condition of the line today. She was not in the least surprised at our description of it, since it gave a gang of men permanent employment just to keep the 'back drains' open along every 4 miles of track. This was especially necessary in boggy areas like Clouna, speaking of which she at once recalled an incident from the Troubles related to that very bog. Martin Devitt, a Volunteer from Clouna, was shot dead near Mount Callan while engaged in ambushing an RIC patrol. His friends managed to drag his body away from the scene and bring it by night to a temporary resting place in 'the bog that's down on the door o' the track' at Russa Bridge, so that he could be buried in the graveyard of his native place. But a spy informed the police, who came by train to search the bog. The coffin, however, had been removed and buried safely the previous night by Devitt's friends.[11]

Later in that same year of turmoil, 1920, this locality was to see more action when the Mid-Clare Flying Column ambushed a military convoy near here on 18 December, inflicting some casualties and provoking the usual reprisals.[12]

But it is not only for its role in the Troubles that Monreal is noted. In the nineteenth century the strong sense of Irishness of the district was well represented by the O'Looney family, particularly by Brian O'Looney (1828–1901), Irish scholar, expert in manuscripts and friend of William Smith O'Brien of Young Ireland. Throughout a long literary and academic career, he laboured tirelessly to promote a new, proud Ireland based on the achievements of the past, and this work was carried on by his nephew Liam.

The old-fashioned kitchen we sat in also played its part, for it was in this very room that the young Patrick Hillery, future president of Ireland, received his silver *fáinne* from Maurice Mullins, husband of a sister of Liam O'Looney and himself a dedicated promoter of the Irish language for Conradh na Gaeilge.

Our visit had been both warming and interesting. We could have asked for nothing more, and we were truly sorry to leave, but we still hoped to get to Ennistymon Station, if at all possible. As we prepared to move off I caught sight of something odd on her old black-metal gate: Gaelic lettering. It was, in fact, a painted-over railway sign. She was still giving us advice and directions: 'The next townland is Cullenagh, and at the bridge over the Inagh River ye'll be in Ahardrue. After that the next cottage is at the main Ennis road at Knockdrummagh.' How could we go wrong after that?

We tore ourselves away from this generous woman and her tiny and historic home, ready to face the worst. But since the line here is now the access road to the cottage, all is clear and our only obstacle was the sharp wind which had suddenly sprung up while we were indoors. A noble valley now lay below us on the left, with the best view we had had in a long time, but the embankment here is high, completely without protection, so we had trouble enough remaining upright in the whipping gusts. We saw some way ahead a cutting, and hurried towards its shelter, but before reaching it we had to cross a high cattle-pass. The wind made it too dangerous to venture close to the edges for a better look, but it seemed impressive, though vulnerable, too. This was quickly spotted during the Troubles, for it was blown up in one of those attacks to which the railway was so exposed.

Rush Bridge it was called, so far as I can determine, and here was the site of the sixteenth milepost. It was pointless to shelter long in the cutting as the wind seemed to be ever-strengthening. Or perhaps it was that we were in a more exposed place than any heretofore. Whatever it was, by the time we began walking the lofty embankment on to Cullenagh Bridge we were literally in danger of being blown away. A greater change from the weather of an hour before cannot be imagined.

Both ends of the bridge were fenced securely, and since it would have been folly to walk the parapets in such conditions we climbed down the 25 feet to the road, from where a far better view was to be had and a crossing made in safety. After this experience of the power of a less than storm-force wind on the exposed embankment we quite believed the account we had heard of a derailment here. It occurred in February 1910, a time of violent gales over the west in general. The guard's van of the 8.30 a.m train had barely cleared the bridge when it was caught broadside by a vicious squall, and two carriages and three wagons were blown off the track when the couplings snapped.

Keith at Cullenagh Bridge, 13 February 1989.

However, the engine and other wagons remained on the line. Even though one of the two stricken carriages slipped the whole way to the foot of the steep slope, all passengers escaped injury except a prisoner being carried under police escort to the petty sessions at Miltown. A splinter of wood injured his foot, but not seriously.[13] A local man, John Hogan, was at breakfast nearby when he witnessed what had happened. He snatched a bottle of holy water and ran to the scene, but there was no need for the water, though he did help in the rescuing of passengers from their dangerous predicament.

The bridge, inevitably, was also the target of an explosives attack during the Troubles, but the charge only partly detonated and no serious damage was done. Today, the metal deck remains and the whole structure is an eloquent reminder of the West Clare to every motorist who passes.

Apart from little intervals of calm as we walked through several muddy cuttings, we had to face the full blast of the wind for over half a mile until we reached Ahardrue Bridge. For in the short distance since Monreal cottage, there had been an almost magical change in the landscape. Gone were the rushes, bogland and sheltering hills; here all was wide-open spaces and well-cared-for fields.

The second cutting after Cullenagh Bridge is driven through rock, notable if only because it is the first such since Applevale. Just beyond this we saw another first: one of the drystone walls so typical of west Clare, built of thin, finely shaped, angular blocks. All the while, traffic roared by just south of us on the main road, while beyond that again the Inagh (or Cullenagh) River meandered towards Ennistymon and Liscannor Bay.

At Ahardrue there should have been three bridges, but we could be sure of only two: those carrying the roads over the lovely wooded river valley north and south of the railway. If there is a railway bridge, it is not visible to a walker on the high embankment. Water we could hear, certainly, far below us, and we concluded that there must be some kind of huge culvert to carry this sizeable tributary of the Inagh/Cullenagh. But as to its design or width we could only surmise for it was hidden under a thick screen of branches. Passing here took us into the townland of Knockdrummagh South. From this point to where it crosses the Ennis road at Knockdrummagh level crossing, the line temporarily takes on a different aspect again, becoming much less open. At one particular set of accommodation gates just yards from the site of the seventeenth milepost we could hardly believe what we were seeing: what looked like a river flowing in one gate, across the line, and out another. No denying it, that was a watery piece of Ireland!

But an escape route was to hand. Road and railway swing so closely together here that they actually meet, so we took an easy option to get us past the worst of the flooding. Without more bother we reached the main road, though not entirely by the line, for a house has been newly built on it, 200 yards from Knockdrummagh no. 1 crossing.

The crossing cottage is still here, not noticeably altered, but much else has changed. A county council compound now occupies a large lay-by close at hand, the road has been extensively widened, and new houses form a little hamlet, some of them built on the line itself. It was pointless even to try to imagine what this crossing was formerly

Knockdrummagh no. 1 crossing. (Photo: Mrs. Collins, Knockdrummagh)

like. Instead, we crossed the road and began our search for any recognisable traces of the no. 2 crossing on the western side. Situated
a mere hundred yards from no. 1, it should have been easy to find.
Opposite Knockdrummagh crossroads we knew we should be at the
right place, but there was only a little boreen leading down to a ford
in the Cullenagh. In the absence of either line or crossing site we had
to conclude that in the process of widening this part of the road, the
council either removed the line, crossing included, or else used it as
part of the new road foundation. Whatever the reason, it was gone, so
we struck out along the road, past more new houses, hoping to see it
in the fields at our left. Keith was first to spot what we were looking
for, just past the houses, and after a spirited struggle over a high
fence we were on course for the first cutting in the townland of Glen
South. It is a one-sided affair in that a chunk was chopped out of a
little hillside to allow the line passage. We were to see many more of
these drumlin-like shapes in the next mile or two, for they are one of
the most notable land features of Ennistymon and its environs.

Seven hundred yards or so away, to our delight, we could see Glen
Castle, and at last we knew our exact location, having passed by it
many times on the road into the town. With nothing to hinder us on
this clear stretch, we shortly came to the point where the Cullenagh
meanders to within 30 yards of the line, and from this raised position
we had a clearer view of it than any yet. It is a substantial waterway
now, at least 30-feet wide, a formidable obstacle to anyone attempting
a crossing. Thankfully, we had no need to, for the only point at which
the railway crosses is at the bridge beyond Ennistymon Station.

As smooth as a lawn, the embankment sweeps forward, its attrac-
tiveness added to by the ruin of the castle overlooking it. What a
fine walkway it would make for the people of the town, was our first
reaction. But why was the grass untrodden? No answer immediately
suggested itself. For that we had to wait until we came to Castle
Hill and the location of the eighteenth milepost. For the moment
we contented ourselves with examining a well-preserved cattle-pass
insofar as we were able from a height of over 12 feet.

Just as suddenly as it approaches the line, the river now snakes away again, almost at a right angle to its previous direction, its near bank marred by some kind of spoil-heaps. On the far side, some way downstream, stands Woodmount House, former home of the Lysaghts, who owned the whole townland. During the latter part of the eighteenth century they seem to have been somewhat unpopular, for the house was attacked on a number of occasions. In 1799 the assailants cut down 4,000 trees on the estate while the helpless owner was forced to look on.[14] The house still stands, uninhabited, looking for all the world as if part of it has been chopped off – which indeed it may have been, since a fire is known to have destroyed a portion of it while the building was still quite new.

The run-up to the castle is at field level and clear, but at Castle Hill all is not as it should be. Our map showed a deep cutting here, directly under the western side of the castle, but our path was solidly blocked by a huge wall of rubble. It took us some minutes to fully take in the prospect – Glen, or Blackwell's, cutting, all 20-feet deep of it, had been entirely filled in. Our only way forward was to climb, and since a close-up view of the castle seemed desirable we went that way. But the sight before us when we got to the top of the former cutting was such that we forgot about our objective for the moment. A whole massive chunk of the western side of Castle Hill was gone, and the cutting, which once ran the full length of the hill, had been wholly obliterated, leaving the land, ironically enough, much as it must have looked before ever the railway came this way. Round about lie piers and other rubble of demolished houses, obviously brought here as fill.

To look down at either end of what was the cutting is to gaze into the semblance of a disused quarry, for the water, prevented from flowing, has collected here in stagnant pools. It seems an inglorious end to what was at one time a considerable engineering achieve-ment. Equally inglorious has been the fate of Glen Castle, which directly overlooking the line now mutely bears witness to the ruin of its younger companion in woe. Built in the sixteenth century as an O'Brien stronghold and still in the possession of Sir Donel O'Brien in 1584, it now stands like a rotten molar, a fragment merely, with no interesting features remaining. Yet up to the early nineteenth century it seems to have been in a good state of repair, since tradition has it that in 1800 a girl from Church Hill named Brody climbed to the top of its walls and placed a stone at each of the four corners. There are other stories, too, though few of them now remembered. In one, an enchanted hare is said to guard a pot of gold buried near the old walls, and despite repeated efforts to capture him, he is still free and the gold undisturbed. Another tells of an underground passage connecting this castle with others in Dough, Liscannor and Cill Stuifin. But the most colourful – and human – of all is surely the tale of the Druid who, driven to desperation by his wife's nagging, flew away from her one day, carrying half of his castle on his back to Glen, the other half remaining with his wife at the home place, Shallee, in Kilnamona, 7 miles away. And of the truth of the story there can be no doubt! After all, the proof is there on Castle Hill for anyone to see, and at Shallee, too!

From the castle, much of the town can clearly be viewed in all its attractive haphazardness, but since the whole area consists of eggs-in-basket type topography we knew we would have other opportunities to see it at closer range, so we made no delay, only climbed down along the rubble to ground level. The going is not easy here in this low, waterlogged corner, but at least the foundation underfoot is still solid. On the left, across the river, is an old woollen mill, but on this side the line finally disappears after several small interruptions. But in spite of this clearance, there is no possibility of losing its course since the stone-arched access bridge to the station is directly ahead. This, Blackwell's Bridge, carries the driveway to Glen Cottage, which is still owned by the same family.

We raced each other to get to the road, delighted to have reached our day's destination at last. But our rejoicing was somewhat premature, as we realised when we looked northward from the bridge to where the station should have been. It wasn't. What greeted us was a new Bord Telecom building and extensive depot. The station yard is no more. So complete has been the transformation that a stranger would find few clues to tell him that this was once a main station of the West Clare system and the second block-post on the line.

We approached the rear of the high perimeter fence down a slope from the bridge, and looking back saw how much disturbed the lie of the land had been, for now the bridge is choked with earth to within 3 feet of the keystone of the arch. Ironically, much of the rubble used to fill Glen cutting came from this very site. Walking along the field at the rear of Telecom, we might look through the fence, but how could we visualise the hustle and bustle of this place in those far-off days when the town was famous for its cattle fairs and butter market? All was silent as we passed. It matters little now that the station-house was built on the up side, that it had two platforms, loading bank, goods' store, a water tank of 2,860 gallons' capacity and many sidings. Too much has vanished.

Disappointed that there was not more to see, we changed our field of enquiry out on to the street. A lucky change it was, too, for no sooner had we passed the Telecom premises than we saw unmistakable stonework. It was the goods' shed, still in fair condition and in process of being restored. The station-house it was, though, that claimed all our attention – or rather, what used to be the station-house, since so resplendently has it been refurbished and added to that one would hardly recognise it. It has been extended back onto the line, and further down the street a dispensary has been built in a similar position, so it is highly unlikely that there will ever again be a clear run through Ennistymon.

A few yards from the dispensary, on the up side, stands a little cut-stone structure akin to a blockhouse. This was the pump house, and though it is now open to the elements, part of the metal hand-pump is still inside. The source of the water for the steam trains was a gravity flow from a reservoir on Beakey's Mountain, some way from the town. But in very dry weather this was often inadequate, and men would be detailed to this little house to hand-pump water from the river into the tank over their heads. One old hand recalls those days: 'Well, the drier the summer'd come the better we'd like it. We used love to be in there. An' often we'd keep pumping when there was plenty water in the tank.' Under cover in the pump house they could

Ennistymon Station, 1953; Glen Castle and Blackwell's Bridge in the background. (Photo: Irish Railway Record Society, no. 10432)

Engine 1C (formerly the Kilrush) at Ennistymon Station. (Photo: Irish Railway Record Society, no. 10096)

smoke and talk to their hearts' content, and two small square holes in
the walls facing the station and the bridge allowed them to keep an
eye out for the supervisor. The holes are still there today.

Right here probably began the insignificant incident that was to
give the whole of the West Clare Railway a fame out of all proportion
to its just deserts. On 10 August 1896 the 12.40 p.m train from Ennis
to Kilkee, hauled by the new 2–6–2T engine no. 8, *Lisdoonvarna,*
took water here at Ennistymon. But weeds in the water choked the
boiler, and by Lahinch the driver, Michael O'Loughlin, found that
he was having trouble proceeding. He did manage, however, to get
as far as Miltown Malbay, but refused to go further for fear of an
explosion. Another engine, the older 0–6–0T loco no. 4, *Besborough,*
was procured to haul the disabled train to Kilkee, but there was a
long delay, and final destination was not reached until 8.25 p.m.[15]
This unforeseen though irritating delay would probably have been
speedily forgotten by the irate passengers but for one complicating
factor: one of those passengers was a certain Percy French, on his
way to Kilkee to give a concert at Moore's Hall – at 8.30 p.m. Owing
to the delay to his person and a further delay to his equipment, the
show had to be cancelled with consequent loss to him of takings
and reputation. He sued the West Clare Railway Company for £10
plus costs, and in a celebrated action won his case, providing in the
process 'an hour's entertainment for the court free of charge'.[16] The
company, of course, appealed the decision but again lost, and it was
as a result of the incident that he composed his famous song 'Are Ye
Right There, Michael?'

Indeed, water seems to have loomed large in the preoccupa-
tions of many people in those years. In August 1902, for instance,
Ennistymon District Council members were most perturbed at a
report that the West Clare Company had erected a windmill near
Miltown (presumably to pump water) 'at the cost to ratepayers of
£150'. Up to this the company had been paying £35 per year for a
water supply but now all that would be dispensed with.[17] No doubt
to the detriment of the council's coffers. How little have the concerns
of local politics changed in a century!

We could have gone on, maybe even reached the Workhouse Halt that day, but what was the point of getting there in darkness? We had covered more ground than on any previous outing and with that we were content. Ennistymon and its delights would wait for us. We certainly did not intend to keep them waiting for too long.

Could we but have foreseen how impossibly wearisome that journey back to Willbrook would be, we would willingly have stretched out in the pump house and slept there, no matter how uncomfortably. The hour's wait under a lamp post on the outskirts of town, the end-less and utterly dark Corofin road, the cold sleety rain beginning to fall, the silence: all these I prefer not to recall too vividly. Suffice it to say that on an empty road in mid-Clare on such a night, walking by the place which is officially 'Russa' but known by the locals as Russia, I appreciated for the first time what the long march from Stalingrad must have been like for the exhausted survivors.

Only two bright specks remain with me from that winter's night: the kindness of the young man who eventually drove us back to Willbrook, going out of his way to do so, and the realisation that in getting to Ennistymon we had exceeded all our hopes.

Day 6

Ennistymon Station to Lahinch

In spite of our previous night's misfortunes we were back in Ennistymon the following morning, a Sunday, and already on the move while most people were at church. We crossed the bridge, shivering at the thought of an early-morning plunge – not beyond imagining since there are no parapets. Neither are the ends fenced, which seems rather odd in view of the fact that access is unhindered at both sides. A more dangerous place for animals and children could hardly be imagined. Completed in January 1887, this three-span structure still looks solid despite the scars of age which the deck in particular is beginning to show. Properly maintained, it could be a substantial addition to the town's stock of tourist attractions, not merely because of its associations with the West Clare but also on account of the fine scenic view which it provides of the Cullenagh.

Directly across the river, in Ardnacullia North townland, is a wide cutting from the lip of which there is an excellent view of the northern part of the town. Nearest to hand is Church Hill with its graveyard and the ruins of the Protestant church built by the Rev. James Kenny in 1778. Used as a place of worship for little over half a century, it was replaced in 1831 by the building which now stands in Church Street; yet from a distance it looks much older than it is, and one might easily mistake it for part of some monastic establishment.

A mile farther north is Ennistymon Glebe, built also in the last quarter of the eighteenth century by the same Rev. Kenny, who was a convert from Catholicism. Even at such an early date did a sense of individualism assert itself in this little town, a waywardness which is still very much in evidence today. Walk along Church Street or Parliament Street, or turn on to the Lahinch road, and you cannot fail to notice the old wooden-framed shopfronts which in other towns are but a memory, replaced by gaudy plastic and neon. In fact, all the main streets have changed remarkably little since the days of cattle fairs and the railway, and the town would now seem to be reaping some of the benefits of this, for tourists are attracted by its old-world appearance and it is probably more photographed than any other town in Clare. RTÉ radio's 1986 documentary, *The Burning of Ennistymon*, was careful to highlight this aspect of the place, but as the title states, it has had a more violent past than its quiet streets might today suggest. For the town was attacked by British forces in September 1920, directly after the ambush at Rineen, 5 miles away, and houses were burned and a number of people shot. The night of terror is well remembered in the area, as is the occasion, towards the end of the War of Independence, when the Black and Tans were finally withdrawing and children from the local primary school jeered them as they went. But the young ones reckoned without the ruthlessness of those men; they at once opened fire in the direction of the pupils, wounding several. It was their going-away present to a town that hated them well.

In the matter of the closure of the West Clare, the traders of Ennistymon were among the most vocal critics of the decision. Not that they had always agreed with the way it was run, or anything like that; on the contrary, even in the first months of its operation they made their voices heard, demanding that freight and carriage costs should be reduced, especially in view of the spectacular success of the line.[1] (In its first four months of operation alone, 39,597 passengers were carried, and profits were £1,351 9s 9d).[2] And the business people of the town were not slow to take the company to court in order to obtain redress for inefficient service.[3] Yet, they never forgot what the town owed to the railway, and as if to emphasise this, William ('Big

Bill') Murphy, Fine Gael TD from 1951 to 1967 and a native of the town, always used the service to get to Ennis and on his parliamentary business, when other public representatives preferred to travel privately. On his election posters, too, he was careful to mention the West Clare and to belabour his political foes, Fianna Fáil, with the accusation that they had neglected and belittled it, calling it 'this toy railway.' If any of those critics had walked the huge embankments overlooking the river here in Ennistymon, they would quickly have realised how empty of meaning were their words. From here, there is a spectacular view of the river and town, and with a minimum of alteration a fine riverside walk could be provided, such as has been done farther downstream, alongside the famous falls.

Another hundred yards brought us to what was known to railwaymen as Piodar's Bridge, named after an old man of that nickname who lived nearby. A metal-deck crossing, still securely in place, it is not even much walked on nowadays since on the far side what was the line is a cabbage garden. But the graffiti artists have been at work on the metal parapets: 'Sid Vicious RIP. Bobby Sands RIP'. Strange bedfellows, indeed!

There is no going farther here. Many new houses have been built in the area once known as the Bog Line, and even in such a confined area we could not locate the cutting and the bridge which carried the road over the railway until we asked directions. A plot of waste ground behind a concrete wall was pointed out. Walk across that, we were told, and we would soon find it. But this, which should be the exit point from under the vanished road-bridge (almost a tunnel if the map is to be credited), is now merely a partly filled dump. By picking our steps carefully we soon passed behind the modern church on the Lahinch road, and that there was once an impressive cutting here was quickly proved. We were confronted by a large shed across the line and an enclosed yard in which madly barking greyhounds had begun to give full voice to their surprise at seeing us. Only by pulling in our stomachs were we able to squeeze by the side of the fence, out of the cutting and on to a high embankment.

The view from here, in Deerpark West townland, is excellent to the north. The church stands in the shadow of the line, as does the convent school, while across the river are the wooded surroundings of the Falls Hotel, once Ennistymon House. The present building is on the site of Ennistymon Castle, a sixteenth-century O'Connor fortress, and even yet some of the older structure may be seen in the basement. The castle belonged to the O'Connors in 1580, but about that time they were supplanted generally by the O'Briens, who continued to be the dominant family in the district up to the mid-nineteenth century. The house came into the possession of the McNamaras in the 1860s, one of which family, Francis, was the father-in-law of Dylan Thomas. Augustus John, a friend of the family, also stayed here. One wonders whether these artistic men were aware that in Ennistymon, about the year 1749, was born one of the best known of all poets in the Irish language, Brian Merriman. He moved to Feakle at an early age, and taught there from 1765 to 1785, but it was his writing that was to bring him immortality. *Cúirt an Mheán-Oíche (The Midnight Court)*, composed around 1780, is his masterpiece, and has proved itself far more durable than the Big Houses of the gentry built at about the same time. He later taught mathematics in Limerick, and died there in 1805.[5] He is buried in Feakle graveyard, close to the grave of Biddy Early. Neither grave is marked. Beyond these few facts, little is known about his life, a fate common enough among the 'mere Irish' in that age.

A track meanders along the top of this wide bank, showing that it is being used as a walkway. It, too, could be profitably developed for the benefit of the town. Think of the safe pleasure it would provide for joggers or strollers, for example. But in spite of such fine occasional stretches as this, our passage was by no means a soft one. There are the usual fences, a very closed-in and flooded area at the site of the nine-teenth milepost, just behind the premises of West Clare Saddlery, and a field beyond that from which the line has been completely erased. Here, opposite Skerritt's garage, the track ran side by side with the road so all we had to do was skip across the dividing wall and walk on rapidly. Not entirely for our own comfort did we do this. As on the outskirts of all Irish towns, new bungalows have ribboned out along the approach roads, and here they are built where the railway ran. In clearing the ground for their construction, the rail bridge which crossed over a byroad here (Madigan's Bridge) was demolished and no trace of either it or the line now remains. West of the last house we came on it again, though just as at Knockdrummagh, chopped off, leaving a good cross-section visible for anyone who might wish to examine the composition of the material used in building it. Access is easy here, as is progress, since the land about is almost completely devoid of trees, even bushes. Those that grow at the side of this long bank are prominent by virtue of their scarcity, so the view to every side is clear. A field away to the north, the road accompanied us, and dead straight ahead, a quarter of a mile off, was Ennistymon Hospital, – formerly the Union workhouse – within its high boundary walls.

To look at it today, a sleepy district infirmary, one could never imagine the suffering and death that were part of daily life here in the years of the Famine. Originally intended to house 600 people, it quickly became grossly overcrowded, as did every other workhouse in those years. For example, in late 1848 there were 1,150 inmates, between sick and able-bodied. Neglect and disease soon reaped their grim harvest in such conditions. Little wonder! In 1847 a mere 1/11d per *week* was the accepted cost of maintenance per inmate, and early in 1848 a report by the vice-guardians of the union found dirt, filth, squalor and vermin to be the norm.[6] The death toll spiralled. In 1848 it was 424, in 1849 977, in 1850 1,048 and by 1851 it had reached 1,589.[7] In spite of this, people still clamoured to get in, which is a fair indication of what conditions were like on the outside. Many of the dead were buried in the workhouse cemetery, but who knows where others found their last resting place? Local tradition has it that Calluragh, north of Ennistymon, holds its share of them and that they were buried wrapped in straw. The yellow meal distributed by the Poor Law Commissioners at the old courthouse in Parliament Street may have reduced the mortality somewhat, but it was only a morsel to the starving thousands, whose primary need was an adequate land-tenure system, not hand-outs in time of crisis.

The only reminder of death that greeted us was the sign 'mortuary' at the gateway nearest the level crossing, and we entered to satisfy our curiosity. But we left after a few minutes without seeing a solitary person – a far cry from the congestion of other days.

Seamus MacCurtin, 'the last bard of Thomond' and one of the best-known hedge-schoolmasters of his day, was buried in an unmarked pauper's grave in 1863 in the nearby cemetery. The year 1900 saw the death here, at the age of 70, of Garret Barry, the legendary piper from Inagh, one of the great figures of Irish traditional music. After a life of rambling, eking out a living wherever he could with his pipes, he had at last to resort to the poorhouse to die. There was no Aosdána then, and it is doubtful even if what he was engaged in was regarded as a cultural activity at that time. We in our own day need not be complacent, either, for it is not many years since Seosamh Ó hÉanaí was forced by lack of interest among the powers-that-be to take his talents to America, and leave to appreciative foreigners what his own countrymen, through ignorance, had disregarded.

During the Troubles the various workhouses were often occupied

Workhouse Halt, 13 September 1953.
(Photo: Irish Railway Record Society, no. 10645)

by one side or the other as barracks, since they were the most sizeable buildings in their areas. This one was no exception. The Free State army used it as a store, and by all accounts the provisions held there were under greater threat from those supposedly guarding them than from the enemy.

The crossing cottage, on the down side, is still lived in, but there is no sign of the little platform on the up side that was used in the early years when occasional trains stopped to facilitate the work-house guardians. This service was discontinued in 1925, and only in mid-1953, with the coming of the railcars, was it recommenced. While it was in operation, it is doubtful whether the inmates were much facilitated by it. An amusing story is told by Monsignor John MacMahon of a summer journey to Lahinch in his boyhood. The engine stopped here, unable to pull the carriages up the slight gradi-ent to Lahinch. However, the master of the workhouse, on being approached, kindly gave permission for his male charges to be used to push, and so they did, successfully.[8] Workhouse rations must have improved substantially since 1847 to allow such a feat of strength. To stir a 35-ton locomotive and carriages, even on the level, would be no mean feat, but to push them up a hill! Obviously, the men were being well fed and held in readiness for such eventualities.

To do the same today would fail even these supermen, however, for just past the crossing is a large cleared area, like a site in process of being prepared for house foundations, and beyond that a sheer step up to higher ground. Excavation has once again wiped out all traces of the line. With a final look around we nodded our farewells to Workhouse Halt, 19½ miles from Ennis, and the last crossing under the jurisdiction of Ennistymon block-station. We were already in Lahinch townland, even if the village of that name was still a mile and a half away.

In that mile and a half there is remarkably little worthy of comment. We came on Lahinsey no. 1 crossing almost unawares, and from here for the first time glimpsed the sea, but not shining like a jewel, as French claimed. But perhaps he saw it in summer. To us it looked as grey as a dull knife. In the field beyond this crossing, it is difficult to find much trace of the line as the ground has been extensively disturbed. Whether it has been reclaimed is hard to say, for long grass, combed in a west-east direction by the sea wind, has covered the entire area to a considerable depth. And so, walking as on a feather quilt, we approached Lahinsey no. 2 crossing with nothing more to guide us than the road on our left and a few rusted paling posts to the right. In the roadway we stood, somewhat perplexed, trying to get our bearings. The map showed clearly enough that the line crossed the road diagonally here, but it is not easy today to believe that it did, for the southern side is several feet higher than the northern. So we climbed, and searched. In a little while we found what we were looking for, running between and behind a terrace of houses, like a little back road, and certainly embanked, because we were now almost on a level with the roof ridges of the houses. Hens and ducks scattered out of our way. We were passing through a farmyard, though well within the bounds of Lahinch. Then we were halted again, this time by a house built on the line, its yard extending back into the field across the track, but we got round it somehow.

There was no passing the next obstacle, however – a whole new estate of houses. All that remains of the line as shown on our map is a little boreen and one of the concession gates. The estate access road occupies the site of the track, while the houses themselves are strung along the down side. This would be an impossible barrier to any attempt ever to reopen the West Clare on its original course. We could do no more than detour onto the public road and travel on thus until, like at Knockdrummagh, we came on the line again in an area that looked as if it, too, was being prepared for 'development'. It is only a brief interlude; in the next field the very topsoil has been torn away, leaving not even vegetation. It was through this wasteland, where once the turntable was sited, that we approached Lahinch Station.

We did not recognise it, even though we had seen pictures of it. Like Willbrook, it has changed out of all knowing. We made enquiries at the nearest house to hand and were answered by none other than

Lahinch. (Photo: Lawrence Collection, National Library)

Mr J.J. Skerritt, last master of the station. We could hardly have come
to a better place or person. He pointed out to us the ruined and roofless hulk of a building just opposite his front door. Did we recognise
it? No. He motioned us towards a picture in his hallway of the station
at the turn of the century. Now did we recognise it? Though there
was much that was different, there were also enough similarities to
show us that we were looking at the remnants of the station-house.
Apart from the yard, it is all that remains here, but 200 yards away,
now in the middle of a walled-off caravan park, the freight shed is
still intact and is being used as a canteen for campers during the

Lahinch station after closure, 7.6.61. (Photo: Roy Denison)

summer season. Only as recently as 1987 were the original sliding doors removed, as they had become unsafe.

We had a closer look at the station-house, noted its odd situation – gable-on to the line – and tried to imagine that night of mayhem, 23 January 1923, when it, together with Corofin, Miltown, Kilmurry, Doonbeg and Moyasta, was visited in a concerted attack by Executive troops and extensively damaged by fire.[9] In its present condition, such imaginings are very easy indeed, for this is somewhat as it must have looked on the morning of 24 January. That attack, at least, was a blessing in disguise, since when the building was subsequently repaired it was also considerably extended.

From the wall of the caravan park we surveyed the desolate scene. Who, standing here today, could possibly believe that this was once, next to Ennis, the busiest station on the whole line, at least in summertime when the tourists came here in their thousands? That there were two platforms and several sidings as well as a turntable? This last was installed in 1953, having been brought from Kilmessan on the Clonsilla–Kingscourt line, and was used to turn the diesel railcars in the peak tourist months when speed was of the essence – a great rationalisation at the time, for during the era of steam locomotives a further 6 miles had to be travelled by the engine to Miltown, where the nearest turntable was sited.

But though almost all pertaining to the West Clare in Lahinch is gone, the fame of this watering place remains, a fame which grew largely as a result of the opening up of west Clare by the railway in the last quarter of the nineteenth century. It is unfortunate, in the light of this, that no suitable memorial to its 'onlie begetter' has yet been erected here, or even proposed, so far as I know.

The name Lahinch in Irish is 'Leacht uí Chonchúir' – O'Connor's grave cairn – and as is usual with place names, it conveys far more of the history or topography of its area than the English translation. For even if we take Lahinch to mean *leithinis* (peninsula), we have a good approximation of reality, for it is indeed surrounded on three sides by water: the Inagh River to the north, the Moy River to the south and the Atlantic to the west. This was originally the territory of

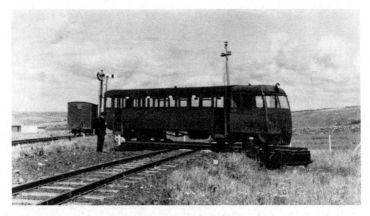

Diesel railcar being turned at Lahinch, 27 May 1954.
(Photo: Irish Railway Record Society, no. 11020)

the O'Connor lords of Corcomroe, but the family fell on hard times during the reign of Elizabeth I and was supplanted by the O'Briens. The various castles in the area – Dough, Tullamore, Liscannor – bear testimony to this change; they were built by the O'Connors but by 1580 were in the hands of Sir Daniel O'Brien.[10]

Dough Castle, at the northern end of the golf course, is now in a very ruined conditionm but its position is interesting. It was built at a strategically important point at the mouth of the Inagh River, where it could control both land and water traffic. Strange to say, it was not demolished by the Cromwellian commissioners, as were so many other tower houses, but collapsed of natural causes, probably not unrelated to the sandy nature of the soil. It is said that an underground passage, filled with valuables, leads from it to Liscannor but that Donn Dumhach, king of the fairies, whose territory the sand hills are, haunts it and woe betide anyone who tries to explore, or even find it.

This whole area between the village and the mouth of the Inagh has for at least two centuries been the gathering place of summer visitors, especially on Garland Sunday, when thousands would collect for the sports and entertainments which lasted all day.[11] It is said that these celebrations once took place at Buaile na Gréine on Mount Callan but that the clergy objected to the pagan connotations of any such frolics on that eminence, and persuaded people to partake in their activities at Lahinch instead. The advice would seem to have been well heeded, and Lahinch and the West Clare benefited accordingly. Much depended on weather conditions, obviously, for almost without fail the local press commented on how fine or rainy the day had been: 'For the first time in ten years Garland Sunday in Lahinch was favoured with fine weather. The ... resort was crowded. Two special trains carried about six hundred passengers from Ennis ... and there was also a large contingent from Kilrush, Doonbeg'[12]

A short distance away, over O'Brien's Bridge, is the ruined church of St Mac Creiche, the banisher of monsters, and a mile further on the little village of Liscannor, once famous for the export of Moher flagstones, but probably best known internationally as the birthplace of John P. Holland, inventor of the submarine. He was born here in 1841 and a memorial has been erected to him near the quay. Another and much more visible memorial, beside St Brigid's famous well, is that to Cornelius (Corney) O'Brien MP in the first half of the nineteenth century and owner of Birchfield House, which today lies ruined a mile to the north-west of the village. Though he aspired to be a philanthropist and an improving landlord, his methods tended to be insensitive, and he was much misunderstood by his tenantry, with the result that he is remembered today as something of a tyrant. Holland, though appreciated more in America than at home, is the more interesting character, if only because his invention was probably the result of his boyhood fantasies about the underwater land in Liscannor Bay. He, like all of his contemporaries, grew up mesmerised by stories of Cill Stuifín, the sunken town, and as he looked out from Clahanes strand, south-eastward down the bay, and imagined the waves breaking over the church spire, he must have wished for a means of unlocking the secrets of that mysterious place.

How the belief in Cill Stuifín originated is perhaps not to be looked for in historical times as much as in the deepest of prehistoric belief and myth. In ancient Celtic mythology, the west was the abode of the ever-young, and certain it is that the surviving stories of the town buried by the waters of Liscannor Bay reflect something of this belief, though often heavily disguised.[13]

A Christianised version of its origin is that St Stephen built a church on a small island at the mouth of the bay 'a thousand years ago', but a huge wave engulfed it, wiping it out completely. Another story tells of a chieftain near Liscannor called Stiofán Ó Ruairc who by virtue of a magic key-shaped wand could cross the bay to Rineen at will. As soon as he struck the water with the wand, it would divide and allow him to pass over. But on one such journey he lost the wand, the waters closed and he was drowned. It was later found inside a fish which had swallowed it, was given to Conán Maol and is buried with him on Mount Callan. A closely related version says that Stiofán Ó Ruairc, whenever he left his town Cill Stuifín, covered it with water by means of his key-shaped wand, which he hid in a secret cave in Ballyvaskin. One day, however, he went off to battle, covering the town as usual; but he was killed and so the key remains hidden. Cill Stuifín will never be freed until it is found.

A more ominous version of the story, at least for Lahinch, tells that a newly married man named Stiofán was drowned when Cill Stuifín sank, leaving behind his bride in the portion of the town left over water (i.e. Lahinch). He returns every seven years to claim her, but she holds a spell over him and so he cannot harm the village. Once, during a terrible storm, when it looked as though the area must be flooded, she was seen to emerge from a fort near the shore and wave a wand in the direction of Cill Stuifín, which was just then moving towards the shore. In a flash it vanished. No one in Lahinch has much anxiety to witness this spectacle too often for, as the *sean-fhocal* goes, 'Leacht Uí Chonchúir atá agus Cill Stuifín a bheidh', or in another version, 'As Cill Stuifín was Lahinch is and Miltown will be'.

Yet a belief persists that Cill Stuifín will be 'freed'. Some say that a boy without hands or feet will find the key, others that it will be discovered by a tailor with eleven fingers and eleven toes. But no matter who the finder is, the casualty will be Lahinch, for on that day it will be drowned.

Some people, it seems, have been granted a vision of that mythical place, but it has always resulted in misfortune. A poor Liscannor man had collected a load of driftwood on the shore when he was approached by a person who asked him to sell it. Delighted, he agreed. 'Where'll I deliver it to?' he asked.

'Out there,' said the man, pointing towards the breaker in the bay. 'Throw the timber that way.'

He did so, and to his astonishment it disappeared, every piece. Some time later, at Kilrush quay, he saw a man in a boat and recognised him as the man who had bought the wood near Liscannor. He saluted him, but the man seemed angry. Jumping ashore, he asked, 'Which eye d'you see me with?' On being told, he blinded the man in that eye. Obviously he had seen more than was good for him.

On very rare occasions, persons have been chosen who might free Cill Stuifín if their courage was not found wanting, but unfortunately none has yet passed the test. A century or more ago, a man riding on horseback from Ennis was accosted at night by many shadowy figures and carried off to a great house. In a room was a vat of whiskey from which he was ordered to drink enough. He did so and then saw a coffin in a corner. He had no more than raised the lid slightly when a horrendous noise began. In terror he let the lid drop but was ordered to drink more whiskey. Again he did so, and tried the coffin once more. This time he saw a golden sword inside and was about to take it out when the noise began again, worse than before. Once more he dropped the lid and ran. At that he was reproached for cowardice and told that if he had taken it out, Cill Stuifín would at last have been set free from its enchantment.

Up to forty years ago, when fishing was still a means of livelihood on this coast, stories abounded among fishermen of cocks heard crowing beneath their boats in the early morning, and ghostly craft seen which would vanish in the vicinity of Cill Stuifín at daybreak. Some fishermen claimed to have brought up household implements such as buckets, keys and, on one occasion, no less than a pot of boiled potatoes! Even allowing for the notorious imagination of fishermen, it is clear that there was something extraordinary here, and it is much to be regretted that belief in it seems to have all but died in this generation.

Track-lifting train at Miltown Malbay. 7.6.61. (Photo: Roy Denison)

We decided to finish this day's pleasant trip forthwith, while we were still in a good humour, and to that end we walked as far as the western side of the village overlooking the rocky shore near the church, hoping to catch a glimpse of the telltale patch of foam out in the bay. But there was nothing in sight except much steel-grey water. In a way we were glad, for we knew of the belief which says that anyone who sees Cill Stuifín will die within seven years. It seemed just then too high a price to pay, even for viewing one of the wonders of the otherworld!

Day 7

Lahinch to Miltown Station

For most of the 6 miles from Lahinch to Miltown, the West Clare track ran at no great distance from the rockbound south-eastern shore of Liscannor Bay, coming closest to the sea at Crag, just south of Lahinch, and thereafter moving somewhat inland. But one is never out of earshot of the breakers, and at some points the whole coastline is spectacularly visible, especially from the Black Hill, near Rineen. Why the line was constructed where it was is obvious: a narrow strip of low land runs along the edge of the bay, and the builders took advantage of this. The road-makers of a previous generation took the same route, and for over half of this journey, road and railway are funnelled in the same direction, sometimes, as at Drummin, coming so close as to be separated only by a single wall.

Two of the seven bridges on this section have been dismantled but the best still survive, the metal-deck crossing at Calluragh South and the stone-arched bridge at Drummin being especially worthy of attention. But more than all else, it is the Black Hill, between the sites of the twenty-third and twenty-fourth mileposts, that makes this journey memorable, for along its flank the line rises to its greatest height on a huge embankment partly cut out of the rock. From the coast road one may yet see the straight but rising scar in the hillside that was the West Clare line. It is not a landmark that will be easily effaced, and anyone interested in the West Clare must visit it, walk it, for it was part of every steam-locomotive driver's nightmares. So steep is the gradient that some of the earlier engines (especially the 0–6–0T models) and, indeed, the Drewry railcars introduced in 1928, managed it only with the greatest difficulty. Its ominous-sounding name, though relating only to physical features, was certainly appropriate. It was a constant challenge, a psychological as well as a physical barrier. And when at last dieselisation removed its sting, it still, together with Clouna and Willbrook, remained one of the best-remembered names on the West Clare section of the system. Michael ('Micky') O'Donoghue – one of the grand old men and legendary figures of the West Clare – in his descriptions of his experiences as a driver in the steam era, always gave the Black Hill respectful mention, and no man knew the line better than he.[1] In many ways, he said, steam engines at places like this and Willbrook were the surest test of a driver's skill, and though he admired the efficiency of the diesel locos (he was reputedly the first man in Ireland to drive one, and he held the all-time speed record on the West Clare: Ennis to Kilkee in 67 minutes on 10 June 1953), he preferred the steam engines and regretted their passing.

Rested and assured, we set out from Lahinch one week later. The Hill was merely a long dark strip in the distance to the south, but even from almost 3 miles off it stood out. Had we heard nothing about it beforehand we might have guessed that it was in some way unusual. As it was, we were looking forward to seeing for ourselves whether it deserved its reputation.

We did not attempt to travel on directly from the station. All we would have seen was the caravan park. It seemed more sensible to leave the car near the church and continue on foot out the Miltown road as far as the byroad to the school. This was the site of Crag crossing, but so many new houses have been built in recent years that no open or undisturbed ground now remains, and it is pointless to hope to find anything here. The main road was the only way forward and, at last, in one of the few open fields left in this part of the village, we saw the line a short way off.

From this point, exactly 21 miles from Ennis and the nearest the line comes to the sea until Quilty is reached, it is easy to see how the track must have looped around the rather featureless hill which overlooks Lahinch to the east. But the haphazard scatter of houses interrupts the view back towards the station, as we had expected, so we faced south where prospects seemed better.

Much building along the Miltown road has meant extensive land disturbance, and before long we were back on the road again, since to follow the line precisely would have meant crossing through newly laid gardens. Having rounded three sides of one such site, we reached a little byroad close to where Hollyhock Lodge once stood, but of the little crossing that was here nothing remains. Worse than that, we had to scramble down a 6-foot slope at the other side of the road before we were again on level ground. Such drastic alteration of the land surface makes it impossible to tell anything about the line along here. Nothing, in fact, has survived apart from a few fence posts and a boundary drain.

A little choked-up cutting leads from this desert into the second of Lahinch's two large caravan parks, and at once the line sinks into a much larger cutting and under a fine stone-arched bridge known as Lehan's.

Engine 5C at Lehan's Bridge, Lahinch, c. 1948.
(Photo: Courtesy of Patrick Hayes, Limerick)

There was no following it here, though, since the way was choked
with briars and littered with debris and wreckage from one of the
fierce spring storms that this region is so prone to. Beyond the bridge
the cutting is wider, and we speedily made our way down into it, glad
of the shelter, for the sea breeze was perishing. From here we had a
good, though restricted, view of the type of terrain ahead: undulating
bare fields, stone-fenced in the main, receding into a treeless horizon.
Then, quite unexpectedly, we were at Crag Bridge – or rather, where
it had been, for the metal deck which spanned the Miltown road is
one of the two that have been removed. Before climbing down to the
road we paused for another look at the panorama stretching away
southward. The line, embanked all the way, loops off to the south-
east like some monstrous snake on its way towards the rugged scenic
area known as 'The Major's Wood', beyond which the ground rises
into the dark ridge of the Black Hill, following the coast into the
distance towards Rineen. It looked daunting enough, but at least the
downhill stretch directly ahead was inviting. We crossed and began
to coast along, but were quickly halted by a vile sight on the seaward
side of the bank. There, in a marshy area at the head of a little bay, all
manner of plastic and other rubbish lay scattered over a wide expanse,
despoiling it utterly and making a stark and ugly contrast with the
shoreline behind. One wonders what the mermaid who used to comb
her hair on the rocks by the sea here would have thought of it all.
Maybe it disgusted her so much that she betook herself to more con-
genial surroundings. In any case, she has not been seen of late.

The huge earthwork over which we were now walking must for
many years have presented a sore annoyance to farmers whose land
was divided by it, for there is no cattle-pass in all its length. This
has been rectified in recent times with the aid of excavators. Two
passages, at some distance from each other, have been cut through
the fabric of the bank, and the rubble used to construct ramps on
either side. Though it has interrupted the continuity of the surface,
the workmanship is not unpleasing. New field-drainage at the lowest
point in the land has also taken advantage of an original culvert, and
so further damage to the bank has not been necessary. This seems

sensible, for it serves as a useful windbreak at this very exposed part of the coast, where no trees would survive for long.

The sizeable cutting which succeeds this long, clear stretch has only one claim to fame, so far as I am aware. Here, on a day of fierce storm almost eighty years ago, several carriages of an unladen special from Kilrush were derailed – literally blown off the track – just after emerging on to the exposed height. But as we passed, all was peaceful. At its southern end, however, flood and mud forced us to take to the fields, from where we were momentarily distracted by an excellent view of Moy House, white and turreted, situated on rising scenic ground overlooking the coast just west of the Moy River. Built by the Fitzgeralds, landlords of the area, in the early nineteenth century, it was later bought by Major George Studdert, whose descendants lived in it until the 1930s. He lent his title to the fine railway bridge which crosses the river a short distance away. Even yet it is known as 'The Major's Bridge' and is, with Toloughlahan and Cullenagh, one of those that should be preserved for posterity. The view from it is spectacular. The public road dips into the wooded valley of the Moy River here, and the coincidence of road and rail bridges only yards apart makes this a memorable place. Unfortunately, most motorists have little chance to admire the masonry and metal deck towering 30 feet above them, so blind are the approaches from both ends. This had been my own experience on all previous passings here, so I was about to make up for lost opportunity.

Getting onto the bridge is no easy task, for it has been necessary to fence both ends strongly, but the lovely surroundings visible from the concrete parapet more than repay the effort. However, if the bank leading on to it from the Calluragh side is clear and passable, the one on the Carrowgar end is quite the opposite. So thickly covered is it with strong trees and bushes that one could not even say for sure how high it is. Picturesque it may look from the road, but to us it seemed like the jungle of the Mato Grosso. We had to fight for every inch of the 150 yards to its end. It would have made far more sense to go by the road, but once in it we had little choice but to struggle on.

No progress is possible on the line for a quarter of a mile from this point. Only a masochist would choose to struggle through the matted blackthorn which carpets it – that stunted, wind-flattened variety peculiar to coastal terrain, whose deadly thorns can rip skin and clothing to shreds in no time. The only cattle-pass we came to was broken, its walls once again well fenced. The farmers in this area seem to be rather expert in this facet of their trade – a sore disappointment to us for we had imagined that progress through west Clare would be rapid. We had reckoned without blackthorns and barbed wire, and it looked as though they would be slowing us considerably.

But it was again time to make enquiries, and some houses close by provided us with the excuse we needed. We quickly gathered a smattering of information from a very knowledgeable farmer: that we were still in the parish of Ennistymon (Kilmanaheen), that the long wood running by the Black Hill to Rineen was once part of the Davis Estate, that Biddy Early visited a herbalist named Nora O'Brien in the area and perhaps learned part of her trade from her. It certainly seems that Biddy cured people here – for example, a man who fell down a cliff near Lahinch – and she was afterwards held in high regard by the people of the place. Of the West Clare he recalled that the sleepers were sold to farmers for two shillings each at the lifting of the rails in 1961, and the land on which the line was built for not much more. But some farmers, it seems, chose not to buy, particularly in places where deep cuttings made much fencing and constant vigilance necessary. These remain the property of CIÉ to this day, he said, as does the responsibility for drains and fences.

Personal reminiscences he had in plenty about the reign of terror in Lahinch and Miltown following the Rineen ambush, and he also pointed out to us the RHO Moy housing development on its beautiful but bleak perch high above the railway. We would have mistaken it for a compound of holiday apartments had we not been told otherwise. He advised us to keep to the road and walk the quarter of a mile to Moy Bridge, that the line was overgrown and the fields alongside marshy. We should have heeded his suggestion; he knew the place infinitely better than we. But, like mules, we chose to do it the hard way, and though we eventually got to the bridge without any mishap we had seen nothing of enough interest to justify the struggle through much dense undergrowth.

The metal deck of Moy Bridge, like the one at Crag, has been removed. Only the stone abutments remain. The reason probably is that it was a particularly low structure, with headroom of no more than 10 feet – hardly high enough to let modern cattle trucks pass. This was also known as Hanrahan's Bridge, and was made a halt in October 1958 – the last halt, in fact, to be instituted before the closure of the system. The line now turns south-westward, more or less paralleling the Miltown road at a distance of never more than 500 yards for the next mile or more, until they swing together again halfway to Rineen school house, whence they curve round the western edge of Drummin Hill and on south to Miltown.

But anyone who has an interest in the unexpected should keep well away from this main thoroughfare, and turn off here for Moy. He or she will not be disappointed. First of all, Moy does not exist, at least in the sense of a village or town. There are hilly little roads in plenty, a church, a community centre, but only a thin scatter of houses. It is, truly, a secret little place, completely different from the nearby coastal strip. These are lofty parts and the attitude of the people reflects this. They are friendly, but you realise almost at once that others like you from the outside world have been here … and have gone. Yet Moy remains that most difficult thing of all: itself.

The ruin of the O'Brien castle at Moymore is probably one of the best-known landmarks in the area, and though not a great deal now remains of it, one can yet see that it was built on a very defensible site. Stories are still remembered which speak of its violent history, and a few of these should be repeated here. One tells that O'Brien, when going to the battle of Dough, locked up his wife and children in a vault underneath the castle to keep them safe from attack in his absence. Unfortunately, he was killed in the fight and the door was never again opened, with unknown consequences for those within. A belief has always persisted that there is some kind of cave under the castle, though no one has ever found it. In 1921 the Moy Company of Volunteers seemed to have struck it lucky when they discovered an iron door, but in the disturbed conditions of the time, they were afraid to blast it for fear of alerting the military. Odd to say, none of the surviving members ever went back to complete the job.

Tales of buried treasure also survive. It is said that the castle was once attacked by the lord of Liscannor Castle, and so unexpected was the assault that the inhabitants barely had time to escape with their valuables. When the attackers found the castle empty, they set out in hot pursuit of the fleeing garrison and overtook them in Ballyvaskin. But not before they had hidden their treasure. And it lies to this day waiting to be discovered.

One of the O'Briens of Moy, Donal by name, seems to have been a rather insensitive, boorish man, a trait that was to cost him dear. On one occasion, at a feast, a bard who was present was placed in a dark room and ordered to compose. He did so, but for his pains he received a bowl of stale porridge and a jug of water next morning. So indignant was he that he satirised Donal on the spot. Only one verse is extant:

No food to welcome the weary guest,
No bed spread down to lend him rest.
From Donal no bard has gifts or gold:
His faith he scorned, his country sold.

Surviving accounts say that the satire preyed so much on Donal's mind that he committed suicide!

In 1600 Hugh O'Donnell visited Moy, and not as a sightseer, either. But whether he captured the castle is not known. In 1656 it was occupied by Captain George Morton, but by the end of the century it had been abandoned and a new residence built nearby.[2] This has all but vanished.

Having once got a taste for these hilly little roads, one will be delighted to continue on past the castle, through Toor and Aillbrack to the graveyard of Kilfarboy, which is quite the most extraordinary of its kind in west Clare. From even a short distance away, it appears to be a village of miniature houses, but a closer look shows that these are vaults. To the right of the entrance gate, in a little enclosure, is an impressive monument to Michael Sexton, the famous bonesetter, who died in 1908. In the graveyard proper are some exquisitely carved grave slabs, both within the ruined church and outside, and in the south-eastern corner is a well sacred to St Joseph, at which rounds are still made on 19 March. At one time, St Laichtín was venerated here, but like other local saints he fell from favour with the passing of local traditions.

This holy place also claimed the bones of two of the best-known Clare poets of the eighteenth century: Micheál Ó Coimín and Aindrias Mac Cruitín. Though they were of different religions, their craft brought them together and they remained on good terms throughout their lives. Mac Cruitín, the last of the hereditary bards to the chiefs of Corcomroe, died in 1749 and is buried in the church in an unmarked grave.[3] Ó Coimín, whose son Edmond later inherited Millford House in the neighbouring townland of Carrowkeel, died in 1760 and was also buried here.[4]

Miltown is a mere 2 miles from here, though the road is narrow and care should be taken at the many blind corners. We, however, were not at liberty to take such a pleasant route, at least on the day in question. We left Moy Bridge behind, and framed by the *V* of the cutting beyond lay the wood we had seen from Crag Bridge as a mere smudge along the side of the hill. As we came closer we saw why it is called the Black Hill: the 'wood' consists almost wholly of blackthorn, flattened into the steep hillside by the sea wind, thereby giving the impression of a solid mass. The visual effect created at this time of bare branches is startling.

As we passed into the townland of Moybeg, the line had almost swung under the hill, and the distance between us and the wood continued to narrow. It is rough land and very neglected-looking. Water, more than anything else, impresses itself on the eye and ear: sodden fields left and right, a hidden cascade tumbling down somewhere through the wood, and the bay off to the west beyond the road. It is no place for the fainthearted traveller. Where line and wood eventually met we found our way barred by a stout fence and beyond that a jungle. We were soon floundering in bog and marsh grass through adjoining fields of jet-black soil, but only once did we pause, at a culvert beneath the line. Here, a cleverly built watering place for cattle had been constructed of west Clare stone blocks and a railway girder (the first we had seen) to keep the beasts at bay and the water clean. As we looked about the desolate fields, it occurred to us that cattle would find far more to drink than to eat in this part of Moybeg.

We came across several attempts at little gardens, all of them looking either half-hearted or washed flat, and they reminded us of tales of devilment and youthful mischief from steam days. So slow were the trains on steep inclines that little wayside gardens like these were a regular target for schoolboys, who would jump out of the carriages, snatch up turnips or stalks of potatoes and dash back on board. With this ammunition they would later pelt horse traffic or pedestrians at places where the line adjoined the road, as at Rineen. Many and many were the complaints received by school principals about such misdeeds by their charges. Speaking of which, it should be said that for many years the West Clare timetable dictated the location of their secondary education for many of the schoolchildren of Clare's western seaboard. Since secondary schools were few in number then, and advantage had to be taken of whatever morning train would get the pupils to school on time, Ennistymon benefited enormously over other towns which might have a greater entitlement to the children if mere distance had been the deciding factor. Hence it was that they came from as far away as Doonbeg, for the most suitable train was going north at that time of the morning.

All this time the only constant thing was the hill, overlooking us severely to the left; the rest was a mixture of inaccessible thickets followed by the odd patch of reclaimed land. Among the stones at three different places we found chunks of yellow scorched brick and knew we were still on target. These were burned-out fire-bricks from the fire-boxes of the steam locomotives, dumped here with ash and other debris as packing for the sleepers. They were a useful guide to us on several occasions in ground that would have been otherwise featureless.

Crossing a little boreen took us into the townland of Carrown-tedaun, but boundaries were the last thing on our minds, for the *fionnán* that chokes most of these fields to knee depth has been joined by bushes which have crept down from the hill in a silent re-invasion of ground that was once theirs. In its present condition it is no fit place for people, but our eagerness to see the Black Hill was what kept us going.

When the line began to rise, it did so gradually at first over 500 yards or so, but then steeply. It is so straight and grown-in by hazel up along the flank of the hill that we had to pause every so often in order to check our progress by looking through the branches, out towards the bay. At every stop there was something extra to admire, until at last the whole of Liscannor Bay and all its coastline lay at our feet. No one with an eye in his head could ignore the beauty of this panorama, but any such considerations were light years from the minds of the wreckers of two centuries ago whose practice it was to light fires on this hill so that passing ships might be lured to their destruction on the rocks. How much misfortune and misery they caused is not known, but it is remembered that at least one of their intended victims fought back. The captain of a Galway-bound ship, seeing the beacon on this hill one dark night, and somehow knowing of the foul practice, ordered the crew to open fire, scattering the would-be assassins. It remains a murky chapter in the annals of the Clare coast.[5]

Today it is the embankment itself that provokes a sense of wonder in the observer. How it was built without benefit of all the heavy machinery available nowadays is something to contemplate. Over 50 feet high for much of its climb, it allows the line to cling to the side of the hill, fully exposed to north-westerly winds from the Atlantic. It must have been an exhilarating sight for passengers in the trains that travelled this way several times a day: cliff-face towering over-head, valley and sea below. Even today, when the screen of hazel has hemmed it in and dulled its impact, it is still a sight to inspire respect for those long-gone builders. Gone, too, is all trace of the cottage and concession gates at the top of the gradient. The milesman who lived here had one major professional worry: ballast was constantly being washed from under the rails and down the hill during heavy rain. So conscientious and diligent was he in his duties that he became the butt of much good-humoured banter from crews on the passing trains. No doubt they appreciated his concern, though, for there were never any serious accidents on the hill.

There was a saying among railwaymen that once you got to the top of the Black Hill you could freewheel into Miltown. Would that it were still so! Our climb was finally brought to a full stop near the summit by what we took, at first glance, to be a broken bridge like those at Crag and Moy. But there was never a bridge here, so we had to look closer. The answer was simple: a new road, hacked out of the hill, and continuing on over it, cutting through the line in the process. Try as we might, we could not find where the line went on the far side of this road. It was as though it had vanished off the hill. Above us only the new road snaked over the skyline, while ahead was a sharp fall to other overgrown fields, but nothing resembling a railway line. Mystified, we picked our way down through the scrub, hoping to come on it, and eventually we did, but some 500 yards off.

Rineen Halt, 1953. (Photo: Irish Railway Record Society, no. 10434)

We were on our way again and moving towards the more hospitable and populated landscape of Rineen. In the next mile, to Rineen school, there is a dramatic improvement in the quality of the holdings and consequently far more houses. Most of them are just one field in from the road, which means that the railway ran by their front doors. Perhaps this is why, in May 1952, a halt was opened a few hundred yards to the Lahinch side of the school. There had been a precedent, of course, since in the first years of the line's operation, trains stopped here on request. At that time, too, this was the site of a ballast siding, but nothing is visible here today that might prove that.

This little halting-place does hold one record of a sort, though one which it could well have done without: it was here that the first fatality on the line occurred, on 28 January 1888, and the event was even more poignant than such usually are by virtue of the fact that the man knocked down while closing a gate was deaf and dumb. Everything possible was done for him, it seems, but he had been badly mutilated and died shortly after.[6]

As we plodded across farm after farm, sometimes finding only a yellowish streak through the grass where the line had been, at other times walking through sections that were well-nigh untouched, we were glad to be occasionally accosted by the owners and questioned, usually most courteously. One such man spoke for practically all when he explained why he had removed his portion of the line: it had split his field into two uneconomic parts. The same was true of most farmers in the locality, he said, and there would be many places where we would not be able to trace it.

At Rineen school we took a breather, and no better place to do so, for it is a building worth considering. Standing solidly like a grey square box, it is one of the most distinctive-looking National schools in the county, and one of the few from the nineteenth century still in everyday use for its original purpose. Sited just inside the townland of Rineen at the stream that marks its boundary with Drummin, it is one of two schools built on the estate of the Fitzgeralds of Moy when the neighbouring Moronys refused to allow them on their property.

That the same Moronys should be so reviled in the parish is not to be wondered at for they seemed to go to extraordinary lengths to assert their property, and other, rights, even at most inopportune times. Frank 'Caoch' Morony refused a site for a Catholic church on his property, and like the above-mentioned schools it had to be built on the nearby Fitzgerald Estate. It is still asserted that Morony told the priest that he would prefer to see two Catholic churches being demolished than one being erected. He need have no worry on that score, the priest assured him; he would never see the new church. Sure enough, before it was completed Morony lost his sight, hence the epithet 'Caoch'.[7]

During the Famine and in the decades after it, they proved themselves unsympathetic landlords, charging high rents and evicting for non-payment at times when the adjoining Fitzgerald and Leconfield tenantry were being treated fairly. This, as much as anything else, fanned resentment, and in the 1880s it came to a head in riot, obstruction and eventually boycott. The year 1888 was most memorable: on one side were the aggrieved tenants, backed by the Land League, and on the other Mrs Burdett Morony, a particularly unappealing specimen of the landlord class. But she had the forces of law and order on her side, and so a clash became inevitable. Military and police in their hundreds were drafted into the district, the Atlantic Hotel became a barracks, and a state of near-siege became almost normality for a time. The original boycott of Mrs Morony and her servants developed into a boycott of the police, and many prosecutions and prison sentences followed. The newspapers of the day were full of the proceedings, and the name and fame of Miltown were noted even in London. All that was achieved by the jailings was to create a sense of solidarity among the people and instil a distrust of the RIC that was to be amply justified a little over thirty years later when one of the worst outrages perpetrated by that force was to occur early in 1920 at a place in the town called Canada Cross.

Why the Moronys, owners or part-owners of so much – Miltown House, Atlantic Lodge, the Atlantic Hotel, Wellington Lodge, and more – should have begrudged the granting of so little is not easy to tell. They seem to have felt no regard for, had no ties with, those they ruled. The price they paid was, therefore, inevitable, given the way events were to develop in the following generation. All those involved in these heated ructions are long dead and the Morony estate has gone the way of nearly all the others, but there has been one survivor in the memory of the general public. It is the song 'Three Brave Blacksmiths' written by T.D. Sullivan to celebrate those men of principle who served jail sentences of 'a week for every nail' rather than co-operate with the forces of landlordism at its worst.[8]

Across the road from the school is as good a place as any to get an accurate impression of the condition of the line. Look back – it is there; look forward – nothing. For as far as we were able to see, all had been swept away. There was little point in walking there, we knew, unless we were interested in nails, bolts and other small pieces of metal debris, for assuredly we would find those in the disturbed earth, but little else. We settled for the road, using the culvert opposite the school door as a sort of starting point. Here and there we stopped to make enquiries, and always the story was the same: the piece of the railway on the property was only a hindrance and so had to be either levelled or filled in. While the passing of the West Clare as a system is almost universally regretted, life has to go on.

Under Drummin Hill, which in places falls cliff-like to the road, railway and highway were separated by only a stone wall, a short way beyond where the twenty-fifth milepost was located. As we ventured into the shadowy corridor we had to step carefully, for proximity to the road has attracted all kinds of debris. Out of this cutting, the line rises steadily, and the hill, which up to this is covered in vegetation, takes on a bare, cliff-like appearance. In places, it has collapsed onto the way. A severe spell of rain might well cause a landslide to block the road here since there is a quite unprotected edge to the railway bank overlooking it, and the cliff is composed mainly of pencil gravel. As we walked this edge, a monument below us drew our attention: a stone plaque commemorating the Rineen ambush, one of the best-known actions of the War of Independence in Clare. From this hill, on 22 September 1920, a party from the 4th Battalion of the IRA, led by Captain Ignatius O'Neill, attacked a truck bringing police from Miltown to Ennistymon. In the ensuing fight, which was soon joined by British reinforcements, six police were killed as against no losses on the attackers' side.

As one stands here today, looking down on the road even from this height (the attackers were considerably farther up the hill), it is hard to believe that the authorities of the time could not have foreseen that this was a perfect position from an attacker's point of view, and acted accordingly to forestall any such assault. Far from taking any anticipatory measures, however, it seems that they did not even trouble to stagger the truck's departure time each day. They paid a high price for their carelessness, both in terms of human lives and the propaganda victory which it undoubtedly was for the IRA.

The consequences for Lahinch, Miltown and Ennistymon, though, were drastic. The orgy of reprisals – burnings and shootings – released against them still remains vivid in the minds of old people. At 7 p.m that night the military invaded Miltown, burning, looting and smashing windows. In the small hours of the morning, when it seemed as if the worst was over, the Tans arrived from their depredations in Ennistymon and Lahinch, and joined by the local RIC they continued the arson, theft and shooting until the following morning. It was a night's work that destroyed for ever any shreds of confidence that the people of Kilfarboy might have retained in the forces of the Crown. They were precious little, for 14 April 1920 had dealt a previous drastic blow to the prestige, such as it was, of those same forces when, at Canada Cross, in the centre of Miltown, a peaceful crowd had been fired on by police and military personnel with the loss of three lives and injury to eleven others. Earlier that day Republican hunger-strikers had been released from Mountjoy Jail, and in Miltown, as in many other towns, crowds gathered to celebrate the event. A bonfire was lit at Canada Cross and a large number of people collected to express their delight in dance and song. All was good humoured until the police arrived close to midnight. They ordered those present to disperse, and then, insanely, opened fire without giving time for the order to be obeyed. At the burial of the three victims at Ballard cemetery on 16 April hundreds of IRA were present while Crown forces were confined to barracks. This outrage did enormous damage to the reputation of the security forces, and at the inquest that followed the jury was uncompromising in its verdict: willful murder. Little wonder that inquests were abolished shortly afterwards and replaced by military enquiries.[9]

It is very likely that the Rineen ambush was a reprisal for this evil night's work. It was a cycle of violence and retaliation that was all too common in the Ireland of 1920.[10] The choice of Canada Cross for the celebrations on the fatal night was, perhaps, deliberate since it had connections with a rebellion of the previous century. In the mid-1860s members of the Fenians would gather here to discuss the news of the day, which at the time consisted largely of happenings in America, such as the Fenian 'invasion' of Canada. When this event seemed to have succeeded, they decided to hold a victory rally here, and ever afterwards it kept the name.

Certainly Miltown, if it played no part in the older history of Clare, as T.J. Westropp said, made up handsomely in the past century for that omission.

The line must have been in a remarkably exposed position as it rounded Drummin Hill. It is difficult to say today what protection it had, since all has again been bulldozed, but looking down the 20 or more feet on to the road one can still feel jittery, so close is the edge to the steep drop. However, this shrinks to insignificance when compared to what has been done a hundred yards on. Our first inkling that we had strayed somewhat from the line came when we noticed a small embankment edge above us. Climbing onto it, we saw a bridge parapet. But there was nothing before us. We were standing on the bridge and it was as if we had reached the end of a peninsula. Yawning ahead of us was a huge gap hundreds of yards wide, where a whole chunk of a hill had been removed and the remnants smoothed into a new shape. The bridge stands, but only just, serving no purpose any more. But what is immediately obvious is that this is unquestionably

Bridge at Rineen, 1988. (Illustration: M. Lenihan)

the most elegant stone-arched crossing remaining on the line today.
All its facings and the underside of the eye are of west Clare stone,
but it is beginning to deteriorate, probably because of damage done
by machines when the bank on its southern side was being cut away.
It cannot survive long even in its present condition unless some
restorative action is soon taken.

As for our course ahead, we could only take to the road and walk
around the huge gap, but before descending from our height we
scanned the seashore a mile west of us at Freagh, hoping to pick out
Aill a' Phúca. It was a forlorn hope, but an interesting tale belongs
to that place and it should be mentioned. As the name suggests, the
púca had made his own of an area near the seashore, and travellers
passed that way by night at their peril. A brave man who survived
one such encounter consulted the priest for advice and was told to
arm himself with a black-handled knife and stick it in whatever
might accost him there a second time. He went back and was duly
attacked, but managed to stick the knife in the creature. The *púca* fell,
screaming, and begged the man to pull it out and stick it again. 'I
won't,' said he. ''Tis fine where it is.' Next day, when he returned to the
place, he found his knife on the pathway, stuck in a lump of jelly-like

substance. The *púca* bothered travellers there no more. A very similar
story is told about the Hag of Bealaha, between Doonbeg and Kilkee,
and in other places, too, sinister nocturnal creatures were met with
and dispatched in like manner.

Freagh Castle we could not pick out, either, probably because
of its very ruinous state, and since we had no intention of making
a detour to find either it or the nearby 'puffing-hole' in the cliffs,
we kept to the road. Freagh Castle does have a connection, if only a
tenuous one, with the West Clare, for here lived Matthew J. Kenny,
who in 1882 was elected Parnellite MP for Ennis, at twenty-one
years of age the youngest member of parliament at the time. His
opponent in the election was R.W.C Reeves of Besborough, one of
the chief promoters of the railway.[11]

A very broken section followed, what with a filled-in cutting, a house
built on the line and farm sheds surrounding a second cutting. We
made some attempts to get down and investigate, but one could
literally disappear here, so deep is the quagmire. A further shallow
cutting, still very wet and reeking of slurry, marks the turning of the
line in a southerly direction, and from here it runs dead straight to
Miltown Station.

We emerged into not only the flat prospect of Fintramore but
also an unexpected blaze of wintry sunshine. It cheered us, as did a
clear view of the line for over half a mile, embanked all the way across
the low bare fields. Off left, the spire of Miltown Church needled the
sky, showing us how near we were to the terminus of the West Clare,
while a bridge ahead served as a marker of our progress. Just beyond
the location of the twenty-sixth milepost, a cattle-pass, 200 yards out,
is still entirely intact, but we had eyes only for the bridge and the view
around. Fifteen-feet high for most of its length, this embankment
would be well worth preserving and might do for Miltown what a
proper use of the notable approaches to Ennistymon could do for
that town. At the bridge we were a little surprised to find the metal
deck still in place, but this is probably only because the road which
runs underneath does not lead to anywhere of great significance and

traffic is not heavy. Though in the townland of Drummin, it was known as Rineen Bridge.

On the horizon, straight ahead, is Downes' Bridge, a stone-arched span carrying a byroad over the line. A further cattle-pass, a few rough patches where the surface has been quarried, and we were in the little cutting leading under it. The cutting at the southern side of the bridge is substantial but flooded. We travelled alongside, examining its rocky sides, not appreciating the luxury of dry footing until we arrived at its exit. Here was a maze of fences and water-logged, quaking fields. We eventually had to crawl under barbed wire and through mud to get back to the line, for only on it could we be assured of not sinking.

Past this obstacle course, the last half-mile was simple. At a slight dip in the way, a culvert sees a stream across and we were into Cloonbony, the townland in which the station is built. We had only to climb the final rising section to be at our journey's end. But before leaving this culvert we searched about it carefully, hoping to find some trace of the wind pump shown on our map. This was probably the 'windmill' that caused so much anxiety to the district councillors of Ennistymon in 1902 (see p. 124-5). Like so much else, though, it has vanished without trace.

But now occurs one of those folds in the land which in extent are not large but which possess a beauty that has nothing to do with size alone. A small river flows here a full 25 feet below the level of the surrounding little hills, and it was this space that the builders of the line had to contrive a crossing for. That they succeeded admirably is unquestionable, and far from spoiling the beauty of this secluded place, their well-proportioned embankment and bridge lend it a light touch of order and symmetry. It is well worth a visit, though I suspect that few people know about it, near and all as it is to the town.

Our arrival at the station was watched only by a flock of curious sheep. Without fanfare, but with a certain sense of achievement, we had reached the end of the first part of our journey. The passengers and crew of the last down train on the evening of 21 December 1888 must also have felt very relieved and thankful as they pulled into the station. For an attempt had just been made to derail it a short distance out. Two rocks had been left on the line but had been spotted in time, so no damage was done.[12] It would have been a poor Christmas present for Miltown after all the stirring happenings of that eventful year.

Miltown Station today is not an inspiring sight. The yard to the rear is deserted and poorly fenced, and the goods' shed on the up side is hardly apparent. Yet on 25 August 1946 this was the scene of a horrible accident, when engine driver Patrick O'Neill was caught between its wall and the train while reversing engine 11C on to the main line. He died shortly afterwards in spite of the ministrations of Dr Hillery, the west Clare coroner.[13]

As we approached the station-house we could almost feel the general air of neglect surrounding the place. The building itself is still in reasonable condition though in need of some renovation. The original verandah shelters the down platform, but a later structure now occupies the place of the up platform and extends right across the line, to almost touch the station-house. It appeared to us to be a block of apartments, though none was occupied. Very likely they are for use in the tourist season, when Miltown takes on a very different aspect to its drab winter exterior. One of the bastions of traditional

Miltown Malbay Station, 1954.
(Photo: Irish Railway Record Society, no. 10868)

cultural activities in Clare, Miltown has long been noted for its musicians, singers and storytellers – people of the calibre of Nora Cleary, Francie Kennelly, Tom Lenihan and 'Junior' Crehan. Only in recent times have such people come to be appreciated by the world at large, and resorted to for their matchless knowledge and expertise. But it *has* happened, and the fame of Miltown has grown accordingly. A far-sighted and energetic group of local people has done magnificent work through publications and lecture series to spread the good news throughout Ireland, but it is the Willie Clancy Summer School in July that brings the biggest crowds of enthusiasts, and from all corners of the world. No mere summer beer festival, this; from its beginnings in the early 1970s it has maintained its reputation for serious musical teaching and practice – no small achievement. Far more light-hearted is the Darlin' Girl Festival in August, but the efficiency, the determination to make things work, is the same. The results are there to prove this.

But before all these modern innovations took hold, Miltown had one other amenity that was bound to set it apart somewhat: its nearness to Spanish Point. The number of lodges on this coastline marked on Ordnance Survey maps of the nineteenth century shows how popular the area was even then with the well-off. This was largely due to the work of Thomas Morony, who in 1810 formed with a number of other gentlemen the company that built the Atlantic Hotel. Only the ruins of this remain today, but in its time it was, seemingly, the last word in luxury.[14] Later, with the decline of the gentry, the resort became a more middle-class haven and a quiet summer retreat for members of religious orders. But nowadays it is used by all, and everyone is welcome who has the means of getting here.

A far cry this from the welcome that awaited the shipwrecked sailors of the Armada when they struggled ashore here in 1588. They were rounded up by the bloodthirsty Boethius MacClancy, high sheriff of the county, executed without pretence of trial, and buried in the sand just below where Armada Lodge now stands. The location of their graves can still be pointed out by older people today, and their memory is perpetuated in the name of the headland.

As to how Mal Bay got its name, there are various explanations. Shaw Mason and Lewis thought it derived from the dangerous and rocky nature of the shoreline (presumably from the Latin *malus*, evil), but it could also come from the Irish word *meall*, which means to attract, but in a deceitful way.[15] Personally, I prefer the story of how the red-haired witch Mal put Cúchulainn under obligation to marry her. He tried to dodge his responsibility by fleeing, but she was not one to be put off, and so pursued him relentlessly until at last she cornered him at Loop Head (Ceann Léime). Desperate to escape her, he jumped onto an offshore rock, and in her efforts to do likewise she fell down the cliff and was decapitated. Her body was later washed up near Spanish Point, hence the name Mal Bay, while her head came ashore some distance to the north at the place now called Hag's Head.[16] Like the story of the origin of Glen and Shallee Castles, how much better this sticks in the mind than some strictly factual account.

It was not only in ancient times that horrible things were washed up, however. During the Great War a ship named *Kelp* was wrecked in Mal Bay. It was carrying hides and tallow, and an outbreak of diphtheria that occurred in the Miltown area shortly afterwards was blamed, rightly or wrongly, on this cargo.

Walking through this former station, one is conscious of the echoes of history. Here it was, on 26 January 1885, that Charles Stewart Parnell turned the first sod of the West Clare to sustained applause from the select dignitaries (including Rev. P. White, parish priest of Miltown, the well-known historian) and the multitude of ordinary mortals present. The formalities over, he got down to the real business of his visit, a good old-fashioned political harangue to the voters of west Clare.[17] They loved every minute of it and, moreover, believed him, for later, after the bitter split of 1891, west Clare returned Mr Maguire as Parnellite member of parliament, one of the few areas to do so.[18]

As we passed under the verandah, all we could hear was the ghostly echo of our own voices between the silent walls. At the road gate, where the level crossing and twenty-seventh milepost once were, a solitary stone building still survives. This was the engine shed, and since it stands almost at right angles to the line, the turntable must have been more or less outside its doors, near the gates. Only later, on seeing one of the many photos taken in 1952, were we able to confirm that here, directly inside the gates, were three lines: the main running road, a passing-loop and a siding to the goods' store. And sure enough, there also was the turntable, exactly where we reckoned it must be.

We crossed the public road and made a brief reconnaissance of what we must travel on our next outing, but there was little to encourage us. Of the line, there was no immediate sign. But since it ran so close to the main street of the town for the next half-mile or so, we thought it no more than was to be expected that there might be much disturbance and change.

We turned a last time to view the station before starting back for Lahinch. Was there something we might have missed? No. All that was we could see. And what of the 10,000-gallon water tank, the turntable, the station signpost announcing 'An Chathair'?[19] Or the siding, cattle-pen and loading bay? All scattered, all gone, never again to be assembled in one place.

A sad transformation, surely, for the terminus of the West Clare Railway.

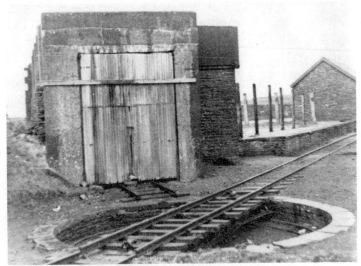

Miltown Malbay locomotive shed, 1952.
(Photo: Irish Railway Record Society, no. 10144)

Track lifting train at Miltown Malbay, 7.6.61.
(Photo: Roy Denison)

There were no kind motorists on all of that road back to Lahinch, a road that was quite dark before we had walked halfway to Rineen school. But the hope of meeting even one kept us going. Had we known that a 9-mile walk lay before us we would probably have done something reckless. The lights of every approaching car merely tantalised us, raising our hopes only to have them die with the fading of the red rear lights into the distance. At Poulaphúca, near the Rineen monument, we tiptoed, hoping that the brave man who had killed that creature had done a thorough job. We would have been in no condition to take him on just then!

Under the Major's Bridge it was pitch black. It would have been easy to convince us, in that dark corner, that there are ghosts. Lahinch was bright, but by then the lights held no attraction for us. We wanted to rest, nothing else, but our legs scarcely knew how to stop. We reached the car, hardly knowing which leg was which. Or caring. Somehow we had got back. Not another thing mattered at that moment.

Part III

The South Clare Railway

Day 8

Miltown Malbay to Craggaknock Station

Only after much persuading and promises of confectionery did Keith agree to accompany me on to the first part of the South Clare Railway the following day. His feet were 'at him' he said. Mine were, too, if only he knew it, but despite our day and a half's work twenty-four hours before, it seemed a pity not to keep up the momentum. So eventually, early on that watery Sunday morning, we faced south-wards from Miltown Station.

A last pause at the station gate allowed us to consult our map a final time before moving into Breaffy North. A mile to the north-west are three interesting houses, which we had no time to visit but wished we had. The first is Cloonbony House, of which only a little remains – a great loss to aficionados of things otherworldly, because it had the reputation of being one of the most haunted houses in Clare.[1] Carrickpatrick House, less than half a mile to the north of it, was also on occasion subject, it seems, to visitors not of this world, but nevertheless provided very comfortable free lodgings for magistrates and other visitors of a legal persuasion when on duty at the Miltown sessions.[2] Aran View, a few fields away, accommodated sixty people during the crisis of the Famine when the workhouse at Ennistymon was grossly overcrowded. Together with Merville Lodge, the Atlantic Hotel and several other spacious houses in the area, it helped to relieve the terrible press of numbers, but hardly the suffering. It is yet remembered that the inmates of this very house were turned out at 7 a.m. every day to fend for themselves. They would go to the shore, to a place called the Rinn, pick sea grass and shellfish, and boil them on a fire of seaweed and driftwood. Even today the mounds of shells, though grassed over, may be seen.

Kilfarboy, more than most western parishes, suffered horribly from the Famine, losing probably a third of its population in the years 1847–51. A contract for the burial of the dead was awarded to a man named Tadhg Diúrnáin, and he carried three loads of corpses per day to Ballard graveyard in his horse and cart. If they were accorded the dignity of a coffin, it was only to satisfy appearances, for it had a false bottom on a hinge, and thus they came to their final rest in a common pit with dozens of others. But all the while, in the midst of horrors almost indescribable, 'leading members of society' in the parish had their eyes fixed on the main chance. The various owners of the houses used as auxiliary workhouses were handsomely paid for the privilege, and some were awarded large compensation for damage to their property – at a time when the money was sorely needed merely to keep people alive. For example, Mr Morony was awarded £700 for repairs to the Atlantic Hotel, and Mr Comerford £130 for Ballykeale.[3] Shocking to us today, perhaps, but a thing of no account in an age when a good hunter was worth more than five Irishmen!

South of the Lahinch road we did not immediately find the line. In fact, we were only able to make headway by travelling along walls for a considerable distance in order to avoid disappearing into unplumbed depths of marsh. Crossing a little back-road saw us into Breaffy North, but no nearer to our goal. Only a scattering of decayed sleepers convinced us that we were approximately on course. But if there was no line to follow, we could at least view with interest the rear of all the houses along the main street of Miltown. And a widely varying and haphazard collection they make, too, showing a side of people's personalities (if houses can be said to reflect much of the character of those who live in them) that they might not always wish to be seen. This was the only close-up view of Miltown that most West Clare passengers ever got.

A short piece of a shallow cutting is almost all that survives of the line until one reaches Flag Road no. 1 crossing, just 300 yards east of the town's main crossroads. The intervening land is very bare and wild-looking, which is unusual so close to civilisation. On the other hand, perhaps we should not have been so surprised, since the ancient name for this region, all the way to Spanish Point, was Bréachmhagh, the plain of the wolf. An echo of this survives in the anglicised 'Breaffy'. Directly behind the football field, part of the line appears again and runs right into a stone wall that we took to be the site of the crossing gates. As soon as we had clawed our way over the wide trench, which has been dug through the line, and up on to the road, we were indeed able to confirm our position. This was Flag Road no. 1, and here were located a set of concession gates that had to be tended by the keeper of the main gates, 220 yards away.

Across the stream, we were in Leagard South, and we noted from our map that for almost a mile, until the line comes abreast of the Mullagh road at Poulawillin, we would be passing through country that looked remarkably devoid of features – few houses, dead straight roads, level fields. As it happened, the map was wrong in two vital respects: field boundaries and location of houses. Bulldozing and new buildings have made nearly all the older Ordnance maps obsolete, and one need only look at old photographs of the railway in places like Lahinch or Ennistymon to see how hugely an area may change in even the space of a single generation.

But Flag Road no. 2 crossing is, thankfully, much as it was thirty years ago. On the down side, it is neatly kept and a garden now occupies the site of the line. Across the Quilty road, the way was completely blocked by a large tyre depot and new house, but that could wait. First the cottage. The kind woman there told us that she

served here during the last years of the railway and that she witnessed no untoward incidents. But a former gatekeeper was killed
while opening the gate here one autumn night. The red gate-lamp
had quenched, and the engine driver, thinking that the way was clear,
kept going. The keeper, seeing a collision imminent, tried to get the
gate open but was struck and killed. As well as being informative
about the various trains that passed here and their frequency, she
was adamant that Miltown is a far more isolated place nowadays
– served by a mere two buses daily – than it was in the West Clare
era. Listening to her reeling off the rail timetable, day and hour, it
was difficult not to agree, despite the cars parked on all sides.

Our reception at the large depot was every bit as friendly and
helpful. Here, we were told of the ghost train at Miltown Station, of
the moving well on the Kilfarboy/Kilmurry parish boundary, which
we would be passing scarcely a mile farther on, and other items of
local interest. As we were being ushered through the wire fence at
the rear of the shed, Miltown dog track was pointed out to us, and
we were advised to 'come back some night if ye want to make a pile o'
money'. We gave no undertaking, but with this to cheer us, we broke
into open country and were immediately in an overgrown cutting.
But the *fionnán* is not what finally made us take to higher ground:
we had gone barely halfway through when it became wet and evil-
smelling. Sewage, it seemed, was getting in from somewhere. We
hurried on, wondering at the laxity of planning laws that allow such
to happen. It was to be only the first of a number of polluted cuttings
that we would meet on the South Clare Railway. Maybe it was our
haste to be away from that place, or the easy nature of the ground,
or even the distraction of the waves crashing on the shore to the
west; whatever the reason, we were at the site of the twenty-eighth
milepost in no more than fifteen minutes. Here, the line swings out
to the edge of the Mullagh road, and just as at Rineen, they run side
by side, though more briefly. Directly west, a mile away, is Miltown
House and Wellington Lodge, home of President Hillery, and just
south of them the old racecourse. Nearby Medina House, off the
coast road, was owned by the White family, and it is claimed that the

Mrs White referred to by Percy French in his song hailed from here.[4] But as will be seen, there are other claimants to that honour.

The cutting which carried the railway under road level here in Poulawillin is now partly filled in with rubbish and wrecked cars, but what finally stopped us was none of these, but the first of two new houses built on fill directly across our way. At least the road was convenient, and so we sat for a moment's rest and map consultation. Before us lay Breaffa level crossing, 28½ miles from Ennis, and south of it the Glendine River with its bridge. We hoped it was intact. Otherwise, a long walk around by Knockloskeraun road-bridge was in store.

As it turned out, we never came to Breaffa crossing. The line has been cleared from the long narrow strip of land beside the Mullagh road, leaving only a faint outline and the right-hand boundary fence. This would have been sufficient guide, were it not for what we found blocking our way: one of those huge V-shaped gashes in the land that pass for drains but are really canals. We climbed warily down to the water, knowing how soft the clay can be on these 45-degree sides, and luck was with us. The bed was solid and we decided to walk along it since it turned a short way off and ran parallel to the line. That was a mistake, for when we emerged some way downstream we had entirely lost the railway. We were still broadly on course, for we could see Miltown power station ahead and Breaffa cottage to our right, but of the line there was no trace. We reached the road, and could have saved ourselves discomfort by merely walking to the crossing and continuing from there. But instead we started across the fields towards the river, gradually correcting our line of progress as we went. We had an easier passage than we deserved, there being no more than muck and high ditches in our way, and even these we forgot as soon as we saw the Glendine River. Swirling, looping in sharp turns and little pools, it rattles along in its narrow gorge as if shepherding stones downstream to its meeting with the Annagh River. Our crossing point, Sexton's Bridge, was intact, but since there were no parapets we hurried over it like men expecting that it might fall at any moment and with only the briefest glance of

Annagh no. 1 crossing, 1954.
(Photo: Irish Railway Record Society, no. 10870)

acknowledgment to the stream gushing underneath. Already, our sights were on a scene more imposing. Here, from a large valley towards which the Glendine cascades, rears a high, ivy-draped road-bridge of one main arch, with others flanking, while nearby, in the lee of Aillateriff heights, a group of mill-like buildings nestles. Over all, the power station stood out like a beacon, white against the sky. Without ever looking to the map we knew that this was Stackpoole's Bridge and Poulawillin Mills. A few minutes' walk and we were at the crossing: Annagh no. 1, 28¾ miles from Ennis. By the merest coincidence, the owner of the cottage is a man from near my home place in Kerry whom I had not met in almost twenty years. He was only too glad to show us the sights, we as delighted to avail ourselves of his offer.

From McMahon's corn and woollen mills in the hollow below his cottage, the village of Miltown took its name in the nineteenth century, and the name of the nearby townland, Poulawillin, still preserves this memory.[5] The bridge, at least 40-feet high, bears the inscription 'Built by John Stackpoole, Esq. July 1811', and has withstood the years with dignity.

These Stackpooles were an influential family, owning substantial property locally, and of them an intriguing story is told. The foal of a seahorse, which had been captured by a farmer at Spanish Point, was sold to Mr Stackpoole and became a champion racer. His neighbours were Fitzgeralds, and Edmund, a son of the family, went to a ball in Dublin, where he fell in love with a girl. Unfortunately, so did an Englishman, moreover one who was an expert duellist. He challenged Edmund, but he, having no expertise in that craft, sent to Clare for his brother Vesey, who was a military man. There was a problem, though: how would he get to Dublin in time to save his brother? He remembered the water-horse, asked Stackpoole for a loan of it and got it. He arrived in Dublin four hours after setting out, with only two stops along the way, at Ennis and Limerick, to allow the horse a drink of wine. He gave the animal into the care of a vet and went to the place appointed for the duel. The Englishman was there, declaring Edmund a coward for his non-appearance, and was about to claim victory when Vesey announced that he would defend his brother's honour. They tossed. The Englishman won, fired first, but missed. Vesey's aim was better.

The vet, meantime, had saved the horse's hooves by placing them in four firkins of butter, but the animal's coat had turned grey, and even Stackpoole did not recognise him when he was returned to him later.

At the western end of the bridge, on the river bank, is St Joseph's Well, which is still the focus of a sizeable pilgrimage each year. Local legend claims that it was once on the opposite side of the river, in the parish of Kilfarboy, but that after water taken from it was boiled, it changed its location to the Kilmurry side, where it remains to this day. Ordnance maps still show it as the well of St Laichtín, and so it was, no doubt, in 1839 when the surveyors were about their work. But in the mid-nineteenth century Laichtín and many other local saints went out of fashion and were replaced in popular devotion by more prestigious names, particularly if their feast days happened to coincide with those of the more 'powerful' figures. Hence St Joseph's Well here. Yet it seems a pity that Laichtín should be forgotten, for he appears to have been a rather interesting person. Patron of the fighting-men of west Clare, he would stand in cold water to his neck, praying for their victory whenever they were engaged in battle. Apparently, his services were very frequently called on! The well is said to have first sprung up when the saint, while visiting the area, found a child who had not been baptised. He blessed a spot on the ground, and at once water for the ceremony gushed out.

Today, even for those not much interested in praying, it is a little oasis of quiet, with its trees, sheltered walks and the river beneath. Not surprisingly, it was fondly remembered by many who had to leave the parish in search of a livelihood:

> *Oh, let me spend one quiet hour the Annagh's stream beside,*
> *Where 'neath the ivy-mantled bridge its noiseless waters glide,*
> *And let me dream where silence falls upon the peaceful scene*
> *Beneath the drooping thorns that shade the well of St Laichtín.*[6]

But not everyone had such regard for the holy place. We are told that a landlord's daughter once desecrated the well and then blithely went off about her business. The saint, however, was not to be mocked. Some time later the same girl was sitting reading at the Black Rock near the Atlantic Hotel, when a huge wave swept her away. She was found later, drowned.

Miltown turf-burning power station, standing disused a few hundred yards to the west, could never have been an efficient operation; it was just not large enough. But it provided useful direct and indirect employment (especially in the supply of turf) in its day in an area that had little to offer but tourism and farming. Hardly a mile south of here, a new generating experiment is now being tried, this time using wind power. The oddly-shaped mast, looking like a cross between a space-age aerial and a giant fly swat, is quite visible from the bridge.

Downstream, near where the Annagh flows into the bay, is Bealaclugga Bridge with its peculiar-looking Gothic arch and castellated abutments, obviously of nineteenth-century construction. But this river crossing has a history that goes back a long, long way beyond that. A well-known story tells that St Senan possessed a bell,

Clog na Néal, which fell to him from Heaven, and that it was used for the swearing of all kinds of oaths. He who swore on it and broke that oath would be forever cursed. A chieftain who was convinced that his servants were cheating him sent one of them to St Senan to get the bell in order to put them to the test. The servant knew well enough what danger he and his companions were in, so when passing here, near the mouth of the Annagh, he 'dropped' the bell into the water. His cleverness did not save him, though. The bell came back of its own accord to perform its function, with dire consequences for the thieves. And so the place became known as Béal a' Chlogadh (the river-mouth of the bell). The nearby Bell Bridge Cottage shows that the owner at least had some regard for this story.

We were quite taken aback by the wealth of history and tradition spanning so many centuries in such a little place. Making a mental note to return at a more leisurely time and examine the area in greater detail, I reluctantly explained to our host that we had to be in Craggaknock by evening, and so we faced for the railway bridge 200 yards from the level crossing. It remains in good condition, only the mass-concrete parapets showing the effects of weathering. The four stone corner piers look quite impressive, as are the on and off embankments, since the river valley is deep here. The Annagh for most of its length, indeed, is a very rapid river, and has cut a deep channel marked by many waterfalls, notably in the area above and below Kildeema graveyard.

Across the bridge, in the townland of Annagh, there was much to admire in the way the river squirmed along in a semi-circle to a huge pool at the base of the embankment close to where the twenty-ninth milepost once stood. A fine place for fishing, without doubt, but extremely deep and dangerous-looking. The current has begun to eat into the foundations of the line, and already land slippage has occurred, leaving a sheer and frightening drop. We kept well back from the edge, not knowing how undermined that side might be, and pressed on into land that was becoming ever more swampy. There was no escape to left or right; the fields were even worse. The power station was behind us now, but a mere field away, on a dry knoll, an old stone-and-brick ruin, surrounded by the remains of extensive out-buildings, gaped eyelessly in our direction. This was once Annagh House, a property of the Stackpooles. Built in the early eighteenth century, it was accidentally burned in 1860 and uninhabited by 1910.[7] Observed in conjunction with the power station and the West Clare line, it presents an interesting if melancholy picture.

Our troubles continued, the swamp developing into a small lake. But for the rushes at the edges of the line, we could have made no progress. We hopped along, from one to the next, a business that demanded total concentration. Then, in lightning contrast, when we squelched through a muddy gap we found ourselves faced with a huge levelled field. The line was being elusive again, and succeeded in hiding from us for most of the way to the next crossing cottage half a mile away. We could do no more than proceed on a median course diagonally across the open space, trusting more to our eyes than to the map. When we did pinpoint the cottage, the rest was easy. We found the line again a few hundred yards from its door, a green streak among the surrounding rushes. Unfortunately, in our attempts to keep on course, we had passed by the odd-looking fly-swat electricity generator. But in any case it was farther off than we had expected; too distant for us to investigate.

We hoped to find out something about this crossing at the cottage, but there was no information for us there as it was uninhabited. However, a certain minimum of information we did have: that this was Annagh no. 2 crossing, 29½ miles from Ennis, and that it was opened as a halt in May 1952; that here ended the section of line under the control of Miltown Station; that Berry Lodge and Cassino Lodge, just north-west of here, were once owned by the Stackpoole family; that the five crossroads of Annagh were half a mile to the south-east.

There was no difficulty in getting to Emlagh crossing, for the way is quite clear and the surface dry. But there was little of interest to be seen, apart from a good example of native ingenuity: a JCB tyre cut neatly in half to make two drinking troughs. At the triple boundary of Annagh, Caherrush and Emlagh, a handsome stone

Annagh no. 2 crossing, 1954.
(Photo: Irish Railway Record Society, no. 10871)

culvert lined with Liscannor flags still carries the boundary stream, but after that it is as well to proceed to the level crossing without any further delay. The cottage is to the west of the road, on the down side, and as we approached, a man passing on a Honda 50 stopped. He was full of information about the area: the power station's last years, the Canadian-designed wind generator and its workings, the decline in population and growth of summer houses, nearly all owned by city people. There was no resentment of these latter in his tone; he was telling us facts only. To finish, and to dismiss himself gracefully, he pointed to Emlagh railway cottage, behind him. 'They're from Limerick. They'll talk to ye.'

They did indeed talk to us – and enthusiastically, too – of this, their new home far from traffic and noise. With permission we stepped carefully through their well-kept garden and into the wilderness beyond where once the thirtieth milepost kept watch. And so began a vicious struggle between us and a large colony of robust briars. That the line was partly dug up worried us not at all, for through a dip in the land the sea showed itself to the north and, more importantly, we were able to make out passing traffic on the Miltown–Quilty road hardly a quarter of a mile away in the same direction. Then Quilty itself was in sight, a little cluster of houses huddled together in low ground near the shore. Here, I was reminded of the yarn of the man who, during the Emergency, set fire to his run-down thatched cottage as the train passed. The engine was burning turf at the time and spewing out sparks, and the cottager, astute enough to realise that a change of accommodation at the company's expense was in the offing, used his matches to good effect.

Ahead of us, an odd-looking fence appeared somewhat like a jump on a racecourse, surmounted as it was by a long post. When we reached it we found that it was no post, but one of the steel rails, only the second we had come upon in all the miles since leaving Ennis. A small stream once ran here, but it has been much altered and enlarged by excavation, and the culvert demolished in the process.

Two hundred yards farther on is another stream, this one the boundary with Quilty East. Here is a more substantial bridge, its stonework and girder facings still firmly intact. Two fields to the north is Emlagh House, another former Stackpoole property, and from here came the William Stackpoole who was high sheriff of Clare in 1784.

Before us, the way looked clear, but if we imagined that the final level stretch into Quilty would be effortless we were entirely mistaken. A wide blanket of thick mud had us supporting each other step for step over a distance of some 150 yards, but still we were not over the worst: the bridge over the stream dividing Quilty East from Quilty West had met the fate of so many others, leaving a 10-foot-wide, 6-foot-deep channel, newly gouged. But in this instance, the kind thought at least was there: a sleeper laid across as a footbridge, sparing us the sticky business of heeling our way down and clawing back up the other side.

It was the end of our purgatory for the moment, and so we walked the final quarter of a mile towards Quilty cross along a fine surface, roads closing in on the line ahead from left and right. Here, once more, is a site for an excellent amenity, with the added advantage of proximity to the sea. We could smell the salt on the air now, and seaweed began to crunch under our feet – debris from the many storms that strike this unprotected coast. With a hundred yards to go to the crossing cottage at Quilty East, the line again disappeared, but we hardly noticed. We had arrived, and a rest was called for. But not before we paused to consider the place where probably the first derailment on the South Clare Railway occurred on 16 July 1892. No. 2 engine, which was engaged in ballast work, left the rails here, but those on board escaped injury. The 'accident', it seems, was not so accidental, for the sleepers and rails had been tampered with by persons unknown. Since an election was in progress at the time and special trains were to be run from Kilrush to Miltown on the following day, 17 July, for an election rally, it was, no doubt, a crude and criminal attempt to prevent certain supporters from arriving to cheer on their candidate.

As we crossed into the road we noted how close the line came to the coast here – closer even than at Lahinch. No wonder it got special mention in the 'Working Time Table' of the GSR, where a whole section was given over to 'Prevention of Derailments by Storm'.[8] The cottage is occupied still, but there was no one at home that day, so we made no delay, only continued on towards the station, 300 yards away. But even from the road it was obvious to us that there would be no passing that way, for an estate of houses now occupies the site of the line. We went as far as we could, almost to their garden walls, without obstruction, but that was all. At a small back-road, once the access road to Sea View House, we called a halt, walked down to the street and took stock.

Quilty, traditionally a fishing village, is completely exposed to Atlantic gales and it was one of these that drove *Leon XIII* of Nantes aground only a mile from here on 2 October 1907. The Quilty fishermen in their *currachs* risked life and limb to bring the crew safely ashore. Let a ballad written shortly afterwards take up the tale:

Those brave fishermen from Quilty town knew what their signal meant
And for the loss of lives to see, it made them discontent.
They crossed the wild and stormy foam, across it they did go
Without dread or fear they gave three cheers, 'Let us man our own canoe'.

However, their good deed done, the remnants of the vessel were fair game. It is a well-remembered event in the lore of the region, the captain's words in particular: 'The best and the worst of humanity I have met in Quilty.'

Quilty Station after closure, 7.6.61. (Photo: Roy Denison)

Diesel locomotive at Quilty Station.
(Photo: Irish Railway Record Society, no. 83601)

The ship's bell hangs today in the picturesque round-towered Star of the Sea Church just west of the Kilrush road, and a display in the porch of the building recounts the events of that stormy day and their sequel – the honouring of the fishermen with medals by the French government. One of these same men, Thomas Boyle by name, lived for over another half-century, and was involved in other notable maritime exploits. During the Great War his ship was torpedoed by a German submarine and he alone survived, floating on a raft for seven days before rescue. And in 1942 he succeeded in bringing ashore the body of a Dublin girl drowned in a storm at Kilkee. Fearless men, the fishermen of Quilty.[9] Also displayed are the texts of two of the ballads written about the events of 1907, 'The Quilty Heroes' and 'Quilty's Heroes'.

We continued on to the station-house, round the sharp bend of the Kilrush road at the seawall. The building is not difficult to find, for though it has been renovated its outline is still recognisable from old photos. Built on the up side, Quilty Station was just over 31 miles from Ennis, and had a single platform and small siding as well as a little goods' shed. In that, it resembled other minor stations like Kilmurry or Doonbeg; what made it different was its exposed coastal position and the danger inherent in this. On 3 March 1897 several carriages of the 10.30 a.m. passenger train from Kilrush were blown off the line between Kilmurry and here, and tumbled down an embankment. That there was no serious injury to any of the two dozen passengers was, as a newspaper report put it, 'really marvellous'.[10] Two years later, on 12 January 1899, at Quilty cross, the 8.30 a.m. train from Ennis was derailed in similar circumstances.[11] Again, no one was seriously injured, but rather than wait for a tragedy to occur the company began to take precautions. A high earthen bank was built at the seaward side of the line south-west of the station, and in 1911 an anemometer was installed to warn of storms. Its high mast protruded from a little wooden hut on the up side a short distance from the goods' shed (which stood at the end of the platform), but the instrument itself was in the station-house, where two differently toned bells awaited the onset of the wind. It became part of the stationmaster's daily duties to take wind-speed readings, and when winds of over 60 mph were indicated only ballasted stock could be used, while at 80 mph all traffic was halted. A gale of 112 mph was reputedly recorded here in January 1927. Ballast consisted of slabs of concrete under the carriage seats.

But the news from Quilty was not inevitably serious. Life had its more jovial and boisterous moments, and these sometimes forced themselves on the attention of a wider audience. Take for example the case which came before the Miltown petty sessions in August 1896. Five men were up on a charge of fighting in a railway carriage at Miltown Station. If they had been going no further, the matter would probably have gone no further, either, but unfortunately they travelled on to Quilty, battling all the way, and there at last action had to be taken. Two of the five were fined twenty shillings each with twenty shillings costs. At the same sessions, a Mary O'Connor was

fined 5/3d for travelling without a ticket from Quilty to Kilmurry, a distance of little over a mile.[12] It was a hefty fine, considering the small journey involved.

A short distance beyond the station, the little gardens of the village petered out into open country, and so we bade goodbye to this little oasis of civilisation in a landscape that is otherwise flat

Anemometer cabin, Quilty, 1953. (Photo: Irish Railway Record Society, no. 10436)

and bare, though we were by no means seeing it at its worst on that bright spring day.

In the mile and a quarter to Kilmurry Station the line makes an S-shape through more or less level terrain, first looping west, then gradually east until it comes side by side with the Kilrush road at Kilmurry Bridge, and finally west again to the station gates. We were almost immediately on a raised section of line, and ahead, on the up side, was the earthen storm-bank, several feet wide at its base and tapering towards the top. Before it was built, the line was totally exposed to the elements and it is hard to see how the builders could have failed to appreciate this obvious fact. Very likely none of the men in charge was from the locality or had stood here near the sea at the height of one of the spring storms that so regularly rocked the area. Now that the protection is no longer necessary, the bank is being quarried for road material and is gapped at many points.

Eventually, it disappeared altogether, though we could still discern where it had lain by the width of the line, which here included its foundation space. But now we were drawing near to a cutting that put all else in the shade, for by the standards of what we had so far seen, it looked massive. Even from a distance of 200 yards we could see that it was cut through the living rock. But already we knew that the worst might be expected, for a stream was even now underfoot, flowing towards us. For the moment, however, our eyes were elsewhere. From our first steps into the shade of the high walls we realised that this, Tromra cutting, was no ordinary undertaking. Its horizontally striated rocky sides begin abruptly and continue in a jagged, solid fashion for practically its whole length. Not surprisingly, we were occasionally able to pick out the marks of the jumpers in the stone.

The first hundred yards allowed us a careful look around, but after that we were gradually forced to the sides and finally to the fields by water and then furze. Climbing the walls of Tromra cutting is like climbing a cliff, for that is essentially what the walls are. We were by no means equipped for mountaineering, nor was clinging to doubtful tufts of grass much to our liking. But we got out, to find ourselves on a football pitch. The contrast with what we had just left could not be greater: here, level and cared for; there, impassable swamp. Yet though the view from our latest perch was excellent, a rather puzzling problem intervened: do the Quilty footballers take it in turn to stand in the ooze of Tromra cutting during matches, and kick back the ball? For surely the ball must sooner or later get in here, since there is no fencing along its edge. Or is it that they are excellent marksmen, all?

New houses line the Kilrush road along here, while off to the south-west, near the shore, we could make out the well-defined shape of Tromra Castle, looking imposing in its level setting. More immediate to us, 50 yards forward, a road built on its own new embankment bridges the cutting at right angles. This recent addition is no mean feat of construction, and it is tempting to assume that the inspiration for its design came from a study of railway banks. It also serves another purpose beside its primary one of roadway: it allows an otherwise unobtainable view back and forward along the cutting.

As we stood in the quietness, it was easy to imagine the scene here almost a century ago: the crowds of men standing on the edges looking down on the labourers below, ready to shout a complaint to the supervisor if they saw any man so much as rest on his shovel, in hopes of seeing him fired and being taken on themselves. So hard was the work that it is yet claimed in the locality that there were no breaks during the working day, not even for meals: 'You had to eat and work at the one time, picking away at a cond o' bread out o' your pocket.'[13]

There was at least one fatality during the tunnelling of this hard 500 yard stretch: a horse-handler. Temporary rails were laid as near to the work face as possible, and the debris carted back in a large wagon. When it was fully laden, a horse would pull it into motion and men would push it thereafter. Here in this cutting, the horse-handler failed to get out of the way in time, and was killed when the heavy wagon ran over him.[14]

Already, out beyond the mouth of the cutting, a long, curving embankment and bridge beckoned us on. But coming to grips with them was not to be so easy. As far as the exit, a caravan park, securely fenced, occupied the land at the cutting's edge, and short of crossing on to the Kilrush road some distance away there was only one way forward: through the miry sink-hole that Tromra cutting had by this point become. We took our chances, slipped down to mud level and began dragging ourselves from bush to bush on the edges of the mire. All went well initially. We even came within 15 yards of dry land. But here our luck ran out – or Keith's did. There were no more bushes to swing from, and the greenest and widest pool of sludge lay still ahead. To turn back when we were so close seemed ridiculous. I felt my way forward, thick evil-smelling slime to my knees, and arrived none the worse for my journey. But Keith was stranded. Nothing for it but to return and pick him up piggyback. It was this operation, of getting from his perch to my back, that was his undoing. In his hurry he misjudged and went in to his thighs. I grabbed, but too late. His wellingtons were filled, trousers, socks ruined. He might now have walked ahead; nothing worse could happen. But it was hardly the moment for such reasonable suggestions. I took him up and, like St Christopher, felt my way forward again through the 'Bog of Eternal Stink', as he was already bitterly calling it. We docked, smelling of something other than roses. It seemed a good time to stop for lunch. After a squeezing of socks and a rinsing of all that could be rinsed, the buoyancy of youth began to reassert itself, and amid much banter about the benefits of mud packs and frequent washing of feet, we ate.

It was with renewed good humour that we set off for Kilmurry Bridge. The lofty embankment leading on to it is a pleasure to walk, and gives what passes for a good view in this flat landscape. Ahead and across a single field to the east is the public-road bridge, clearly visible and a fine solid example of the mason's craft, as is the railway bridge itself. From even a little way off this latter might well be mistaken for a cattle-pass since it has no parapets. Only when one is crossing it does its true size become apparent. This, as well as being called Kilmurry Bridge, was also once known as King's Bridge, and the stream flowing underneath is the Ballymackea River.

What then was the metal-parapet bridge 300 yards away, we

wondered. Our map showed it to be a road-bridge – and Sullivan's Bridge is the only such in Shandrum townland, which we had crossed into at the river. A little byroad runs beneath – an access way to Kilmurry graveyard and well worth a visit for its interesting and finely sculpted grave slabs. The church, like all Irish churches dedicated to the Virgin Mary, is relatively modern but in a ruined condition. In a nearby field is Tobermurry, Our Lady's Well, which was once much resorted to for cures. But even in 1839 O'Donovan found that no rounds were being performed there, 'to the great shame of the Dalcassians'. In that same year, Fr Anthony McGuane, parish priest of the combined parishes of Kilfarboy and Kilmurry, built one of the three churches of the parish at Mullagh. His younger brother Patrick served under him as curate and became parish priest of Kilfarboy on his death, at which time the parishes were divided. Fr Anthony is still remembered in the folklore of the region as a man of great powers and as one who had the gift of prophecy. He once said that 'when taxes become as high as the rent the Great Dragon will arrive in the east. It would be better for men to be taken to their God before that day comes.' Certainly, the Ireland of today goes far towards fulfilling the first part of the equation. Whether the EC does the rest remains to be seen.

Sullivan's Bridge is so low that it is a wonder it has not already been removed. It has been struck several times by passing vehicles and the stonework has begun to crumble, particularly the corner piers. If it is not urgently attended to, part of it may well fall and injure a passer-by, and then there will be the usual chorus of howls for demolition that usually attends such accidents.

At the end of the off embankment stood the thirty-second mile-post in the good old days, and from here to where the line begins to rise towards Kilmurry Station, the going is tough. Furze has invaded the line, and only for a narrow corridor kept open by cattle, our task would have been far more painful than it was. On the rising ground we had to abandon the shallow cutting in which the track was laid and take again to the fields, as a stream now flows there, brushing the long *fionnán* like disembodied hair. A far cry it is from the day when the guard's van was sent hurtling down along this slope, having been struck by an engine during shunting operations in the station. Nothing will ever again hurtle down here except water.

But now the road was before us, and having squeezed through the usual barrier of sleepers we were face to face with Kilmurry Station, the first staff post on the South Clare Railway, 32½ miles from Ennis. The station-house, on the down side and in Kilclehaun townland, is in beautiful trim, probably better cared for than when it was in semi-state ownership. Its surrounds are neatly kept and the location of the siding can be clearly distinguished. Its goods' store, now painted green, is intact and being used – the same shed that was often piled roof-high with bulky 8-stone bales of carrageen moss in the days of the railway. Picked by local people during the spring tides, it was bought by a district agent, stored here and shipped out when quantity justified. Guinness, Jacob's biscuits, fertiliser and farm machinery were other regular items of cargo unloaded here, and there was a constant to-ing and fro-ing of shopkeepers, publicans and farmers to the station, since Mullagh, 2 miles to the east, as well as Kilmurry, was part of the station's hinterland. (On Ordnance maps its official title was 'Kilmurry and Mullagh Station'.)

The role of the West Clare in the modernisation of agriculture in Clare has never been researched, but it was not negligible. Even on Sundays farmers would travel long distances to examine for themselves some of the latest machines, especially of the hay-saving variety, on temporary display at Kilmurry Station before being collected by their new owners. The same thing happened, no doubt, at every rural station along the line.

Yet the early days of Kilmurry Station were not auspicious, for it appears that the people of Mullagh took a very dim view of the proposed route of the line at the time of its construction. They felt that their own area was the more logical site for it, far more so than the more sparsely populated region 2 miles to the west. On 6 June 1889 a large meeting was held at Mullagh with representatives from all the surrounding parishes, and an organisation was formed, 'The Mullagh Railway Association', to press their claims. Other counsels prevailed,

Kilmurry Station, 1952.
(Photo: Irish Railway Record Society, no. 10146)

however, and so they had to content themselves with the inconvenience of the journey to Kilmurry every time a delivery or collection had to be made. By the 1940s and 1950s, though, all old resentments seem to have been forgotten, for the station was constantly busy with an up and down goods' train every day, plus a morning and evening passenger service. (Pity the poor stationmaster, a man of noble title but little dignity, for he had to load and unload merchandise either alone or with whatever help his family might afford him.) This was later augmented by a midday passenger train to Kilrush two days per week.

One of the more amusing aspects of the West Clare during steam days was the easy-going attitude of almost everyone involved. Happenings at Kilmurry were no exception. At this station the driver of the Ennis goods' train would change places with the driver from Kilrush. If his train should happen to arrive in early and there was no shunting to be done, he would go the short distance to Kilmurry, have his few pints and then bring back a billycan of porter for the other driver, who would do likewise for him at another time. No one ever seems to have suffered too many ill-effects from such procedure, and looking back, it seems to give a human touch that is all too absent in the efficiency-mad services of our harried age. Or is that merely to hide inefficiency behind a veil of sentimentality?

As we pulled away from the station, a large house on our right, Clonmore Lodge by name, attracted our attention. It is claimed that the Mrs White of parcel fame from Percy French's song once dwelt in a previous house on this site, but who can tell if this is true or not? Certainly a family of the Whites lived here,[15] but others also have claimed the honour, as we have seen at Spanish Point, and since French is long dead it is now unlikely that the identities of his characters will ever be conclusively proved.[16]

Three hundred yards away is another level crossing, Kilmurry no. 2, which was tended from the station, and beyond it, sliced through a hill, is a very impressive-looking cutting. This one we had been looking forward to seeing, for it was in this place, on 2 October 1920, that the body of Captain Alan Lendrum RM, was discovered wrapped in a sheet in a rough coffin. The intention obviously was that the body be delivered to his relatives, for the coffin was labelled 'Kilkee'.[17] He had been shot, perhaps unintentionally, at Caherfeenick, on his way from Kilkee to the Ennistymon petty sessions on 22 September, the day of the Rineen ambush, and his body buried first in the sand near the seashore. But it was later brought here to Kilclehaun to put at rest the minds of his next of kin. That Kilmurry and Mullagh escaped the dire consequences endured by other towns after the ambush and Lendrum's disappearance was probably due more to oversight on the part of the military than to any leniency or sense of justice.

At a cottage nearby, an old man was observing us closely, so we introduced ourselves and explained our purpose. He was able to confirm for us much of what we already knew and to point out to us many sights that we would have passed by. One such was Mount Callan, its partly wooded slopes a dark blotch 7 miles away to the north-east. Engine no. 5, which now stands at Ennis Station, was named for this much-frequented hill, the forerunner of Lahinch as the great summer gathering-place for celebrations on Garland Sunday. St Patrick's Day and Easter Sunday also drew huge crowds to Buaile na Gréine, on the southern slope of the hill, up to the mid-nineteenth century, but eventually with encouragement from the Catholic clergy the celebrations were channelled towards more worthy pursuits (e.g., praying at the blessed well at Mooghna, near Ennistymon, and at St Brigid's Well, Liscannor) and accessible locations.

Large amounts of scholarly sweat have been devoted to explaining the history of Mount Callan's ogham stone and Leacht Chonáin, the supposed burial-place of Conán Maol Mac Mórna, one of the greatest of the Fianna; but nothing conclusive has come of these labours, and the theorising which began with Theophilus O'Flanagan in 1785 still continues.[18] Folklore attributes great importance to Mount Callan and the area about. On the hill, it is said, will be found the key that will free Cill Stuifín from enchantment, and it was to nearby Doo Lough that St Senan banished the monstrous Cathach from Scattery Island. In more recent times the same lake had a new addition, for it was to these dark waters that Captain Lendrum's car was driven after his death in 1920, and here it remained submerged and rotting for many years, the victim of souvenir hunters and a ghoulish reminder of the Troubles.[19] By an odd coincidence, Doolough Lodge, a mile west of the lake, was visited in 1910 by the newly crowned George V, in whose service Captain Lendrum was later to lose his life.[20]

Since we had no time to visit Tromra Castle, which had tantalised us several times since we had left Quilty, we did the next best thing: viewed it through the powerful binoculars with which the old man kept the coastline within his grasp. One of a number of strongholds which protected the lands of the O'Briens, Lords of Aran, it was built in the fifteenth century and has survived remarkably well, considering its turbulent history. It remains, a dumb reminder of the political and military power that was once based here but has long passed away. Even the city of Galway was glad to pay an annual tribute of wine to these O'Briens for protection against the 'ferocious O'Flahertys'. It was an alliance that lasted until the reign of Elizabeth I, when the Aran Islands were finally captured by the same 'ferocious' clan.[21] Edmond O'Flaherty plundered the castle in 1642, an act which cost him his life, for he was later hanged by Coote, governor of Connaught, who himself was stabbed to death by Murdoch O'Flaherty, nephew of Edmond. To look at the neat grey flagstones today, one would never dream that they were once the cause of so much bloodshed.

Near the castle is the site of Seafield Lodge, which was burned in 1922. It was, in the eighteenth and nineteenth centuries, the home of the Casey family, many of whom were prominent in the affairs of the county. James J. Casey, born here in 1831, is probably the best-known member of the family. He attained high legal and parliamentary office in Australia as solicitor-general and minister for agriculture in Victoria.[22]

Jutting into the Atlantic beyond the castle is Seafield peninsula. Barr na gCros it was called in Irish: the headland of the crosses, from the custom of burying the dead temporarily here in stormy weather when rough seas did not allow them to be transported to the graveyard on Mutton Island, half a mile offshore. One of the ships of the Armada was wrecked here, and Boethius MacClancy is said to have executed a hundred of the Spaniards on the island.[23] How Mutton Island came to be is vividly documented by the Four Masters, who state that about the year AD 799 a tidal wave drowned all this coast. From their description it might be concluded that some kind of earthquake causing land subsidence was the culprit. This may also have been the origin of the Cill Stuifín legend.

In 1921 the island was used as a place of detention for offenders under the Sinn Féin courts, but otherwise it has for many years been uninhabited except for occasional fishermen. Even these are now few and far between, and the coast off Seafield, which at the turn of the century supported almost two dozen three-man *currachs*, is deserted for most of the year.[24] The fish-curing station lies unused, and the barter trade in kelp, carrageen and fish between the people of Seafield and the merchants of Mullagh is only a distant memory.

We returned the binoculars to their owner and gratefully accepted his invitation to have a 'drop o' tea'. We had had notions that we might get as far as Craggaknock before dusk, but he did his best to dispel them. We would make good time, he said, until we reached the Annageragh River, just beyond Cloonadrum school, a mile away. But there we would have to make a wide detour by road, for the railway bridge is gone. This less-than-comforting news should have decided us to leave it for another time and get back to Miltown with the day-light, just for once. But no. Such a fine day was too precious to waste, and so we told him we would try it regardless. 'Well, mind yerselves goin' through that cutting, so. That place isn't right ever since your man was found there inside in the coffin. There's even a light seen there in the night, sometimes.'

There was nothing even remotely haunted about it that spring day as we walked through. A vicious breeze blew away all thoughts of ghosts and hurried us on our way. After its impressive entrance, Kilclehaun cutting falls back gradually, but it is still more than 12-feet deep for most of its 500-yards' length. In parts it widens to almost 50 feet, but all this was of little help to us. Flooding, fencing and the familiar furze defeated us at last, and once more we had to do our mountaineering act and drag ourselves up and out. From its edge it was easy to see why farmers objected so much to the railway's passage through their land when, as here, it divided fields so decisively. That deed is being reversed now. Again, before us was another road embanked across at right angles, just as in Tromra cutting. It is an inevitable development, for no farmer can afford the long detours and consequent delays that such mighty gorges put him to.

From here to the cutting's end, there was no great difficulty, and getting onto the embankment beyond involved only a little deviation to avoid a long expanse of briars compacted and burnt white by the salt wind. On the bank, the chippings were quite undisturbed, and accompanied by their crunch we rattled along at a fine pace. There is a grandstand view of the country around from here, and the huge bare fields, some of them boggy, took us by surprise. Somehow, we had thought of west Clare as a place of little stone-walled plots. Nothing could be further from that idea than this area, though the impression of size may be magnified by the scarcity of trees. Reeds, though, are here in plenty. It was the first time since Ballygriffey, almost 30 miles back, that we had seen any. In long bands they meander with the streams, all the more impressive for being almost the only tall plants in sight. Just past where the thirty-third milepost stood, an elegant stone-parapeted culvert carries one of these streams off southwards towards the Annageragh, and as we finished inspecting it we were treated to an even more welcome and enticing sight ahead: at least a quarter of a mile more of clear embankment just like that between Drummin and Miltown Station. Rearing solidly out of marshy ground, it looks like a Dutch dyke. As we walked it we thought it somewhat surprising that it was not being used by farmers as a road, but the ballast lay there, quite undisturbed, and that suited us very well. This pleasant section ends in a cutting through which the line curves to the right and out of view. Though it was wet and over-grown, as usual, nothing substantial held us up, not even a huge drain opened off the line to the right and every bit as wide as the cutting itself. One could conceivably mistake it for a branch line were it not that the recent claw-marks of the machinery used to dig it are still so visible in its sides. We were tempted to follow it, if only for a little way, but mindful of how much daylight we had left to us, we passed on – and straight into a solid wall of furze. Once more we resorted to the field above. But the sequel at least was happy; for downhill from us was Cloonadrum school in clear view, with the railway cottage next door that was once the home of the grandfather of Brian Mullins, member of the famous Dublin senior football team of the 1970s. We walked down through the tree stumps and rubble along the edge of the cutting, and I recalled an account told to me about what the labourers who worked here endured. The weather, it seems, was extremely hot while work was in progress during that summer of 1891, and the men, parched and sweating, begged permission to get water from a nearby well but were refused, with the threat of dismissal should they do so. And as at Tromra, the crowds of onlookers standing above considerably lessened the possibility of strike action. (Folklore records that there were five unemployed men for every worker, all waiting on any opportunity that might offer.)

Towards the end of the cutting, a signal post stood at the down side, but now there is nothing here at the boundary between Kilclehaun and Cloonadrum except another of those new crossing roads which are such a feature of the line between Quilty and Craggaknock.

Our first suspicion that Cloonadrum school is a school no longer was raised when we came to its little playing field. It was overgrown as no such field is ever overgrown where there are busy young legs to trample it. But the building was still painted its original Department yellow, and was modern. When we asked at the crossing cottage (still occupied by its original railway owners), we were told that, like so many other one and two-teacher rural schools, it was a victim of falling numbers and the obsession with 'big is beautiful' of the early 1970s. It is now a holiday home.

Our chief worry was whether the river ahead was passable without the long detour by road. However, as soon as we were told that a foot-plank was in position downstream from the bridge we felt more able to give our full attention to finding out more about the district around. Just above Lissyneillan Bridge, the Annageragh River is joined by two other smaller streams. It is as pretty a place as one could wish to see, especially near the large cascade on the main river, where fish-passes allow salmon access to the upper reaches of the river and so on to Doo Lough. This little enclave between the Kilrush and Doonbeg roads goes unnoticed by the vast majority of motorists, but this merely proves that the driver's seat of a car is a very poor place from which to see the countryside.

A mile and a half upstream is Knocknahilla House, owned for generations by the O'Kelly family, one of whom was killed at the battle of Culloden in 1746. Two members of the Fenians, each with a price of £1,000 on his head, stayed in the house in 1867, enough surely to make Mr Kenny, a former owner of the property, turn a few times in his grave. He voted for the Union in 1799.[25] A few fields away is the graveyard which was opened during the Famine. It is but another of the bitter reminders of the devastation caused by that scourge in the parish of Kilmurry–Ibrickane, whose population was reduced from 10,700 in 1847 to 5,387 in 1850.[26]

At the far side of the river, if we manage to arrive safely, we will be in Lissyneillan, which takes its name, they tell us, from a ringfort of the same name, into which certain people are supposed to have been 'carried' by the Good People at night. A quarter of a mile away, on a hill overlooking the northern bank of the river, is the ancient and now disused Kilclehaun graveyard, unusual in that it is unwalled and has no access road. Needless to say, like all too many Irish graveyards, it is in a dismally neglected state. It contains a holy well dedicated to St Brendan at which a cure for eye ailments may be obtained by visiting it on nine consecutive days, bringing away moss with which to bathe the afflicted parts, then returning it on the ninth day.

On 13 August 1955 an unfortunate railway accident occurred at Cloonadrum.[27] The crossing gate, though it had been opened at the train's approach, was loosened by the vibrations and swung closed as the guard's van passed, splintering the planks of the little wooden outshot where Peter O'Brien was sitting and injuring him severely. Only when the train reached Craggaknock Station, a mile and a quarter away, was it noticed that anything was amiss. When he did not appear, the van was searched and he was discovered dying at his post. Two circumstances which made his death all the more tragic were that he was shortly to be married, and that he was not supposed to be on duty that week, but was standing in for a friend who was on leave.

It would have been easy to remain longer, talking with the hospitable owners of Cloonadrum cottage, but the light had begun to fade and our 'bridge' was waiting for us, as was Craggaknock.

Only gradually, as we left the crossing behind, did the river valley reveal itself, with the embankment reaching out blindly towards the opposite bank. We saw at once that we were unlikely to get an adequate view from the edge of the abutment where the span had been removed, so we took a steep track off the bank and down into the river meadow at the valley bottom. From here, the full extent of the feat that was Annageragh Bridge instantly impressed itself on us as incomparably the most forceful structure we had yet seen on our 33-mile journey. Almost 40-feet high the stonework stands, stark now, yet beautiful. This was one of the few bridges put out of commission in 1961, when the line was being taken up – hardly surprising when one considers its height. Beside it we looked, and felt, insignificant. A hundred yards downstream, sure enough, was the crossing-plank, but there was much, much more besides, and none of it to our liking. Floods had washed down a mass of trees, and they were lying in a tangled heap against it, making passage impossible. Even if it had been clear, only a ropewalker or a fool would have attempted using it just then, since it was narrow, slippery and the current underneath looked menacing.

We turned, defeated, to retrace our steps to the level crossing, with only a quick detour to look over the edge of the stone abutment (which had been walled off) sheer down to the river below. Back at the cottage, our faces must have betrayed our disappointment; we were at once offered a drive around by Lissyneillan Bridge to the next level crossing, a mere half-mile away but just then completely out of our reach. It was more than we would ever have asked for, but we accepted, delighted at the generosity that prompted it. But the helpfulness did not end there. The man of the house, when we arrived at Lissyneillan crossing, told us that he would drive around to Craggaknock Station, wait for us there and then bring us back to our car in Miltown. He would hear of no refusal. He had already spotted Keith's wet trousers and understood the probable cause; himself a water-keeper with the fishery board, he was accustomed to such. Again we accepted and in order to cause no undue delay we decided not to walk the 400 yards back to the bridge. From the crossing we could see the whole way and there appeared to be nothing remarkable in this almost-straight stretch. Instead, we turned our attention southward, determined to make the three-quarters of a mile to Craggaknock the fastest we had yet travelled.

There is a gradual curving of the line to the south-west here, but no obstacle more substantial than fences – and after the Annageragh River all things look easy! Three hundred yards on, at the site of the thirty-fourth milepost, we passed into Craggaknock West townland, and right of us was an area which our map showed as divided into many allotments, a hint that there was once a large population of smallholders in the region. Little now remains of either that population or the plots they cultivated.

Another culvert we had no time to examine and passed by, but 200 yards on was a more substantial road-bridge. It is becoming dangerous, concrete crumbling from the girders at the sides, and though the middle looked safe enough we crossed cautiously. Some distance off, though it was indistinct in the gathering gloom, we could see the outline of another bridge spanning a cutting, but no more than that. We were beginning to find it difficult to see our way, and by the time we reached the cutting the ground was also against us – water, furze and more water. We could probably have negotiated it slowly if we had had time to spare, but we had none and so were content to walk along beside it for as long as we could. It is no mean depth, almost 20 feet in places, and when we crossed onto the little road leading over the bridge to the solitary house on the western side of the line, we could see that it continued for some distance more. The knowledge that we would not have to walk back to Miltown made it possible for us to delay a few moments to speak to the owner of the house, an Englishwoman who has lived here for many years. She described for us her problem with the men engaged in raising the line in 1961. They removed the girder parapets of this, Chambers' Bridge, her only link with the outside world. But she eventually forced CIÉ to erect replacement concrete walls, which remain to this day.

It was almost dark now, but we could still see Craggaknock Station 500 yards off. For nearly all of that way the cutting runs, becoming shallower until, as it reaches the road crossing, it is a mere 2 feet under field level.

Thus gently ended our longest day's walking yet.

The driver was waiting as he had promised, and since we had

no wish to delay him any further, we put off any examination of the station until our next visit. In any case, the darkness would not have allowed us to see much.

With, oh, what relief we sank into the car! But only as we passed Kilmurry, Quilty and the other places we had travelled earlier in the day did it really come home to us how far we had walked and how horrible the journey back would have been on foot and in darkness. We said it quietly then, but I repeat it now: thank God for charitable people.

Day 9

Craggaknock Station to Sragh Siding

It took us only four days to recover from our long march. Even Keith, after a bout of misgivings, decided to go west again, but on the understanding that we would give a wide berth to any large, unfathomed pools of mud. And so we arrived at Craggaknock Station on the morning of 27 February.

We walked along the single platform, on the up side, and noticed the stone edging, still intact and just as it must have been when passengers boarded and alighted here. A flower garden now occupies the place of the line. Little besides remains to tell of Craggaknock Flag-Station, 34½ miles from Ennis. But then, there was never very much here except the station-house itself, not even a goods' store. Anyone with business to transact had to go 2 miles north to Kilmurry Station or to Doonbeg, almost 2 miles south. Yet, surprisingly, in spite of its seeming remoteness, takings from passenger traffic here were as high as at Kilmurry or Quilty.[1] Today, there are few houses within a mile's radius of it, and only one of these was dignified by being named on our map. This is Craggaknock House, a plain early nineteenth-century dwelling, less than a mile to the east.

We were cheered somewhat to see the way clear and straight for a considerable distance before us, and took full advantage of such a hopeful beginning. 'Tosach maith leath na hoibre', as they say. From a distance of a half-mile or so we looked back and realised even more

Craggaknock Station, 1954.
(Photo: Irish Railway Record Society, no. 10873)

clearly than from closer range how small and isolated this place really
was. It is little wonder that it has sunk back into complete obscurity,
now that the railway is gone.

The land we were now passing through is poor indeed, rushy
and brown, and the first house we passed was abandoned. A hard
and unrelenting struggle it must have been that forced a house to
be deserted like this, especially in Ireland, where the love of land
is likely to be in inverse proportion to its usefulness. Little wonder
that even the milesmen along here tried to supplement their wages
by supplying turf, one of the few commodities freely available. Some
of them, though, seem to have been over-enthusiastic at this kind of
work, to the detriment of their railway duties, for they were reported
by a member of County Clare Farmer's Union on 14 February 1922
as 'cutting turf for sale during working hours'. There was an inves-
tigation, but no charges. During my travels I quoted this case to an
ex-railwayman who had himself been a milesman in the 1930s at a
wage of 35/- per week. His answer was typically forthright: 'God
blast 'em, but hadn't they little to be doing, reporting a poor working

man, an' during the Troubles, too. Wouldn't you think they'd have more to be thinking of.'

At the entrance to a cutting just south of where the thirty-fifth milepost stood we took a last look back. With Mount Callan in the distance looking far nearer in the clear morning air than it really was, the station seemed to have shrunk into the very ground. Since so little more was to be seen we turned to face what was to be one of the strangest places on the whole line. Almost at once we were in water but we hardly noticed; what held my attention were several masses of frogspawn, the first I had seen in nearly twenty years. We stepped gently to avoid injuring it, conscious of how hard hit frogs and other wetland creatures have been in recent times by drainage and recla- mation works of all kinds. If we had known then what manner of place this was, we would have stepped far more carefully. Higher and higher the walls loomed as we advanced, and the water became progressively more like a lake. We began to notice more of the flora around us: water lilies and other plants normally only met with in lakes. But in spite of this oddness nothing could have prepared us for what next greeted us. What up to this had been very definitely a cutting now suddenly fell back, on the left, into a broad amphitheatre with cliffs on all sides rising sheer out of the water. As we stood there gaping, we could not even guess what the purpose of this large area might have been, but a rumour that we had heard concerning 'The Big Hole' in this cutting came to mind. Seemingly, a deep well was dug here when the cutting was made so that the steam engines could take water on board when passing. Only much later did I dis- cover that this was but half the story. In 1913 a quarry was opened here to supply ballast, and a record still exists of the purchase of a stone-crusher, delivered to Ennis Station for £125, to be used here. This crusher was operated by none other than the legendary Micky O'Donoghue, and so began a career that was to be both long and illustrious, spanning half a century. Only a short siding was neces- sary here since the quarry was so near the line, but there was a constant problem with seepage. Eventually, as the quarrying went more than 20 feet below the level of the line, a windmill had to be erected to pump the water out. So its present-day condition is not at all surprising.

This cutting held an unwelcome surprise for a gang of enterprising railwaymen during the Troubles – or rather, the second of two surprises on that particular day. The Kilrush-bound passenger train had been held up by the IRA in the cutting just north of Cloonadrum crossing, and the passengers robbed of all but their petty cash. But four milesmen soon came on the scene with their bogie and began to ferry them to Doonbeg Station. After several journeys they themselves were held up in this very place by the same robbers, who had brazenly stayed close to the scene of the first crime, and were relieved of whatever the grateful passengers had been able to pay them. They were then dumped into 'The Big Hole' for their trouble, to swim as best they might. We had no ambitions to do likewise so we kept close to the up side and were able to feel our way by it, and on into level land 300 yards away, where another ruined farmhouse, its thatch half caved in, mouldered in its overgrown yard, one more reminder of decline and decay in this part of Clare hardly two generations ago.[2]

Further south, a loose string of houses indicated a road ahead, and since we had already crossed into Cloonmore townland, it was safe to

Lifting the West Clare near Kilmurry. 7.6.61. (Photo: Roy Denison)

presume that we were only a short distance from Clahanes crossing. Almost a mile away to the west we could clearly hear the hiss of the sea out at Doughmore Strand, beyond the sand hills fringing Doughmore Bay. Without our map we would have thought them to be spoil-heaps left behind after some vast drainage scheme. This part of the shore is named White Strand on most maps, and is a huge holiday attraction, but it is as well to know that the safest swimming beach in the bay surrounding Doonbeg is at Killard, on the west.

Before reaching the crossing, there was one further check to us: a ruined culvert, a grossly widened trench and a field where all the contours of the line had vanished. But as we walked through the furrows newly ploughed, it was easy to distinguish, like a dark vein in the surrounding clay, a 5-foot-wide ribbon of clinker and gravel running to the road wall. In that turned-up ground we saw more pieces of rusty iron than at any other place, an indication that there is plenty of it buried along all of the line.

The cottage was being busily renovated but the new owner could tell us little. An old man next door was more knowledgeable. We were at Clahanes crossing, right enough, he confirmed, though it was sometimes called Cree. This is understandable since Cree village is only a mile to the south-east. In 1889, the inhabitants of the place were no more pleased than the people of Mullagh at the prospect of being bypassed by the railway, and made their dissatisfaction known, too, but they were still disappointed for all that.

Two miles away, at Drumellihy Westby, Thomas the Chevalier O'Gorman lived out his last years after an extraordinary career in France. Native Irish speaker, scholar, collector of Irish manuscripts, member of the Irish Brigade and friend of Louis XV, he lost everything during the French Revolution and returned to Ireland penniless to exist on the charity of relatives. He died here on 18 November 1809.[3] Also in Drumellihy Westby is one of the best known of Clare's places of pilgrimage, Our Lady's Well, which is still very much frequented by persons seeking cures.

As for the country ahead, we would pass through four crossings all of the same name, before we got to Doonbeg, he said; Caherfeenick nos. 1, 2, 3 and 4. But had we heard anything about the 'stuff' being washed up all along the coast? We had indeed. Even the Dublin-based media were by now realising that a wreck far out in the Atlantic had begun to yield up its cargo to the shore, and reports were beginning to surface nationally. Many intrepid or lucky people had profited, but there were also dark hints that Revenue spies were on the prowl, so no one was much inclined to boast too loudly. Yet an atmosphere of excitement had been of late a palpable thing in these parts, added to by the prospect of striking a blow 'agin the government'. It even seemed to many that the happy days of smuggling were once more in full swing. That such happenings are relatively commonplace along this coast is amply proved by occasional newspaper reports down the years. For example, in 1874 the *Clare Journal* recounted a very similar case, in which timber and barrels of oil were driven ashore after a spring storm.[4] The poor fishermen-farmers of the coast were delighted, of course, but the coastguard and other agents of the Crown tried as usual to spoil the fun, and were quietly obstructed and thwarted at every turn. That attitude, at least, has not changed with the passage of time.

A hundred yards south of the cottage, a little lane that has seen busier days crosses the line. Clahanes no. 2 gates stood here, but they were no more than small concession gates and were operated by the keeper of the no. 1 crossing. The section immediately beyond was much overgrown, but the surface was firm so we came to no harm. There would be little chance of passing here in summer, though, when these briars would be at the height of their glory and in prickly mood.

We picked our way forward, and a slight fall of ground became noticeable, giving us a view of road traffic half a mile away at Caherfeenick. Hardly surprising, this view, since we were now on the Clahanes Bank, a constant trouble spot for laden steam trains from the south. The gradient here is not as obvious as at Willbrook or the Black Hill, yet it was enough to give the place some measure of notoriety.

Whoever cleared away the line in Carrowmore, which we shortly crossed into, did a thorough job. It is no recent 'development', either, for the fields have a settled look about them. On a number of occasions, at the meeting points of several fields, we might stand temporarily at a loss, but always there was some indicator: a metal fence post, a sleeper, a lump of clinker. There was also the gapped and dilapidated earthen fort immediately to the west of the line, shown on our map, though unnamed. This is surprising, for it seems to have been very extensive.

In the field beyond this fort, the line reappeared, much to our relief, and having forded a little stream, we stood once more on a definite track. As we scrambled across we became aware that we were not the first to do so; delicate footprints led to the water's edge and away from it on the far side, the tracks of a badger if the large claw-prints were anything to go by. It was not the only trace of wildlife we met. At a swampy cattle feeding-place just beyond the site of the thirty-sixth milepost we came on a scene of butchery – a succession of frogs' carcasses in every stage of dismemberment. Something more positive was at hand, however, to distract us: Caherfeenick no. 1 crossing, a mere field away. Once more, as at Clahanes, the approach was across a ploughed-up field. Here, during the Troubles, an attempt was made to sabotage the train by removing part of the line. A warning was received in time, though, and no damage was done.

The road we had now come to was obviously only a by-way; the crossing cottage was still 150 yards off. Yet our attention was held by the stream that runs at the roadside here. It has been enclosed by a beautifully built culvert for 10 yards on either side of the crossing, the only covered portion being the 5 feet of the crossing point itself. Stone-lined even on its floor, it is safe to walk through, even under the covering slabs, where the girders are exposed. Yet its only claim to fame is that it is an excellent example of high-quality stonework that eminently served its purpose. The stream channelled here forms the boundary of Caherfeenick North townland, and this crossing was the first, and smallest, of the four Caherfeenick crossings. In spite of our enthusiasm for exploring every inch of this small masterpiece we soon felt we should be going, for our behaviour was beginning to cause some concern to passers-by.

The cottage at Caherfeenick no. 2 crossing is one of those places that stick in my mind, not because of anything remarkable in itself but because of a tiny and little-known incident that occurred here over seventy years ago. The woman in charge of the crossing had gone to open the no. 1 gate, shutting her little child in the cottage for the few minutes she would be absent. He managed to lift the latch with a broom handle, however, and waddled out and towards the rails. Fortunately, the fireman, Tom O'Donoghue (a brother of Micky's), was alert. He stooped down from the footplate, threw the child back and so saved his life. The company awarded him £3 for his quick thinking, but he had something far more valuable – the lifelong gratitude and friendship of the family he had served so well. The child, Tom Shanahan, grew up to be a railwayman himself, and is still alive today and delighted to tell of his close shave with death.

Caherfeenick no. 2 cottage had not changed greatly since its railway days and was still occupied by its last gatekeeper, who had both good and bad memories of his time of service. He recalled all too vividly the nights spent sitting up waiting for specials that did not arrive until hours later, sometimes in the dead of night; for if a previous train was flying a red flag behind as it passed through the crossing, he would know that another train was following, though not its precise time. The raising of the rails in 1961 he particularly remembered for the hard work involved. He was continuously absent from home for twelve hours a day, since he had to cycle to Cappagh, Kilkee, Rineen or wherever he was needed, and all for £7 per week. He would recall for as long as he lived the bitter wet and cold of February mornings, 'an' wet or not, you had to work in them same clothes all day.'

With these sobering words to balance any romantic notions we might have about 'the good old days', we took to the line again but not at once, for a huge level range has replaced the half-dozen small fields into which this ground was once divided. Every so often we had to gauge our position by checking backward and forward, but there is little danger of going astray between Caherfeenick crossings nos. 2 and 3 since they are only a quarter of a mile apart.

The road at no. 3 is reached through the usual fence of sleepers, and the cottage is 20 yards away, on the down side. It is as though time had stood still here, for the little house is in pristine condition, everything as it was when first it was built. Even the sombre brown paint on all the timber-work looked right, as did the bucket of water on the window sill and the slates mortared at the joints. One would almost expect the rails and sleepers to be lying in their accustomed place before the door, so old-world does it all look, but a fruit garden now occupies the bed of the line. We expected the owner to be an old person, but not so. A relatively young man greeted us, explained that it was his parents who tended the crossing for many years, and recalled for us some of the stories told by his mother about the turbulent days of the early 1920s, when the IRA regularly held up trains in search of mail or useful equipment. More recently, others had been this way, detectives in wellingtons, poking the line in one of their periodic searches for the armaments of the new IRA. It is doubtful whether many of that party would have known that on the road at these gates Captain Lendrum was shot on the morning of 22 September 1920 while travelling to Ennistymon from his home in Kilkee. He was not the only person to die here. An old beggarman also met his end at this spot, through a simple enough accident. He had got a lift on the running board of a car that was too crowded to fit him inside, and as the vehicle bumped over the rails he struck the pier of the crossing gate, was knocked off and killed.

But Caherfeenick no. 3 has a more recent and cheering claim to fame: it is the home place of Michael O'Halloran, MP for Islington, London, one of the many emigrants who have achieved an eminence abroad that would almost inevitably have been denied them at home.

As we began to go we were told, as a parting shot, to watch out for 'The Crown', near Doonbeg Station, a place where northbound steam trains usually had difficulty when fully laden. At once, the Clahanes Bank came to mind: 'The Crown' must have been at the southern extremity of the long, slow drag up to Clahanes crossing.

For the next half-mile, the line, though in places wet and rushy, is at all times passable. The land about is rough, with few houses and only the roar of the sea to relieve the silence. At the southern end of Doughmore Bay, near Doonbeg, is an army firing range, but the only people likely to be in that area as we passed were salvers of timber and other wreckage. Halfway between us and the shore, on a knoll surrounded and protected by marshy land, stood Caherfeenick, the fort from which the townland derives its name, but we were too low down to be able to discern what condition it is in.

At the site of the thirty-seventh milepost we left the line to speak to an old man who had been recommended to us as having a good knowledge of the railway and the district around. He was at home and, typical of west Clare people, willing and able to talk. For over eighty years he has lived here and was able to recall for us most of the main events in the life and death of the railway in the country between Kilmurry and Sragh. The generations of drivers, guards and firemen that passed here down through the decades he also remembered. One of his earliest recollections was of Black and Tans travelling in a special carriage behind the guard's van, hoping to surprise any of the IRA who might try to hold up the train. He recreated for us Doonbeg Station in its busy years, when jobbers came from as far away as Meath and there were constant cattle trains from Kilrush and Kilkee as well as from the four major fairs in Doonbeg itself; and he described for us its decline and final downgrading, due largely to the growth of marts and the coming of motor-truck transport, which delivered merchandise to shopkeepers' doors, thus dispensing with the necessity of going to the station to collect it. The changeover from steam to diesel he summarised in a brief sentence: 'Quicker transport and better comfort', and still vivid in his mind was the day in March 1952 when he, together with a sizeable crowd, went eagerly to Doonbeg Station to watch the first diesel railcar pass through. A small, pale Scotsman – 'if he was seven stone he was a ton' – he recalls as being the engineer sent down to train the local drivers to operate the new machines.

Other rationalisations he witnessed, too, such as the spraying of the grass and weeds at the sides of the permanent way by a machine mounted on a locomotive. Previously, such work was done by gangs of men and went on constantly during the summer months. With the new technology the whole route from Ennis to Kilrush could be done in two days.[5] Though sorry to see the line close, he was philosophical, regarding it as no more than another of those changes that are inevitable. But one consequence of its going that even yet angered him was the condition of the roads. We soon found out why, for when we left his house to walk the public highway to the next crossing, 500 yards away, we had to travel in a zig-zag fashion to avoid the potholes and craters pitting what was left of its surface. Bad as the line might have been on occasion, it could have been not a whit worse than this piece of moonscape.

We arrived, though, without injury at Caherfeenick no. 4, where the railway met and crossed two roads at a T-junction and the townlands of Caherfeenick North and South come together. The former gatekeeper, then still living in the crossing cottage (but since dead), recounted for us an incident to which the passage of the years had lent humour but which at the time it happened was anything but funny. It involved one of the two 'light specials' – trains of empty wagons – which were hauled to Kilkee for the Christmas fair every 26 November. He and his wife were at their supper, having completely forgotten about the train, when it passed the window 'an' stopped on the wrong side o' the gates.' He told also of the indecent haste with which the line was raised: 'They closed it the last day of January 1961 an' started takin' it up the first day of February.'

Less than a mile away is Doonbeg, 'the long village', as it is known, and he pointed out the remnants of the early-sixteenth-century tower house standing by the bridge over the Doonbeg River a short distance from its entry to the bay. Perhaps accommodation was scarce in the village in the nineteenth century, for as late as 1893 T.J. Westropp noted seven families living in this tower. It is also still said in the district that a hedge-schoolmaster occupied a room of this ruin and his salutation to any beggarwoman who might happen the way was 'ramble up, decent woman'. Not even Mae West could have put it better! Under one of the blind arches of the nearby bridge is a dark

Doonbeg Station, 1953.
(Photo: Irish Railway Record Society, no. 10437)

little 'room', still visible to this day, where 'Mary Belfast', another old woman, lived. Certainly it would appear that the eastern end of the village was the interesting part in those long-gone days!

To the north-west of the village is Doonmore Castle ('the big fort'), now very ruined but the scene of much contention in its day. After several changes of ownership at the end of the sixteenth century, it was attacked by the Earl of Thomond in 1599 and its garrison hanged, though they had surrendered.[6] The same fate befell the garrison of Doonbeg Castle during this campaign. A short distance farther along the coast is Killard Church, which has had an equally chequered history, as both a Protestant and a Catholic place of worship. It did not, however, survive the attentions of the Cromwellians in 1651.

In this corner of south-west Clare between Doonbeg and Kilkee – what one might call the beginning of the peninsula which stretches westward to Loop Head – there are little secluded villages with names that sound quaint and distant even to people in east Clare: places like Bealaha, Coosheen, Farrihy. As yet, they have been only lightly brushed by tourism, but that cannot last. They are too attractive to be left to their own devices for long. Unfortunately, when that time comes only the ghost of a population will be left to benefit, for emigration has again wreaked havoc in these parts, and all the advances that have slowly, painfully, been made over the past quarter of a century look set to be wiped out in half a decade.

On the Skivileen river-bridge, just south-west of Caherfeenick no. 4, we had to pick our way through a heap of junk and metal debris, the remnants of a collapsed shed. Levees protect both banks of the river, which is at least 15-feet wide here, and the line runs over a culvert outside of each levee, so in all we crossed three bridges in quick succession. We had arrived in Mountrivers townland, and Doonbeg Station was a mere 300 yards away, across the Miltown-Kilkee road. The usual barrier of sleepers marks the crossing site, but of the other surrounds much has changed since a public house and its car-park now occupy what was the station yard. We made our way by the side of it through a little lane to the station-house, a long, plain single-storey building on the down side, which remains much as photos show it to have been in its working days. Only one thing is missing: the floral displays that brought great praise and several prizes to Doonbeg under stationmaster Michael Hanrahan in the late 1930s and the early 1940s.[7]

Fifty yards down the line is the goods' shed, also relatively unaltered, and as we walked back along the platform edge we could clearly make out where the large siding was. However that may be, the fact cannot be disguised that the lifeline of this little hamlet was cut when Doonbeg Station, second block-post on the South Clare, 37¾ miles from Ennis, closed. It is unlikely that its busy days will return. And so has been fulfilled the prophecy of the priest who promised his recalcitrant parishioners that if they did not refrain from picking seaweed on the Sabbath, and attend at church as required, a day would come when carriages would travel down across the quaking bogs of Sragh to carry off the sand from the sand hills of Doughmore. The carriages may have come and gone, but trucks still cart away the sand!

We were on the point of continuing towards Sragh, our day's

proposed destination, when an interested local man engaged us in conversation. On hearing of our quest, he offered to take us to where Captain Lendrum's body was hidden before being carried to Kilclehaun cutting, an offer too good to be missed, especially since he would drive us there and back.

As we bumped northwards for 2 miles along the ruined and tortured roads to the place, we began to recognise landmarks we had seen earlier. Shortly after Clahanes school we came to what appeared to be the seashore but in reality is a lake separated from the sea by only a narrow corridor of land. This is Lough Donnell, debouchure of the Annageragh River, and it was in the sand by its edge that the unfortunate Lendrum was buried, having been shot 2 miles away. Even in bright spring sunlight, it looked to us a melancholy place. It must have seemed infinitely more so on that night all those years ago when a small group of men arrived here on their grisly business.

Back at Doonbeg Station and before striking out again, we paused to get a photo of the little goods' shed. Keith posed willingly enough in the doorway, but nearly leaped out of his skin in terror when a bull tethered inside let out an unmerciful bellow. I had much trouble in convincing him that I did not contrive the incident as some kind of

Goods' shed, Doonbeg Station. (Illustration: M. Lenihan)

joke! He muttering darkly, we continued along the platform edge to where it dips down into the grass, and here it was that I convinced him that there was something odd that needed to be considered: why should Doonbeg platform have been so long (at least 150 yards)? There was no obvious answer, of course; all we could do was be thankful that it has survived intact, even if it is now rather useless. Four fields to the west stands Mountrivers House, another former Studdert residence and for a time an RIC barracks. 'Honest Tom' Steele, Daniel O'Connell's great friend and 'Head Pacificator', is said to have lived here for a time in 1814.[8]

As it emerges from the station precincts the line passes through a slight cutting, but we avoided walking there. A bad smell of sewage and the thick mud underneath the surface grass hastened our departure into clearer country beyond. The public road and the railway run parallel for 1½ miles south of Doonbeg Station, never more than 200 yards apart. The line along here has been very much injured, quarried in some places, bulldozed in others, but we never quite lost it because at all times we could use the road as a marker and reference point. At a little embankment just south of where the thirty-eighth milepost stood we paused. Someone had dug out a portion of the bank, and though it is not a kind of action to be much recommended it at least allowed us a view of the composition of the line here in Mountrivers. We noted especially the 6-inch-thick top layer of ash and burned material, and could gauge from it how much the sleepers were packed with such stuff.

A humped three-arch bridge carries the road over the meandering Doonbeg River where it makes the largest of its loops to the west, and 200 yards downstream the railway bridge crosses. It is not exceptional, yet fine of its type and somewhat odd in that its deck is made of sleepers rather than metal or concrete. For a few minutes' walk on its southern side, the line is intact and not much the worse for wear, apart from the very choked side drains. A short boreen leads off left here to a tiny creamery on the roadside, a building that at first glance appears to be deserted. However, a large shining stainless-steel bulk tank by its gable seems to refute that impression. Here also we passed through a crossing where there were probably only concession gates on a passageway into the bog. In the field on the far side, an optimistic farmer had spread manure on the line. We wished him every success and a good crop of nuts and bolts!

In no long time we reached a stream and crossed the first of many culverts in Sragh, which is probably the wettest townland in all Clare. Surprisingly, most of these crossings we passed by had fallen victim to the spate of land-improvement projects in this area in recent years.

Happily, this particular boundary marker and former site of the thirty-ninth milepost has been spared. It is of two channels, and though one lies choked with debris, the other is quite sufficient for even the heaviest floods. Its most impressive feature is the four-inch-thick roofing-slabs overhead. The comment of a man in one of the wayside cottages was before me as I measured the stone. The culverts, he said, had to be built of 'the best of stuff' because the weight of the steam loco alone was over 35 tons, and it might be pulling as many as twenty wagons. These flags that have survived in situ look as if they might withstand the falling of the sky itself.

The story beyond this is less happy. In the 500-yard stretch to the

Sragh siding, 1953. (Photo: Irish Railway Record Society, no. 10438)

Culvert, Sragh townland. (Illustration: M. Lenihan)

point at which the road veers off sharply towards the south-east, the line is no more. Only a broken row of metal fence posts, appearing intermittently, remains to tell of its passage. The slight embankment from the divergence point of road and railway to the level crossing 200 yards away looked somewhat akin to an elongated farmyard, with silage pit, shed, electric fence and many, many cattle-prints. But not a sign of a farm dwelling, unless it might have been a brightly painted house a short way off to the east. Probably the best-known example of this type of colour scheme in all of Ireland is Mahony's house at Moyasta, 3 miles farther down the line. Having caught and dazzled the eye of some professional photographer, it is now featured on a picture postcard as a typical example of west-of-Ireland vernacular paintwork.

As practically the last act of our day's walk we stopped to rest at the little road which once crossed over the line to run on westward through the bogland. It surprised us more than a little when the map showed that we could go all the way to Kilkee by travelling it if we chose, and quite directly, too. From close at hand it looks no more than any other of the little byroads to the private turf banks which abound in Sragh. Yet this was Sragh Halt, 39¾ miles from Ennis and southern limit of the jurisdiction of Doonbeg Station. It was from here that vast quantities of turf were transported during the Emergency and afterwards, a trade that gave a measure of hard-earned prosperity to this region. As well as a hut for the keeper of the gates and siding, there was a small platform on the up side and it seems that passenger traffic to Kilrush was quite substantial from the time of the opening of the halt in May 1952 up to the closure of the line. However, the fading light of a short spring evening was not the time for further exploration. That we postponed for our next visit.

Darkness most absolute overtook us long before we arrived at Craggaknock. But we had other things to worry us, besides. Potholes, for example. To try to avoid them merely led us into others, and at last we abandoned ourselves to whatever lay underfoot. We got there safely, eventually, but it added considerable time and effort to a journey that was already quite long enough. More than once, along those unfortunate roads, we asked each other the simple question: how might one solve the basic logistical problem of having a car waiting at the right place after a day's walking so that the long slog back to the morning's starting-point might be avoided? Not so easy as it sounds, for without previous knowledge of conditions on the line, one has no way of knowing how far one may go in a day. In any case it was a problem we never solved.

Day 10

Sragh Siding to Moyasta Junction

Probably in no other town in Ireland except Cooraclare is the oath 'by the skin of the dingo' used. In the early months of 1874 there was great excitement in this community, for a large mysterious animal, supposed by 'all the zoologists' to be a dingo, was causing havoc among the flocks of the parish, and farmers were at their wits' end.[1] However, the trail of depredation seemed to have been brought to a sudden halt on Tuesday 21 April at Gower, a mile south of the village, when a large beast was shot.[2] Much to the disappointment of everyone, the dingo turned out to be only a mastiff.

Unfortunately, the world was still not safe for sheep, for just as life was returning to sleepy normality in Cooraclare, the 'dingo' struck again. And again. Newspaper reports of its nocturnal visits continued to thrill the public well into June, and all kinds of speculation as to its identity were indulged in.[3] Some thought it a wolf, some a bear, others an evil or tormented spirit. Whatever it was, we are no wiser today,, for, just like Jack the Ripper, it vanished as mysteriously as it had come, leaving an enigma that still cries out for a solution.

Lewis, in 1837, barely acknowledged the existence of Cooraclare, but this slight has never inhibited its people from making a name for themselves both at home and abroad. Among its illustrious sons are counted Conor McDermott, renowned schoolmaster; Martin Meaney, US general; Fr Anthony Hickey, papal adviser; and in its ancient church, at Kilmacduane, lie the remains of Chevalier O'Gorman.[4]

At Sragh Halt we were 2½ miles due west of Cooraclare. A week's interval had allowed some checking of historical and topographical details, and armed with these we were all set for the trek to Moyasta. We had begun somewhat later in the day than usual because we felt confident that with only 3½ miles to travel we would have plenty of time, even allowing an hour to examine the Loop and the various crossings at Moyasta. We should have known better. Even if we had never heard of Sragh Bog, our maps might have told us that in such a landscape, after thirty years of neglect, the railway would be in very poor shape.

As it happened, this was indeed the case, but for reasons quite other than what we would have expected. The line itself has survived remarkably well, considering the nature of the ground, and bears out General Hutchinson's remark about its being the best constructed of the narrow-gauge railways inspected by him. But great changes are occurring at the edges of the bog, with reclamation constantly pushing the serviceable ground forward at the expense of the wetland. The railway line has, unfortunately, got in the way of much of this improvement and has suffered accordingly. This is understandable enough, but every time we passed the wreckage of yet another smashed culvert we wished that the 'improvers' had been more discriminating in what they chose to destroy. We did not forget to search about for the platform and siding, but our efforts yielded nothing. South of here for as far as we could discern, the line also is hard to find; only for the odd sleeper and fence post strewn haphazardly here and there, one might be convinced that talk of the West Clare's presence was all a fable.

We began, making the best of a bad job. But there is nothing to delay one along here or hold the attention for long. Even Lochnavar House, slightly to the east – the only dwelling named on our map – is no more. Once owned by the ubiquitous Studderts, it was demolished in the early 1970s after the Land Commission had divided the estate.[5]

A small flooded cutting saw us on course again and we had to wade through quite deep water before emerging on to a little road where a lone abandoned house was the only sign that anyone had ever been here. But at least a view of the line curving off in a wide arc to the south-west was heartening, for there seemed to be no serious obstacles. Our map was not as encouraging, though. The little tufts denoting swampy ground occupied a great deal of it, and the very place names told their own story: in all of them '*móin*' figured prominently. Why this route was ever chosen for a railway is not easy to tell. Perhaps it was the best of a number of bad options, for the land to east and west is not appreciably better. Whatever the reasons, much fill was needed for this uncertain surface, and there is at least one known example of considerable subsidence. Photographs still exist that show engine no. 4, *Besborough*, on its side in Sragh, and of course rumours still persist that it was never recovered, but now lies buried in the bog awaiting salvage by some lucky finder. The accident happened on 13 May 1892, before the South Clare Railway had opened for traffic.[6] There were no injuries to the crew, fortunately, and though there is no record of the engine being raised and re-railed, it must have been, since the later career of the *Besborough* can be accounted for very completely.

As we walked along a slight embankment we began to appreciate the immense task of those men who pushed the line through here a century ago. Merely to keep the water at bay was no small feat. Mr Barrington, engineer to the South Clare Railway Company, was putting it mildly when he said of this place that 'some difficulty has arisen due to the boggy nature of the soil'. The culvert close to the fortieth milepost site deserves particular mention, for it is stone-arched but with red-brick facings. Built diagonally to the line, it is another of those forgotten minor masterpieces that may so easily escape the eye of the casual passer-by.

Walking in bogland in winter or spring is outside the experience of most people nowadays, but when one adjusts to the flatness of the surroundings, it is not without its compensations. There is a huge silence, and the sky seems all the more limitless since hills or

Culvert, Sragh. (Illustration: M. Lenihan)

mountains have been pushed far back to the edges of the conscious eye. The eternal water and the rushes sharpen rather than dull the sight, for the distinctions and variations in shape and colour are endless. It might truly be said that no place is more deceptive than a bog. A visitor to Sragh might pity the sprinkling of people who live here: how do they live? What is there to do in such a place? He might well save his sympathy, for it is a fact ruefully admitted in more 'civilised' Kilkee, Kilrush or Doonbeg that the inhabitants of this drab-looking backwater are exceptional for their strong sense of community and distinct identity, traits fostered, doubtless, by the hard struggle for survival.

Only the sod walls keep off the water in areas where the line is at the level of the bog, and this they no longer do effectively for they are breached in many places. A small rise in the general water level would completely flood the way. This was well illustrated for us as we tried to get through a shallow cutting and found ourselves in water to the knee. Even more disconcerting than the never-ending water is the lack of definite landmarks in the flatness of the bog, so we were much relieved to see a road quite near us on the left, more especially

since the map showed that it would accompany us all the way to
Moyasta. For over a mile we could follow its progress through gradually rising ground towards Moanmore Church, sited on a little hill on
the near horizon, and the first real waymark since the bridge we had
passed over at the Doonbeg River. To our right ahead, what seemed
to be a high isolated bank of turf stood at right angles to our line of
travel. As we moved closer, we saw that it was a road, but certainly
the strangest one ever, for it sat comfortably on a 6-foot-high ledge
of bog, the outside of which had been cut away almost to the road
hedge. How it remained intact is not easy to say, but it seemed solid
enough when we climbed on to it. In fact, from above one would
never know that it was other than an ordinary country byroad.

Our map was proving to be of little use in the identification of
the many small roads through the bog, so we were glad to come on a
farmer foddering cattle. He pointed out the boundary of Sragh and
Moanmore at a shed built on the line a little farther on, calculated
how far we were from Moanmore Lough, and told us something of
the turf traffic on the bog during the 1940s and 1950s. From about
1941, in the absence of regular coal supplies, turf came into its own
and Sragh took on a new significance.[7] Cattle wagons were often
used for hauling the turf, and the locomotives latterly burned it as
fuel – to the terror of every farmer for miles around: 'they nearly
burned what hay was in the country'. At least one case is on record
of the wagons of turf themselves being ignited by sparks from their
own engine.

At the townland boundary, the quality of the surface improved
dramatically, and the reason was not far to seek: the side drains had
been well maintained. If this can be achieved in the middle of a bog,
what might not similar cleaning do for other less-wet places? Here,
since the shed occupied the whole breadth of the line, we were forced
into the adjoining fenceless bog, and from there the true austerity of
the place came home to us. There is no shelter whatsoever against
rain or storm; it would even be difficult to build walls, for how would
one find a firm foundation? For this reason, the few houses that have
been built here in recent times stand in a row on the line itself. It

was the only solid place available. The bog approaches the very back door of each house, and the front gardens, though they face towards the road, are of pitch-black soil that is more peat than earth. We approached somewhat nervously for several angry-looking dogs had gathered to protect their territory, and there was no avoiding them. In fact, we would have to pass directly by the front door of each house, so we felt more than grateful when one of the owners appeared to scatter the dogs and give us permission to proceed. From a distance we waved our gratitude and hurried to put even more space between ourselves and the snarling beasts. So anxiously attentive were we to doing so that Moanmore Lough took us quite unawares. But we did not slacken our pace until we had reached the shallow cutting which runs by its southern shore. Here, forced to slow for the usual reasons, we had a chance to view this, one of the largest lakes in the south-west of Clare. If truth be told, it is a poor-looking thing, more an overgrown boghole than a proper lake. Yet the map shows it as a substantial body of water, at least 600 yards in length from north to south, though far less than that in width. We hoped it might improve as we moved on, and examined it from a different angle, but we were disappointed.

Here, at the forty-first milepost, was another level crossing, but little in the way of traffic can have passed here except in the turf-cutting season.[8] In quick succession we came on the debris of four culverts before we reached Moanmore crossing. The first we passed without examining. Whoever demolished the second one exposed a cross-section of the line, and we were able to photograph the kinds of stone and gravel used in its formation. A close examination could very well indicate where they came from, for certainly they had to be brought in from some distance away. We were at least partly prepared for the third by a 500-yard tract of levelled ground where only one small island of line has survived, a rectangle now fenced off and used as a hay yard. We reached the canal where the culvert had been, only to find a single abutment standing, still discoloured brown, showing the height the water once reached. It is at least 2-feet lower today.

Now, facing on to the last short stretch to the cottage, we were expecting no further obstructions, but it was here that we met one of the largest trenches to date, at least 8-feet deep and 10-feet wide. It too had a surviving stone abutment, on the northern side, but nothing else to indicate its original span. It would have been a dangerous jump, so we took the long and cautious way down. We reached the cottage and the road at last, but all that greeted us was desolation, for the site was a wilderness, the windows of the cottage boarded up and its slates beginning to fall away. It was the first derelict railway house we had encountered in almost 42 miles of walking, and a sad demise for a cottage whose foundations Mr Barrington, SCR Company engineer, in his report to the shareholders on 1 March 1891, described as 'completed'.

To where the forty-second milepost stood, and for some distance beyond, the ground is very passable and one will find ample opportunity to look around and view what the surroundings offer. Alas, there is little apart from the church, and even this has no particularly notable features. More and more we found ourselves concentrating on the minutiae of the line itself – the condition of this or that set of crossing gates, the side drains, elevation over the accompanying fields, and so on. So casual did we become, so accustomed to easy going, that we were struck speechless when out of the blue a full-scale river barred our way. And there was no bridge. It was a setback we had not reckoned for, since the map showed it as only another stream, whereas in reality it was anything but. Swift and deep it rushed along, offering no visible crossing place. We could have travelled east along its bank to the road-bridge some distance off, but we decided to try a nearer way, its junction with the Moyasta River 30 yards to the west. After a fierce struggle through furze and briars we located a narrow part where, by supporting each other forward, we could ford it. But it is not a safe crossing, especially when the river is high. Certainly, for anyone with leisure time to sit here, this little river junction is a place of seclusion and quiet, but we were hardly in a frame of mind conducive to such tranquillity as we trampled our way back to the line. On the Moyasta side of the divide we paused a moment to look back in baffled resignation at the few feet of a gap that can make all the difference. A hundred yards on, as if to warn us against further complacency, the river came so close to the line as to be almost touching it, before veering away again at right angles, about its own unseen business.

But now we were on the home stretch and even two further broken culverts and a thicket of flourishing furze succeeded only in delaying briefly our arrival at the junction. From the point at which the river returns from its rambles to rejoin the line, it is noticeable that the side fences seem to draw back, giving the line an impression of width that is difficult to vouch for on the ground but which photographs of this place during the railway's working days show to be accurate. For here was the divergence point of the Kilrush and Kilkee lines.

We had arrived at Moyasta Junction, 43 miles from Ennis, and the sad scene before us put me in mind of the comments of another arrival here ninety-five years ago: 'we came to Moyasta Junction where the scene became exciting, there were so many blue, green, red and white lights, and so many trains lying about. It looked like a small edition of Clapham or Willesden Junction ...' The lights are long gone, and the trains; the only movement to greet our arrival was the traffic on the Kilrush–Kilkee main road. We pulled ourselves onto the platform, glad to be back to a semblance of civilisation, and began our exploration of 'the mysteries of Moyasta'.[10] Facing us near the northern apex of the triangular platform stood a small stone building, its door still intact. Inside were the remains of the pump which pushed water from the river to the 3,600-gallon tank on its roof. Of this tank no trace now remains. Was it in this house also that electricity was generated in the early years of this century? We could not be sure. But that Moyasta Junction was the only station on the whole system which had its own generating capacity there is no disputing. The plant, however, was dismantled after CIÉ took over from the GSR, so little evidence is available today to enable this facet of the station's history to be recalled.

A closer look at the rest of the platform revealed some interesting

Moyasta junction, 1952.
(Photo: Irish Railway Record Society, no. 10149)

Engine 5C with down goods at Moyasta, 5 February 1955.
(Photo: Irish Railway Record Society, no. 11303)

details: the right-hand side, the line to Kilkee, was in quite good
shape, whereas on the Kilrush side both line and platform were
so overgrown as to be almost unrecognisable. We continued along
the clear side to the station-house, which is still occupied. It is an
unremarkable building of its type, but its crossways position, gables
to both lines, plus a number of alterations, makes it appear more

unusual than it really is. The three water columns that once stood around it – one on each corner of the platform – are gone, but the shell of a concrete tank from which water was pumped to the larger roof tank is still in position 10 yards from the station, on the Kilkee side.

There was little else to be seen, so a choice had to be made: would we examine the Loop – the through line between Kilrush and Kilkee, which ran along the edge of Poulnasherry Bay – or continue on to one or other of the two terminals, each 5 miles away? Since a decision of this nature is best made in comfortable surroundings and preferably with some refreshment in hand, our next act was well-nigh inevitable: we adjourned to Taylor's hostelry, the focal point of Moyasta 'village'.

It was a wise decision, for not alone did we pass close by the famous pink-and-green postcard house on our way there, but the owner of the tavern is knowledgeable in matters relating to the railway, and has a large collection of memorabilia, especially photographs, which he willingly allowed us to look through. We were even provided with a quiet corner of his large lounge to satisfy our curiosity to our hearts' content. Indeed, the lounge itself is a kind of memorial gallery to the West Clare, for pictures of people and places associated with the line occupy every convenient space. It was a fascinating opportunity for us, who had been seeing only the ruins of the railway, to get glimpses of it when it was a going concern.

It was originally from the Taylors that the land occupied by Moyasta Station, platform and yard was bought in 1890 for £95, and it was the same family who bought back much of it when the service was terminated, so there is a continuity here that is probably unique in the annals of the West Clare. But the *sine qua non* of establishments like this is quality drink, and many of the most humorous tales of the railway have drink as their lubricant and Taylor's as their centre point. Take for example the case of the two Cork brothers, gangers during the construction of the line in this region. So unpopular did they make themselves with their men that they were eventually chased off the works and pursued to Taylor's, where the proprietor, in order to avert bloodshed, hid them in an upstairs room and then plied the irate navvies with drink to soothe their grievances.

Or the amusing episode of the milesman who was fired three times – on the one day! He was a connoisseur of porter (he even had a recipe of his own: mulled porter with a sprinkling of ginger) and partook as often as he could. On his great day he was admitted to Taylor's early in the morning and was fired for lateness on arrival at work. The ganger, an easy-going man, rehired him after morning tea-break, but he was fired again when he left early for a liquid lunch. He got a second chance after the four o'clock tea-break, but his stressful day led to his going for more porter less than one hour later, so he was finally fired as from then, this time permanently. Sorry for himself? It was his boast and glory for as long as he lived!

A further proof of the quality of Taylor's porter involved an even more typical West Clare incident, when a driver and fireman who had had a serious argument became so averse to each other's company that they abandoned the train, passengers and all, in Sragh bog and walked their separate angry ways to Moyasta and Taylor's, only to be reconciled there later. That such an incident was not untypical is proved by a report of 4 October 1892 in which it was stated that drivers, firemen and guards were in the habit of leaving their trains at Moyasta and visiting the local hostelry. The manager of the railway company, Mr P.K. Sullivan, stated in his reply that he 'investigated the charge and is satisfied that the allegation is without foundation'. Spoken like a true bureaucrat!

But there are enough such tales to fill a small book. We could profitably have stayed at Taylor's for longer than the two hours we did, but we were anxious to see the Loop, and to find out more, if we could, about this railway 'republic', this 'island state of the narrow-gauge', as one impressed traveller called it.[11] We emerged into the glare of daylight and turned right by the gable of the premises, down a little laneway leading towards the tide. Almost at once we came to another lane at right angles to it, where stands the last of a row of twelve thatched houses that can be seen in many of the old photographs and which have vanished within the past thirty years. A sign of changing times and improvements in housing, perhaps, but also an indication of the decline in population Moyasta has suffered through the ruin first of its turf trade and finally of the railway. Beyond this lane is the only level crossing on the Loop, called in the railway manuals Moyasta no. 3. The cottage is still in use, but the little platform, on the up side, where so many thousands of Kilkee-bound passengers entrained, looks neglected and forgotten.

From here we gazed out on the sloblands of Poulnasherry Bay. As the Irish version of its name (Poll na nOisrí) indicates, it was once known for its oysters,[12] but though it is still much frequented by shellfish pickers from Kilrush and farther afield, oysters no longer feature in their take. A sizeable triangular-shaped inlet of the Shannon, 2 miles long by 1½ wide, it is bounded by Moyasta on the east, Blackweir on the west and Cammoge Point to the south. Looked at on the 6-inch map, all its shores appear to be bounded by railway, but that appearing on the southern shore is merely the trace of the ill-fated 1860s line on which rails were never laid, though they had actually arrived by ship at Kilrush for the purpose.

There are extensive mudflats at the western end, near Blackweir, and the area is rich in wading and marsh birds. But the one thing noticeably absent is boat traffic on any part of the bay. This is a modern 'development', for in the nineteenth century this was one of the main points on the lower Shannon for the shipping of turf upriver, especially to Limerick.[13] It was from this trade that Moyasta first gained prominence. Some of the channels used by the turf boats still exist in Carrowncalla, on the eastern shore of the bay, and extend as far north as the Loop at Moyasta Junction; others have been filled in. An alternative though more laborious method of loading was to transport the turf in small boats – 'cots' – to the larger vessels anchored further out the bay.[14] All such operations have long ceased, however.

Our efforts to proceed the short distance through a shallow cutting along the Loop to where it joins the Kilkee line were frustrated by scrub and bushes, and we were forced almost on to the shore before we could go ahead. But once we reached the main line, there was no further difficulty. The way is clear right to Moyasta river-bridge – the 'Red Bridge' – and beyond. From the long stone-faced embankment leading to the bridge, a fine view of the bay may be had, particularly on a clear day. The metal deck and stone abutments alike are in good condition, though some large pieces of masonry have been thrown into the water. Not so fortunate has been the stonework of the embankment on the side facing south into the bay. A storm seems to have torn out a section of the limestone blocks, exposing the earthwork near the bridge and causing some subsidence of the top surface.

It is easier to return along the main line to the thatched house in the laneway and proceed from there past the crossing cottage on down the Loop to the Kilrush end. Reclamation was in progress here during our visit, but at least the overgrowth had been removed and we could see clearly the dimensions of the line. Hardly a hundred yards from the junction with the Kilrush branch we noted traces of a second, parallel, line immediately to our left. Here also lay a mound of solidified tar, the sole remnant of the sleeper-tarring plant that was once sited here.

In all, the Loop is approximately 600 yards in length and was extremely useful for allowing a direct passage to through traffic, especially from Cappagh to Kilkee. A glance at a map will show what a cumbersome operation this might otherwise have been. However, with the decline of steamer traffic on the Shannon after the turn of the century and the consequent eclipse of Cappagh, there was less occasion to use the Loop, and by the last years of the railway it – together with the Kilrush–Cappagh extension – had become redundant.

There was precious little else to see of railway vintage. We inspected the sites of the three other level crossings, of course, all within a radius of 200 yards of the station-house, but as at most other such places, there was nothing, for at Moyasta, just as at Knockdrummagh, near Ennistymon, road widening has changed utterly the lie of the land.

Yet we turned for Sragh pleased with ourselves, and not least because for once we had daylight to see us safely over the pocked

West Clare track-lifting train. 7.6.61. (Photo: Roy Denison)

road, which was as bad as any we had travelled heretofore. In fact, by comparison with many of the roads of west Clare, the remnants of the railway line are in enviable condition.

Day 11

Moyasta Junction to Cappagh Pier

When we next arrived at Moyasta we were in high good humour. First, to be able to park here by a main road, halfway from whichever destination we might choose, was a veritable luxury after the obscure roads we had been through on every day's walk so far; second, we had reached, with any reasonable luck, the penultimate stage of our journey, and would that evening be looking out on Scattery.

We made a brief courtesy call to Taylor's that morning. Really, it was just an excuse to have a 'quick one' before setting off into the biting March wind, though we convinced ourselves that what we needed was a last quiet moment to make up our minds on which terminal to start for. Logically, perhaps we should have gone to Kilkee first since that town was the true terminus of the West and South Clare Railways, the Kilrush section being a mere branch line; but I chose to go south-east for the quite arbitrary and personal reason that all my mother's family for generations had been familiar with the river port. Between Tarbert, their home place, and Kilrush, there was constant coming and going across the Shannon for centuries, and I distinctly recalled her telling of how my grandfather had narrowly escaped drowning in the 'Shannon disaster' of 1893.

We went back to the station gate, the site of Moyasta no. 1 crossing, where the line passed over the Moanmore road, ready to start from there. But the 200 yards between this and the main road, where the forty-third milepost and Moyasta no. 2 crossing were situated, was so overgrown as to be wholly impassable, so we did the only thing possible: made the necessary detour. Not one in a thousand of the motorists who now hurtle along this wide road each day knows it, but here at Moyasta no. 2 occurred one of the few serious accidents at the junction, when a young boy, trying to save the gates from an oncoming train, was knocked down and killed.

A century ago, on 26 July 1888, this same road was thronged with people, but on different business entirely. That morning, a small army of police, military, officials and landlord's men set out from Kilrush on their ugly business of eviction. Their destination that day was Moyasta, and the victim was one Matthew McGrath. Admittance was duly demanded to his house, was refused and the infamous crowbar brigade went into action. It took the battering ram forty minutes to force an entry, but Matthew's son Pat, his daughter Anne, and a neighbour, Kate Keogh, retreated to the loft, pelting the emergency men with stones, boiling water and porridge. They were soon overcome and severely beaten, but the women were quickly released, whereupon they cheered for Parnell and the Plan of Campaign. The crowd cheered back, and the large force of police made a fierce baton charge.[1] There were no deaths that day, but the episode added one more grievance to the long list held in the people's mind against the forces of 'law and order', a list that was to fall due for bloody payment just over thirty years later.

McGrath was taken to Kilrush bridewell but not without a fierce struggle. Three times he managed to break the handcuffs before he was finally subdued, thereby ensuring himself a place in the memory of the people even to this day.[2] He was later sentenced to eight months' hard labour, and upon his release on 6 March 1889 was immediately rearrested. The charge: breaking his handcuffs![3] Not so lucky was his mother. She died a few weeks afterwards, and the coroner's jury stated clearly their opinion that her illness was due to the eviction of her husband and the imprisonment of her son.[4]

The McGrath eviction was only one of 22 carried out on the estate of Captain H.S. Vandeleur in that July of 1888, but it was a turning point, for it received extensive press coverage and a photographer from the company of William Lawrence was present to record the proceedings for posterity.[5] Trouble had been simmering in the region for two years before that, and evictions had already occurred in Kilrush town in October of 1887, with a resulting boycott of the police and two police resignations in protest at the behaviour of the authorities.[6] In May 1888 Fr Gilligan of Kilmurry McMahon had been jailed for a month for attending a banned meeting, the first priest to be prosecuted during the land agitation in Clare.[7] So by the time the July evictions got seriously underway, the battle lines were clearly drawn. On one side were the landlords with their bailiffs, agents, sheriff, emergency men, the RIC and the army (almost 500 of the last-named were needed for the Vandeleur evictions alone), and on the other the tenants, their priests, the National League and the vast majority of the people of the locality (up to 10,000 were present at the Moyadda eviction on 19 July). At the time it may have seemed that the forces of the establishment carried the day, but it was a pyrrhic victory. Within three years the evicted tenants were back on their farms and within a generation they would own those same farms. And the Vandeleurs, and their 20,000-acre estate? Gone, as is Kilrush House, their spacious home. It was burned on 26 March 1897 and never rebuilt.[8] (Consistent to the very end, Vandeleur was evicting tenants in Kilrush town that same day for non-payment of ground rent.)

From the road to this line's meeting point with the Loop is very straightforward going; we reached it in minutes. The dividing bank is still prominent though much overgrown, and two culverts, one very damaged, allow a small stream access to the bay. Why it was necessary to build two is difficult to see when the watercourse might have been diverted a few yards south and guided under the single amalgamated line.

On the night of Tuesday 28 October 1902 a 'most determined attempt' was made to derail the 6 p.m train from Ennis right here. The points had just been passed when the driver felt a continuous jolting, stopped the engine and found a large stone – 58 pounds weight – on the line. A local boy was later arrested on suspicion of the deed. His father had that day been sentenced at Ennistymon to a month in jail for assaulting the stationmaster there.[9]

A short way forward we were brought to a halt, but by another of those drainage canals cut through the line. A few feet beyond it we came on two sleepers protruding 3 feet out of the tidal debris at the foot of the railway bank. These are the sole remains of the hut enclosing the lever which operated the points for the Loop. In the early years a key and staff worked the lever, but latterly Annett's locking system was used. There was a similar hut near the junction of the Loop with the Kilkee line.

South-west from here, for a quarter of a mile, the line curves gracefully along the edge of the bay a mere foot above high-water mark. It would be more accurate to call the embankment a causeway here, since on the landward side, also, are signs that the sea invades the low fields adjacent to the line. There were some fences to contend with, but we had only to step off the embankment momentarily to pass them. All in all, it was pleasant to walk along here, the sea breeze in our faces and a firm surface underfoot.

Heavy machinery was at work in that townland of Carrowncalla North as we passed. A deep drain was being scooped out at the eastern side of the line, and the spoil being used to construct a sod wall on its seaward face. Though mud and debris were everywhere, no serious injury had been done to the fabric of the bank, which acts here as a breakwater. By the right-hand side of the line, opposite the first farmhouse along the way, was a large stagnant pool, the only evidence yet we had seen of the channels used by the turf boats of the nineteenth century. At least 12-feet wide, it stretched off southwards, parallel to the line, for as far as we could see. We walked on the intervening bank along here to view the channel more clearly, and were surprised at its depth, over 15 feet. Through the mud in its bed a little rivulet was flowing, joined just ahead of us by another from the east, which was insignificant in itself but whose massive channel has been hacked through the embankment. It stopped us in our tracks and for a considerable time, since its sides were slimy with stinking tidal mud and took careful negotiating.

The calls of the seabirds were our sole accompaniment as we started along the last straight run before the line curves southwards again and out of sight, leaving the boat channel to arrow its way ahead directly to the bay. The cottage at Carrowncalla no. 1 crossing was recognisable a short way off, but before we reached it we had to pass one other excavation of the line. Here, however, a pipe had been run through the earthwork and the surface repaired, so there was a minimum of trouble in getting by. Even from close at hand it seemed that there might be someone living in the cottage, but its windows were shuttered, the door securely locked.

One hundred and fifty yards to the west, a bridge carries the road across the boat channel and towards the water's edge. Since we were so near at hand we investigated. It is stone-built, therefore not recently constructed, and from here the channel runs direct to the tide. But there was something odd: the opening of the bridge is a mere 5-feet high – no bigger than a large culvert – so how could boats possibly have travelled under it and on up to Moyasta, particularly if laden? It must have been added later, when the transportation of turf was over.[10]

The narrow neck of land outside the channel, on the western side, continues on out the bay and comes to a head at Ilaunalea, 500 yards away. From here in 1863 it was proposed to build an embankment across the mouth of Poulnasherry, by way of Black Island and Ilaunbeg, to Kilnagalliagh, on the western shore. It was a daring plan and probably would have succeeded but for the ill-advised attempt to close the mouth of the bay in the face of winter tides. The rest is history. Today, the eroded, scattered remnants of the earthworks can be seen only at low tide. If the line had developed as proposed, its only junction would have been here, not a mile farther north, at Moyasta, and the station-house would probably have been where the lonely Carrowncalla no. 1 level-crossing cottage now stands.

We had a choice now: either to proceed back to the cottage and from there onward along the 'new' line, or to go out across the narrow peninsula to Ilaunalea, see what remained there and then continue along the remnants of the 1860s earthworks south-west for half a mile to where the old line rejoins the new at an accommodation crossing. The tide being out made up our minds; it was an ideal opportunity as we might not come this way again.

The causeway joining Ilaunalea to the mainland was, if not man-made, at least deliberately buttressed with stones brought there, no doubt to make a safe passage for the railway that was to cross this fragile neck of land. At high tide nowadays, only a narrow strip on the landward side remains clear of water, and this might make one who is unfamiliar with the flow of the tides rather nervous; it would be a bleak place to be stranded, for no matter how short a time. However, Ilaunalea itself is at all times over high water, so there is no danger of drowning, at least! We were fortunate to be able to trace now, at low tide, a long tapering stub of gravel pointing north-west from the tip of the headland – all that remains of the old embankment on this side of the bay. Very little else can be distinguished farther out. Until recently a lone railway girder protruded from the water 200 yards away, at the 'Wicked Gap', as a marker of the channel, but even that has disappeared.

Turning south-east, we climbed to the highest point of the 'island', the spot where any line from Ennis would have had to join a Kilrush branch, and looked along the remnants of the old bank, very wide but worn to within 2 feet of tide level and broken in several places by out-flowing streams. Inside this is a lagoon with mud and reeds aplenty, and to the east, along the shore, the line we left at the cottage. We would be able to keep it in sight at quite close range for all of its length until we rejoined it later. Directly opposite us, at the site of the forty-fourth milepost, we noted that it ran at the water's edge over a short causeway, but fell back a field's width from the slob thereafter.

Our worry was whether we would be able to cross the streams that broke the bank ahead into sections, but as we approached the first – the boat channel – we were relieved to see that it was no more than 2-feet deep. Beyond, the going was straightforward enough to allow us to observe our surroundings closely: the jagged chunks we were walking on (certainly no seashore stone), the highest point reached by the tide, the opposite shore. It was infinitely more interesting than the West Clare line 200 yards away, which, even from here, we could see was very overgrown. A second stream from the lagoon was no deeper than the first, and we forded it without difficulty, though at high tide we would have to swim here.

Shortly, we were treading solid ground again, the only part of the bank which has not been eroded. Bushes took over at once and there was no avoiding a walk along its seaward side, amid the wrack. But since no time had been wasted on our informative detour we were not unduly concerned by the slow going here. Eventually, we had to get on to the top of the bank, if only to measure how close we were to the 'new' line. A culvert seemed a convenient place to start, and it pleased us to find that the corresponding culvert on the West Clare was merely yards away. It was time to change, and there was delightfully little trouble in doing so.

On the old familiar ground again we ran into muck almost at once; cattle have made their own of this place, whereas the 'old' line is too overgrown even for them. But salvation was at hand ahead; on and across our path was a farmyard and a tractor at work with silage. Hopefully, we introduced ourselves to the farmer, a man who turned out to be most knowledgeable. He gave us much local information, among it some that mildly confused us. Looking out along 'the old bank', as he called it, to Ilaunalea, he told us that we were mistaken, and the map also, that Ilaunalea was the small island to our left, a short way into the channel and known as 'Lána' to local people. This, according to the map, is Ilaunaclaggin, but he, who had lived here all his life, had never heard such a name. The headland we had just visited, where the old line ends, was Mulqueen's Point, he said. It was worth hearing all this from him because, as we had found on a number of previous occasions, even the Ordnance charts are not completely reliable; sometimes names of places have changed, but sometimes also one suspects that the original information obtained by the surveyors was faulty. He warned us that the line ahead was both muddy and overgrown, and that if we wished to see something far more interesting nearby we should walk down the small road from this crossing to the shore and continue by high-tide mark until we reached the narrow mouth of the bay, where a ferry once operated, linking Kilrush with 'the west', and where thirty-five people were drowned on 12 December 1849 when one such craft sank.[11] The passengers were nearly all paupers who had spent the day in Kilrush in search of food and were returning empty-handed when they met their end. The newspaper that reported the story was bitterly critical of the fact that not a single magistrate visited the place, 'where 35 dead bodies were lying exposed to public view', and had words of praise only for Captain Kennedy, the Poor Law inspector, who took it on himself to see that coffins were procured for the dead.

The oyster beds he also knew about – their former location, extent and the reasons for their disappearance – and he confirmed for us what we had already observed: that the bay is now a quiet place. It is especially so in comparison with how it was even in his youth, he admitted sadly.

The little road to the shore extended only as far as the stones and shingle of the beach. Tractor-prints led from there to the point at which the old road from Kilrush to the ferry took up again, and from then on the way was clear. Southwards and south-east, the Shannon lay open and wide as we reached the end of the ferry road and the bare, lonely stretch of water where once such frequent crossings were made. From here, there is a fine view of Cammoge Point and places west, but neither slipway nor jetty as a reminder of the boats that operated here. Only the tantalising gap remains where once there was a thriving trade. Silence has replaced the bustle of a land as yet unemptied by famine, disease and emigration.

Thirteen and a half centuries before that terrible accident of 1849, the great St Senan also crossed at this place, but in most peculiar circumstances. Senan's father, Ercan, owned land on both sides of the bay, and one day asked his son to drive his cattle to the western farm as he himself was too busy to do so. When Senan came to the mouth of the bay the cattle refused to swim, so he reached out his hand and at once the waters divided to let him and his herd pass, dry. When safely ashore at Cammoge he ordered the waves to close and promised that never again would the water of the bay be stopped. Had those in charge of the 1860s debacle but known of this legend they might well have concluded, as William M. Murphy did later, that the safer course by far was to go round the bay.

As we walked the undulating straight road back to where it met the line at Carrowncalla no. 2 crossing we could not but notice a sprawl of old buildings right of us, almost on the shore. Looking from a distance exactly like a scene from the marsh episodes of *Great Expectations*, the house was vaguely sinister, even in daylight, its hipped gable turned coldly to us, its face fixed on the river as if expecting the arrival of secret visitors. The actor Oliver Reed now owns it, so we were later told. Just north of the crossing, very close to the railway, stands Ferry Lodge, one-time home of William Dalton, paymaster of the West Clare, but it was to the crossing cottage that we directed all our attention.[12] The ground is spongy here; even the side drains appear to be tidal, perhaps not surprisingly, since, according to the map, spring tides cover much of the land directly south of the line. From a little cutting close to the site of the forty-fifth milepost, a different angle of the sinister old house on the shore became visible, as did, for the first time, the flashing beacons on the twin stacks of Moneypoint power station 5 miles to the south-east beyond Kilrush; Fionn Mac Cumhaill's goalposts, as they have been aptly called.

The river, now visible on three sides, made a pleasant companion to our walk through this part of Carrowncalla South, but only briefly; a substantial cutting soon blinkered all but a narrow view directly ahead. The side walls here are at least 12-feet high, and we were hardly surprised to find the surface underfoot deteriorate rapidly into squelching bog, very like part of Rineen cutting. But something more dangerous was brought sharply to our notice: barbed wire. We jerked to a halt, our faces only inches from the rusty strands strung at shoulder height from side to side of the cutting. It had happened us on at least two previous occasions, so we should have been more alert. Considerably more warily we moved on, towards a large, green building sitting squarely on the line out beyond the cutting. As soon as we reached level ground, something entirely unexpected drew our attention completely from the line, and sent us fumbling excitedly for our maps. Only by degrees did the picture presented to us register for what it really was: Scattery Island, Inis Cathaigh, monastic home of Clare's greatest saint, Senan.

We climbed a high bank to get a clearer view, and the longer we studied the island the more it looked to us like a large submarine, prow high, stern almost awash, slipping silently down the Shannon, the round tower its periscope and the nearby cathedral its conning tower. In the subdued March light we could see just enough of it to make all the romance and legends associated with the place come uncannily to life. At any moment, it seemed to us, the Cathach himself, the enormous serpent who ate Senan's smith Narach and was banished to Doo Lough for his trouble, might emerge from his old home, shake the water from his great mane and come prowling about some unfinished business.

The island is uninhabited now but its history has been long and largely bloody. Yet it began auspiciously enough, with St Senan's founding of his monastery here about the year 540. Seven churches there were, and the round tower, and though the congregation was large, there was not a single woman in sight, for Senan, like most early Irish saints, had his little oddities. One of these was his strict refusal to allow any female to set foot on the island.[13] Whether this rule was relaxed after his death in 544 we do not know, but that Scattery grew enormously in importance as time passed is attested to by its being made a diocese, moreover one with jurisdiction over parts of Kerry and Limerick as well as south-west Clare.

The coming of the Vikings at the beginning of the ninth century heralded a period of gradual decline. The monastery, originally built on the island for security, now found that position its most fatal weakness, and time after time it was plundered until the Vikings themselves settled here in the mid-tenth century.[14] This merely drew the ire of Irish kings on the sacred place, and so the raids continued, the burning now being done by the Irish themselves. Even Brian

Boru paid a destructive visit.[15] The Normans in the fourteenth century and the English in later ages kept up this unhallowed tradition, and yet the island's population somehow managed to survive the pillage and bloodshed, temporarily swelled every year by throngs from the mainland who came in early March to celebrate the 'pattern' day. Strange to say, the festival intended to honour the great cleric was suppressed not by the British authorities, but by another cleric. One of the first acts of Fr John Kenny when he was appointed parish priest of Kilrush in 1827 was the abolition of the Scattery pattern on the grounds that it gave rise to drunkenness and unseemly behaviour.[16] But as regards the inhabitants of the island, it was only in our own relatively peaceful era that the ghost was finally given up. The last people left in 1978, and since then, except for occasional curious sightseers and islanders visiting their former homes, Scattery lies empty. Yet, though it lacks people today it has no shortage of relics of the past that are eminently worth visiting: the buildings alone date from the sixth to the twentieth centuries. In its now peaceful environs, surrounded by the mark and the bones of sixty generations, one is made very conscious of mortality, but of the timelessness of human aspirations, too.[17]

The green structure barring our way was a thing to be got by quickly, after the prospect of Scattery. It appeared to be a sort of reinforced mobile home, but since its windows were all covered securely with what looked like ships' hatches, we could make ourselves no wiser. We passed on, to a pleasant little bay where the water reaches to within feet of the line, a secluded place which looked as though it might attract many visitors in summertime. Our view of it was soon blocked as we entered another cutting, but there was no help for this since the tide was full, preventing us from walking the shoreline. Tough going it was, too, in that cutting, what with briars, mud and the banks shutting out much of the light. As we emerged we were pleasantly surprised to find ourselves quite close to a road and some houses. The 200 yards to the road were grassy and passable, but the land to the left, so recently a sizeable hill, had already dipped abruptly, and we approached the crossing over an embankment, cut through by a culvert 12 feet below where we were walking. But before we could reach the houses we were stopped by a concrete wall across the line, which could mean only one thing: bridge gone. We were right. Before us was the gap where Brew's Bridge once stood, and across the road a new house, built almost on the line. We had better make enquiries, we decided.

An invitation to rest and have a bite to eat was gratefully accepted, and in the course of twenty minutes' conversation we heard much that interested us, some of it to do with the railway, some about the area in general. The headland jutting into the estuary directly in front of the bridge is Baurnahard Point, and the *cabhail* there was once a bailiffs' hut. It is many years since those gentlemen resided there, either because poachers have turned honest or more probably because there are just no salmon to catch any more. But lest it be thought that decline of fish stocks is a completely modern phenomenon, listen to what a newspaper of 1874 had to say of a drastic fall in the numbers of fish caught in the spring of that year: 'Since the legislation and use of the drift nets the fishermen on the Lower Shannon are catching all the best fish ... [whereas] ... the more wealthy proprietors on the upper waters are catching very few'. What has modern technology done, after all, except move the problem a few hundred miles out into the Atlantic?

The gruesome days of the Famine are still remembered here, with the terrible mortality in Kilrush workhouse etched on the minds of the people even yet. In 1847 alone, 1,070 people died there, and in 1850–51, a date by which most people consider the Famine to have ended, the toll was higher still, 1,700. During all this unprecedented misery, mass evictions went on and large quantities of corn were exported from Kilrush port for the benefit of those same landlords who were literally condemning their fellow Christians to death in their thousands.[18] Prominent among them was Colonel Crofton Vandeleur, chairman of the workhouse guardians and far more concerned with finances than with people's lives. Through his actions during these years, the Vandeleur good name was first tainted, a trend that was accelerated during the proprietorship of his successor,

Captain Hector Vandeleur, who brought the family to ultimate ruin by his actions in 1888.

So vicious was the behaviour of most of the landlords during those five terrible years that it even came to the notice of the House of Commons, largely through the exertions of Captain A.E. Kennedy, the Poor Law inspector assigned to the Union. An able administrator and thoroughly conscientious, he worked tirelessly at the almost insuperable problems thrust on him, and when at last (probably through the machinations of Vandeleur and some of the other guardians) he was transferred in August 1850, the people he had striven so consistently to help wept at his going.[19] Grim times, indeed.

Also clearly remembered here are the various boating tragedies that have occurred down the years, such as the Cammoge ferry drownings of 1849, the Shannon disaster of 1893, and the loss of three people sailing to Querrin in the late 1940s. These, together with the deaths of many individuals in the river, especially in recent years off Tarbert pier, make a sad litany, but one to be expected on a great waterway like the Shannon.

But there is humour, too, and much of it at the expense of the West Clare. Did we know, our hosts ask, that one of the engines in the early years was christened 'I'll Walk Beside You', after the famous John McCormack song, because it was so slow? In the same vein is the story about the innocent poor man from Sragh who rode his donkey into Kilrush and was asked by an acquaintance there, 'Musha, how did you come in, Johnny?'

'Yerra, I thrun me oul' leg across th' oul' ass.'

'Why in the world didn't you come by train?'

'I never thought about it, sure. But, d'you know something! That's the way I'll go home.'

His business done, he led his ass back to the station, tied it to a buffer at the rear of the train, and, knowing nothing at all about tickets, sat in.

They came to Moyasta, and while the train was stopped and tickets were being checked he decided to get out and see how the ass was doing. There was no sign of the beast. Scratching his head, he went to the driver: 'Tell me, sir, by any chance you didn't see e'er an ass pass you out, did you?'

On a different tack again, had we heard that the 'Michael' of Percy French's song was Mike Talty from Kilrush, the fireman on the train in which French was travelling on the famous occasion? But in all these tales and anecdotes the humour is kind, the banter of friends about a friend. Less lovingly remembered are those who carried away the line, together with Brew's Bridge, in 1961. But all the memories are tempered by realism: a train will probably never again pass this way.

As in every other place where we had lingered to talk and question, we had to tear ourselves away reluctantly at last, particularly since we wished to have enough time to spare to see Kilrush at our leisure. However, there was still much to be pointed out: could we see the hills off to the west? The outermost is Kilcredaun, with Rehy Hill inside, while Carrigaholt of the fine castle, where Lord Clare's Dragoons trained (and still do, by moonlight, it is said), lies between them, almost 7 miles away across the water.[20] At half that distance Querrin Point was visible, hooking into the river, while Beale Bar over in Kerry appeared much nearer than it really was. A short distance away we would pass a stream that divides Carrowncalla from Leadmore West.

As we pulled through the rear fence – a little hut, constructed solidly of sleepers, its door hanging crazily on one hinge – was brought to our attention. Built as a tool shed and shelter for the linesmen on wet days, it has survived them all, become a sort of mute memorial to their vanished labours.

The section beyond Brew's Bridge is easy going and quite impressive where the line rises to a little embankment, no more than 5-feet high but very wide. Also very exposed, as was discovered during a violent storm on 12 January 1899, when two carriages of the morning train to Kilkee were blown off the track. There was only one passenger on board at the time and he escaped uninjured, though traffic on the line was interrupted for the rest of the day, as were telephone communications.[21] Another derailment took place here in the 1940s, but on that occasion a storm was not to blame.

We were soon hemmed in by thorn bushes, and by the time we came to a recognisable landmark – a farmhouse and its sheds, once owned by a former inhabitant of Scattery – we were well beyond the stream that marked the townland boundary, and we had no inclination to go back and search for it. The tide was now a mere field away, Scattery looked amazingly near, and we wondered whether the 'Red Stones' were on that shore just south of us. We were curious because it was there that St Senan worked one of his miracles. He had come out from Scattery to say Mass on the mainland but on landing discovered he had left his Mass book at home on the island. Rather than go back, he asked a passing man to go and get it for him. The man agreed, but said that he had no transport, whereupon Senan lifted a flagstone on to the water, where it floated. Warning the man to make no sudden moves, he set the stone in motion and off it went to Scattery, where the book was waiting. Just as surely, the man was transported back to where Senan stood, and we can only imagine his speechless state as he came to land at the 'Red Stones'. Yet this miracle was by no means unique in west Clare, for farther west St Cuán was also given to trips on such unlikely transport.

Something that would have floated us over the sea of thorns on all sides of us would have been very welcome just then, but alas, there was no miracle, only our strong boots and much expenditure of energy. When we at last escaped, it was only because the next landowner along the line had seen fit to clear away everything, the embankment included. All the way to Leadmore no. 1 (or Shanakyle) crossing, the very level of the land has been lowered by at least 2 feet. But the side ditches remain, so in effect what is here is a long, narrow field, running dead straight to the road, where the forty-sixth milepost stood.

The very name Shanakyle ('the old burying-ground') is synonymous in these parts with the Great Famine,[22] as we found out when we called at the crossing cottage, where the woman who kept the gates for almost thirty years before the line closed still lives. She had heard many stories of the workhouse inmates who were buried here in a huge anonymous pit without ceremony or benefit of clergy. The miserable coffins were deposited in tiers and covered by only a sprinkling of earth to await the next gruesome consignment. Yet these were the lucky ones! At least they had a coffin. Perhaps half of the thousands who died in the Kilrush Union were buried with only a shroud of straw tied with a *súgán*. An unnamed writer to a newspaper of the time well summed up the feelings of the people at this final humiliation:

> *Aye, buried like dogs are the Poor-House Dead*
> *In this Christian land, without shroud or shred*
> *Of a winding-sheet on the wasted frame –*
> *And this Godless thrift is our Guardians' aim!*[23]

Other horror stories, too, survive about this place, such as that of a man named O'Connell who fell into a coma in the workhouse, was presumed dead and carried with a cartload of corpses to the grave pit. As usual, the coffins were thinly covered with earth and left so to await the morrow's quota. That night, however, a man passing by the graveyard heard moaning, and on investigating located O'Connell's coffin and released him. He lived on, it seems, for a further twenty years. There were probably many others who were mistakenly buried after only the most cursory of medical examinations. In recent years, a monument has been erected over the mass grave, a tardy memorial to all those nameless ones.

To enter Leadmore no. 1 cottage was to get a brief glimpse of the past, for the interior of the house was quite unchanged from how it would have looked in West Clare days. An old railway clock, the open fireplace, a drawing of engine no. 5 from 1892, all testified to a lingering regard for old times, though the owner was quite adamant that she had no regrets over the passing away of the railway.

On the Kilrush side of the crossing, the going is wonderfully easy for a short distance; in fact, the line is now a tarred road. For once we were enabled to walk without having to pick our steps, and so could look about as we wished. The graveyard was only a field away to the north, while slightly ahead and curving into the river was Skagh Point (or Scuff Point, as it is called locally). It was from here that ballast was obtained for the railway until, in 1904, a dispute with the Crown over royalties led to the removal of operations to Ballygriffey. In the nearby fields, close to the graveyard, in October 1887 a crowd of about 200,000 people gathered to protest against the proposed evictions in Kilrush town, this site probably being chosen because of its connections with the terrible evictions of forty years before.[24]

Before long we saw the reason why this road is so well maintained: a new town sewage-treatment plant, standing in its own enclosure near the shore and looking like some sawn-off pyramid. It looked very well indeed, but we investigated it no further; Kilrush held out more appealing prospects for exploration. The paved road went only as far as the plant gateway, and we ran into much troublesome mud in the wide cutting beyond. There was no climbing along the capacious side banks, either, for they were dotted with sheltering cattle, and Keith, with Doonbeg goods' shed still vividly in mind, refused to go that way.

Hardship brings some rewards, however. When we emerged from the cutting, a fine view of Kilrush awaited us, together with its harbour, and Cappagh further south. And best of all, only one last straight mile of line separated us from the town. As at Moyasta, the railway skirted the high-water mark along here, but the mud and reeds of Kilrush Creek make it a less than inspiring sight. For the first few hundred yards of riverside embankment, before the land bulges out into a little triangular promontory, there was all the usual tidal rubbish. But there was also Skagh Point, wagging its long finger into the harbour as if admonishing Watch House Point on the other shore. Finally, there was Cappagh pier, our destination, tantalisingly close, a mere half-mile away as the crow flies. The long road for us, however! And it was improved not a whit by having been extensively dug up. We struggled on, past the urban district boundary – which is nowhere indicated, of course, except on the map. But even that gave us a sense of having reached, if not our final objective, at least its outer suburbs, though in truth the only parts of the town clearly visible to us from this particular low point were Cappagh and Soldiers' Hill, both on the far side of the harbour.

Once more, the line runs by the slob here, its well-laid foundation stones actually stained by the mud. We had plenty of opportunity to examine them in detail, for several times we were forced to climb down along them in order to bypass fences. Had we taken a little detour to the north instead, we would have been able to see Pella House, one-time residence of Admiral J.F. Studdert, an eminent commander in Nelson's fleet and friend of Daniel O'Connell and other prominent men of the early nineteenth century. From its grounds, the coastguards kept watch over the estuary during the First World War, when an intrusion or even an invasion by the Germans seemed possible.[25]

At the exit of another cutting, a huge stone building jutted to the very edge of the line before us. A mill or factory it surely was from the style of its architecture, and not built in recent times, so the trains must have passed through the narrow gap between its corner and the cutting wall on the left. If so, there was certainly no scope for passengers to poke their heads from carriage windows. The stone edge would have made a very neat guillotine, indeed. Past this corridor, the surrounds open abruptly to the right into a yard, recognisable as that of a seaweed-processing factory from the piles of that commodity lying about. But not a soul was there to make us any the wiser.

One would hardly recognise the line here, concealed, cut through by a deep boundary trench, and finally obliterated altogether as it approaches the border of Kilrush townland. But 200 yards on, even this poor remnant was swallowed up in an enormous blank concrete wall. And it was here that the down signal for the lead-in to Kilrush Station was situated, the map informed us! A green light would have been most welcome at that moment. We approached as one might have approached the Berlin Wall before it was opened, with a sense of trepidation, a feeling that here everything stopped, and that a secret that we vitally needed to know had been locked securely away behind this impenetrable screen.

Of vital help to us was the fact that the wall straddled what was still a deep cutting; by getting on to the lip of the left-hand side we would be able to bypass it. Having scrabbled up onto the field and walked past the blockage we discovered a coal yard and another high wall 50 yards away. A neat, ready-made depot! How varied are the uses to which the West Clare has been put. In this yard, as well as coal, there were two buildings which we immediately recognised as of railway provenance, though what their function might have been we could not say just then. We later found out that one was a carriage-shed, the other an engine house. In this latter, the steam-riser worked his night-time shift, getting the fire-box cleaned, the fire stoked and the coal bunker filled for the early-morning passenger train, just as his opposite number in Ennis was doing at an equally ungodly hour.

We quickly passed the second high wall and out beyond the yard, where the hill on the left rapidly falls away until, 200 yards ahead, we could see where it came to the level of the line itself at a road junction. Directly below us to the right was a row of houses fronting on to the quay, and in the back garden of one of them an elderly man stood silently, watching us, sizing us up. We slithered down the grassy slope, partly to explain our unusual arrival and even more in hopes of answers to some of the questions we were anxious to ask. A courteous old man he was, but fiery and unafraid to express political heresies, as we quickly found out. He set the tone by his answer to our introductory apology for maybe startling him: 'Indeed ye didn't. I seen a lot stranger things than ye passing here.'

As it happened, he was only too glad of an opportunity to speak his mind on what he saw as the lunacy that had brought the country in general and the docks area of Kilrush in particular to its knees. This run-down area all around us here was once the vital end of the town, but 'there's nothing left now only the bones'. He made the very sensible point that a country that decides to dispense with regional railways must have good roads to replace them, and he poured scorn on the so-called planners who put all their hopes in road transport in the early 1960s, but hardly strengthened the existing roads, let alone provide extra roads to carry it. 'Brilliant men gone astray' was his

verdict on the Fianna Fáil government of the time. 'They sold everything for money' – he weighted the word 'money' with contempt – 'an'
they're still looking for money! An' they'll never have enough money,
no matter what they'll sell!' His message was abundantly clear. We
could have stood an hour listening to him, so pleasant is it to hear a
heartfelt and non-party-political estimate of public representatives.
But the first signs of evening would soon be on us, we still had much
ground to cover, so at the risk of seeming abrupt we had to steer our
host towards some factual details. We were at Merchants' Quay, he
said, and a siding of the railway ran to the large store at the quay's
end a hundred yards south of us. The railway yard and station were
just ahead, but first we would pass the railway cottage at Leadmore
no. 2 crossing. As his final word, he warned us not to expect too much
at the station, that 'there's terrible changes in that place since the
railway was closed'.

That should have been sufficient warning to us, but we, who
had seen only photographs of the station-house in its days of glory,
nestled cosily in the shadow of Glynn's huge mill buildings, could
not reconcile what he was telling us with our own notions of what
should be there. Within minutes, the crossing cottage was to hand,
unlived-in, though quite well cared for, and with a prominent stone
plaque proclaiming '1892', probably the date of its construction. A
tarred road now lay before us, and here began problems, and the first
hint that the old man's warning had been well founded. Quite simply,
no matter how closely we looked we could find nothing to guide us
on to the former route of the line. It was gone. We took a sighting on
the station-house, down almost on the creek to our right, and began
to pick our way along a direct route between road and tide. But what
has befallen this intervening ground? Nowhere, in all our travels, had
we come upon a place which looked so like a bombed site. Rubble
and debris of all kinds lay strewn over these flat acres to the very
edge of the quay, and a few scrawny ponies wandered through the
desolation that was once Kilrush railway yard.

How could one tell now that there were formerly as many as ten
sidings here? Even all traces of the dock crossing gates, just 20 yards

from the station gates, have gone. Words can hardly do justice to the poignancy of the scene.

Uncomfortable, even dangerous, though it was to have to pick our way through this wasteland, we did it, still hopeful of finding something. We might as well have gone by the road; there were no wonderful discoveries, no magical ending, only the station-house, standing, as always, just across the road from Glynn's mills and round the corner from Merchants' Row and Frances Street. But it seems to cringe now, so alone is it in the midst of its forlorn surroundings. We stopped to stare, almost to commiserate, though we had intended to pass right on, see some of the town and call on our way back from Cappagh, if light permitted.

A fine red-brick building it must have been one time, but even though one half of it now seemed to be occupied, the other part was semi-derelict and appeared to be a mere garage or store shed, if we were to judge by the large doors in the eastern gable-end. What might have brought so historic a structure to such a pass was a story we could not resist, no matter what constraints of time were upon us. So we once more entrusted our hopes and expectations to the hospitality of Clare people, and, as usual, were not turned away empty handed.

We were taken by the owner on a guided tour of the premises and shown all there was to see, which was little enough in comparison to what had been either removed or destroyed. When the house was sold after the closure of the line, it was gutted and used as a truck garage, and only in recent years has it been re-established as a dwelling house. It will be a long process to restore it fully, but the present owner is determined to do so.

In spite of the hardships it has suffered, the building still possesses some charm and much of its original timber-work, a tribute to the quality of the materials used in its construction. By the gable-end where the large doors hang, traces of other demolished structures tell of a larger building than now exists, but too little remains for one to be certain of their function. At the rear of the house as it now is we walked along the former platform, but found no evidence of the verandah and its fine decorative cast-iron supports that we had noted in pictures from the Lawrence Collection. (Even by 1954 this had been removed, as photographs of that time show.) Nor can the quay be seen from here any more. A shed, built in the mid-1960s, fills the space where four separate lines ran, and obscures all view of the river. Even the location of the turntable, two water-columns and the 3,800-gallon water tank can no longer be made out.

At the western end of the station we looked across the wasteland we had arrived through and it was hard to imagine the activity that was a daily (and often nightly) feature of the place for almost seventy years: the shunting, the offloading and the transfer of cargo. Hard also it was to visualise the terror of railway guard Michael Ryan whose foot became wedged between the rails here during shunting and whose cries went unnoticed as he was run over and killed by wagon no. 27 on 10 March 1933. His tragedy, in a sense, symbolises the tragedy of Kilrush itself, for in spite of the coming of the Moneypoint power station, it has well-nigh expired almost unnoticed. A town of broad streets, fine houses and great natural endowments has fallen on lean times, and a harbour from which great benefits might still be expected now lies choking to death in mud and silt.[26] One can only hope that the proposed multi-million-pound marina and its ancillary projects will help to revive a town that deserves far better of native government than it has got over the past half-century.[27]

Frances Street, close by the station and at over 98 feet the widest public thoroughfare in Kilrush, was named for the wife of John Ormsby Vandeleur, who devoted much of his wealth to improving the town in the early nineteenth century. To an outsider it may appear rather odd that even today the town boasts two streets – the other being Vandeleur Street – dedicated to a family that hardly sided with the people in the darkest hour of their history. But the reply of a true townsperson would probably be that not all the Vandeleurs were like the last of them, and that a family should not be condemned for the excesses of its worst elements.

What we were most anxious to see was the workhouse, at Ballyurra, half a mile north of the town centre, but there is little left

Kilrush Station. (Photo: Lawrence Collection, National Library)

of the original complex except some of the 'Famine walls' built in
exchange for food in order to satisfy the economic dictates of the
1840s, which decreed that nothing be given away free. On a 6-acre
site and opened in late 1841 with accommodation for 800 inmates,
it was quickly overwhelmed by the sheer scale of the misery caused
by successive potato failures. In December of 1847 a crowd of about
3,000 people besieged the building seeking aid, and had to be dis-
persed by police and the army.[28] In December of 1849 the streets of
the town were rent by the shrieks of starving mobs, and it was some
of these people who were drowned in the Cammoge ferry disaster
while returning hungry to the west on 12 December. But the worst
was far from over. By June 1850 there were 5,000 people in the main
workhouse and its six auxiliaries, among which was numbered the
nearby Broomhill House, one of the oldest dwellings in Kilrush.[29]

The temporary fever hospital, set up in 1847 to try to curtail the
spread of infection, was soon nicknamed 'The Slaughterhouse' from
the numbers who died there – over sixty patients per week at the end
of that year. In the main building, conditions were little better, which
was hardly surprising, with up to five people to a single bed and no
fires to provide warmth during the coldest part of the winter of 1849.[30]

Kilrush Station: view from goods' bank.
(Photo: Irish Railway Record Society, no. 10748)

That there were not far more deaths was probably due to the exertions of Captain Kennedy in the face of the parsimony of the guardians.

Most shocking of all, perhaps, in that outrageous chapter of our history was the mortality among children. Most of the thousands who died in Kilrush workhouse were under the age of fifteen, and the manner of their deaths was described graphically by a visiting clergyman: 'I have seen many in the act of death, still not a tear, not a cry. I have scarcely ever seen one endeavour to change his or her position. I have never heard one ask for food, for water – for anything; two, three or four in a bed, there they lie and die, if suffering, still ever silent, unmoved.'[31] To us, who have seen on television children die before our eyes in similar circumstances, that description rings all too horribly true. It may also partly explain why the people of Ireland have been, per capita, the most generous in the world to the victims of such catastrophes.

But it was not the workhouse that saw the greatest crowds gather in Kilrush. Half a mile away to the east, Ballykett Fair Green was, several times during the nineteenth century, the scene of large public meetings, most notably in July 1841, during O'Connell's Repeal agitation, and again in October 1887, when evictions were about to begin. But perhaps the greatest assembly ever seen in Kilrush took place when Fr Mathew, the 'Apostle of Temperance', paid his first visit to the town in November 1840 for the dedication of St Senan's Catholic Church, the foundation stone of which had been laid in 1838 by none other than Colonel Vandeleur. Up to 20,000 people gathered that day, some from as far away as Kerry, and there were huge numbers of enrolments into the temperance fold.[32] All that now remains to remind us of Fr Mathew's great work is the Temperance Hall, still marked in old Ordnance maps, near St Mary's Convent.

One mile east of Frances Street is the provocatively named town-land of Rape-Park, but this appellation has, not surprisingly, fallen into disuse since few of the citizens of the place are very anxious to give it as their address. Alive and flourishing, however, is the memory of St Senan. A few hundred yards south of the Kilkee road near Leadmore House is Senan's Well, at the place where the Cathach landed when he was banished from Scattery. In his vexation he took a bite out of the ground, but at once the holy well sprang up, where-upon the poor monster, seeing that there was no defeating the power of the holy man, departed quietly to his exile in Doo Lough. Four miles to the east is Molougha, Senan's birthplace, to which people still travel to pray and be cured, particularly of ailments of the eyes.[33] His sister St Imy is remembered in the place name Killimer, where a modern church is dedicated to her. Nowadays, Killimer is best known for a much more secular institution: its car ferry to Tarbert, on the Kerry side of the Shannon. It runs daily all the year round and is one of the most successful of its type in Ireland.

Directly east of the road down to the ferry is Besborough, former home of R.W.C. Reeves, one of the chief movers in the bringing of railways to Clare and whose wife turned the first sod of the South Clare Railway at Kilkee on 9 October 1890. No more than half a mile away, in Burrane cemetery, lies the tragic Ellen Hanley, the Colleen Bawn, whose murder in 1819 caught the public imagination and provided the inspiration for Gerald Griffin's novel, *The Collegians*, Boucicault's play, *The Colleen Bawn*, and Benedict's light opera, *The*

Lily of Killarney.[34] None of these fictionalisations captures the true horror and sordidness of the killing of this young girl or the pathos of her burial far from home in a grave lent for the purpose by Peter O'Connell, a scholar whose own life ended also in disappointment.[35]

Farther up the estuary is Clonderalaw Bay, with its castle where the formidable and much feared Máire Rua McMahon was born about the year 1615. She it was who said during the Confederate Wars of the 1640s when her husband was brought home mortally wounded to Leamaneagh Castle, 'We want no dead men here.' She married at least three times, her third husband being a Cromwellian officer named Cooper. By such means did she save her son's inheritance from confiscation. Poor Cooper, it seems, lived only for a short time afterwards. Some stories have it that he lost his balance while walking on the battlements of the castle, others that his hand 'slipped' while he was shaving! One way or another, he ended up very dead, indeed, and Máire Rua went on to enjoy her now-secure position until her death in a hunting accident many years later.

As always, it was time that beat us. As we turned from Toler Street back into Frances Street after our futile visit to a workhouse that no longer existed, the first gloom of evening was upon us and lights were beginning to be lit. We quickened our pace, and it was this very reaction that brought to my mind the story of the old country-women from Sragh. They would come to town on Saturday to do their shopping, and in the evening would be returning to the station, laden down with parcels. One of the railway guards, a mischievous man, never failed to take advantage of this. From whatever pub he happened to be drinking in he would watch out for their passing, then slip out, cap in hand and race past them, hell for leather. They knew from his uniform that he was the guard, and presuming that the train was about to start, they would try to rush, scattering their purchases in the panic to get there on time. And no matter how often he did it they could never afford to ignore him, just in case that one time he might be in earnest.

We avoided the station this time and steered directly for where the metal river-bridge crossed the creek diagonally 200 yards away. It is no longer in place, having been removed in the early 1980s, we were told, because it had become dangerous owing to lack of maintenance. This we found surprising in view of the excellent condition of many of the other metal-deck bridges we had passed. Maybe the salt air of the estuary was harder on this one than on others farther inland, yet why, then, does Moyasta Bridge still stand proudly, in face of the very same salt conditions? We crossed by the road-bridge a little upstream, and from here it was obvious that, even if we had been able to proceed, it would have been only for a very short distance, because the line runs almost at once into the perimeter fence of Doherty's timber yard.

We were now on the Cappagh road, and since for 500 yards the line is completely inaccessible we had to be content to follow the boundary wall of the huge providers' yard and wait until we came to the westward-facing section of Cappagh road where the high wall falls away to shoulder height to reveal the harbour again. Much of the promontory hidden by the high wall and occupied on its eastern, landward end by the timber yard seemed to be littered with scrap metal and other junk, and it took us only a moment to realise that the line must have run far closer to where we were standing. But the sole place it could have passed is directly inside the road wall, since beyond a narrow collar of dry land just here there is only slob. We kept to the road, checking at frequent intervals to make sure that there were no dramatic changes in the landscape, but only the gradually emerging, muddy and overgrown bed of the line greeted us each time.

It is hardly surprising that the Kilrush–Cappagh stretch of the South Clare should be in such poor condition. It was, after all, used only very infrequently from the 1920s on. A reporter, who was on the last train to travel this journey to Cappagh in January 1961, claimed it had been only the second train to run here in forty-five years, and he described the tracks to the pier as 'rusty and rotting'.[36] This is confirmed by a photograph of Cappagh Station taken in 1953, which shows grass several inches in height growing up through the sleepers and ballast.[37]

We passed by these poor remnants without attempting to set foot inside the wall, but soon even these petered out at the point opposite Soldiers' Hill, where the land, widening out into the harbour, has allowed houses to be built. From here to Supple's crossing, which leads on to Watch House Point, only intermittent short, overgrown fragments of the line remain. A small golf course occupies much of this area, and though the map showed that the route was to the rear of the course, nearer the creek, we had no means of checking whether it was still intact, and so had to walk on to the crossing. Here, from the bank of a large, reedy pond, we could look back and see that some, at least, of the line has survived, though much obscured. Before us, over the open field, to where it meets the right-angled turn of the Cappagh Road, we followed it with certainty until it was lost in a playground lately constructed in the little triangle of ground between tide and road. Signal post and track are alike gone, of course, but it is easy to pick out the route from here: sharp left and then straight on for the final 250 yards to Cappagh pier. Because of the high road wall on the left, there is a view only to seaward, and a lonely enough prospect it was in the disintegrating light to look out into Scattery road and see the dark bulk of both Hog Island and Scattery itself, with never a single inhabited house on either.[38]

Cappagh pier was silent, too – devoid of all life except for the constant lappings of the sea. We approached the terminus with sinking hearts. Here, once, ran a main line and a passing-loop which serviced the platform on the up side, but now the only remnant, apart from the stone platform edging, is an ugly concrete shed. We stepped onto the pier through an open door space in the protecting wall, and gazed along its darkening length. Out at its head was the goods' shed, once a familiar sight to steamer passengers, but there was little else to delay us here; the two parallel rail sidings are gone, though the stone surrounds of the turntable that turned railway wagons singly to the right, onto the pier, is still visible in the roadway. In West Clare days, there was only one siding to the pier head; the other was added by the GSR for greater convenience of loading and unloading. The pier itself has had a busy history. Begun in 1764, it was extended in the

1820s, again in the 1830s, and from it turf has been shipped to Limerick, fish to Billingsgate and people to America.[39] But it was not a place for dawdling on this bitterly cold March evening, so we turned our backs on Cappagh, the southern extremity of the West Clare Railway.

In so doing we also consigned to the darkness other places we had been looking forward to visiting; the square, for example. No more than 500 yards from the pier, it lies derelict now but was once the home of British military power in the region. During the 1888 evictions, the Berkshire Regiment was stationed there.

Beyond Cappagh Lodge, to the south-east, lies Aylevarroo Bay, and beyond that again Moyne, the embarkation place of those lost in the Shannon disaster of 1893. On 15 August sixteen people from the Tarbert area who had come to Clare for the day were drowned on the return journey, a leaky boat being the culprit.[40] The balladeers were not slow to grasp the opportunity:

> From Moyne quay they sailed away, for Tarbert they were bound,
> But little was their notion that that night they would be drowned.
> They steered towards Carrig Island but the sea began to roar;
> The screams and cries did reach the skies when they found they were
> no more.

41: *Cappagh terminus, 1953.*
(*Photo: Irish Railway Record Society, no. 10439*)

Loco F501 on the lifting train at Miltown Malbay, 7.6.61.
(Photo: Roy Denison)

Now, a century later, they are all gone, evictors and evicted, rich
and poor, those who perished in the tide and those who died peacefully in their beds. Gerard Manley Hopkins was stating a much
ignored but terrible truth when he, writing in that same age, said
that people, together with the little lives they inhabit, 'both are in an
unfathomable, all is in an enormous dark Drowned.'[41]

Engulfed, thankfully, in only the ordinary darkness of a cold
spring night, we began our walk back to Moyasta.

Day 12

Moyasta Junction to Kilkee

Owing to continuous poor weather, it was the end of March before we could get back to Moyasta. But when we did, the prospect of finishing our trek in one more day's walking was a powerful incentive to make a last determined push.

The journey may fairly be said to divide neatly into two sections: the first, to Blackweir, being almost totally along the northern shore of Poulnasherry Bay, while the second is more inland. On neither part are there any insurmountable obstacles, though all the usual inconveniences and unpleasantnesses are plentiful. But perhaps the most singular fact about this area is the narrowness of the neck of land that separates Kilkee from the upper reaches of Poulnasherry – no more than a mile and a half at most. Without doubt, a time will come when all of the peninsula from Kilkee westwards will be an island, though the great-grandchildren of our grandchildren will hardly see that day – unless there be another eruption like the one the Four Masters describe![1]

Our previous impression of Moyasta Station was not much modified by this second visit. It still appeared woebegone, and all the more so on such a grey day. At the end of the stone platform edge, and before launching out into the day's first trial – the overgrown 250-yard section to the Kilrush–Kilkee road – I felt it necessary to cheer Keith for the journey ahead with an account of a little incident that occurred here in 1904. A male passenger was short-taken on a train that had just pulled into the station, but being unaccustomed to public conveniences he behaved in an entirely natural fashion, i.e. sprayed away from the carriage door. The only problem was that he fired in the wrong direction – onto the platform, where people were coming and going. The upshot was that the poor man found himself in court charged with indecent exposure and committing a nuisance. If there had been only men present on the platform that day, the judge might well have smiled and dismissed the charge. Unhappily for the defendant, there were members of the 'fair sex' present, and since it was incumbent on the law to protect all such from even visual molestation, an example had to be set. And it duly was: a fine of 10/6d was imposed, with 10/6d costs.[2] He was lucky. A century earlier he might well have ended up an amputee.

I wished I had more amusing stories, if only to keep our minds off the marshy ground we now had to toil through. But of this place, where even the *fionnán* is washed flat, there are no stories extant. It does seem to give credence, though, to the notion, still held to locally, that the station's originally proposed site had to be changed because it was found that the land selected flooded at high tide. We passed the remnants of the concrete water tank and the site of both the hydraulic ram and forty-third milepost, but only the river to our right seemed really to belong here.

At the road, because of the considerable alterations of recent years, including the building of a new bridge, we were not seeing Moyasta no. 4 crossing as it looked in West Clare days. Yet, there is no difficulty in distinguishing the exact crossing-place, for across the road the line emerges from the wall and runs by the river on a substantial bank, altogether a most pleasant walkway, past the junction with the Loop, until the 'Red Bridge' is reached. Here, despite a trying breeze, we paused to view the mudflats and the brownish water of the bay. On a calm summer's day, what would be more delightful than table and chairs set here, a chat among friends and a cool drink in the hand! In 1884 Mr Barrington, the engineer, picked this location because 'it had a good hard bottom and there would be no difficulty in getting a good foundation'.[3] The understanding at that time was that W.M. Murphy would build the 8½ miles of line from Kilrush to Kilkee for £40,000 and of that sum £1,800 was to be allocated to Moyasta Bridge. Even today, it seems a ludicrously small sum for such a fine piece of work.

The skeleton of an old boat, its sailing days long past, clawed the mud under the stone facing of the off-embankment, and from the western end of the causeway we were heartened to see that our passage would be easy for some way ahead. The line curves gradually southward here before settling into a westerly direction for its 2-mile run to Blackweir, and since almost the whole of this is by the shore, there is no protection whatsoever against the wind. There is scarcely anything of interest until a little causeway is reached, close to Moyasta West no. 5 crossing. Up to this point, the surface is at first smooth and firm but then deteriorates gradually into quagmire. We could do no more than walk the fields alongside, and only joined the line again where it rose into an embankment at the water's edge before becoming a causeway across the head of one of the deeper stone-faced indentations on this northern shore of Poulnasherry.

A culvert allows the tide access to the slobland north of the line, a necessity since a small stream flows to the bay here. Just beyond this we had, for the umpteenth time, to again retreat to the fields. From here we noticed a very perceptible rise in the ground ahead, a thing that had hardly been discernible even at Willbrook or Russa, where such might be expected. This surprised us for we had heard nothing about any gradients, severe or otherwise, on the Kilrush–Kilkee portion of the system.

We progressed well nonetheless, even through the final muddy cutting leading to the crossing cottage 200 yards farther on. To gain access to the road we had to cross into the yard, round a turf shed built on the line. The house is certainly the original building, and little changed on the exterior. The roof beams still protrude from under the eaves as they did in all the others we had seen which had not been altered.

An unpleasant scene awaited us west of the road though. From a wide gateway, through which trains once passed, we could see that

'The Red Bridge', Moyasta. (Illustration: M. Lenihan)

the large field ahead had been levelled, and that for at least 400 yards
there would be no distinguishing features to guide us. All we could do
was take a sighting on a tree in the distant hedge and strike out into
this, the largest open space we had encountered since Moanmore.
Halfway across we passed by where the forty-fourth milepost had
stood sentinel, but no one now counts the miles from here to anywhere. At the boundary we searched for traces of cut stone or culvert
foundations but discovered none. Only a solitary metal fence post,
half buried, pointed us onward. Another huge field greeted us west
of the ditch, yet here, peculiarly, the line was undisturbed and, like a
pale-green carpet rolled out to welcome us, it ran through the grey
clay on either side. We happily availed of it and speedily came to the
next ditch, 300 yards away, where a huge drainage canal lay in wait.
There had certainly been a culvert here, for the beautiful flat flagstones
lay strewn useless aside. As we rested to take stock before facing out
into another bare, windy field ahead, it was only too obvious how
little protection is here against winds from the bay. The map showed
a ruin on the foreshore directly south of us with the intriguing name

of Bohaunagower, 'the little house of the goats'. What might have warranted its inclusion by the Ordnance surveyors was a question we intended to ask the first person we met. There was no sign of any living creature, however, as we crossed this latest thoroughly levelled field, or of anything to delay or interest us, and it was almost with relief that we approached the overgrown field attached to Bawnmore crossing cottage. A greater contrast there could not be between the two sides of a single ditch: the land to the east flat and open, the other so neglected as to be almost impassable. We soon saw why: the cottage was utterly in ruins, and a farmhouse near to hand by the shore was in no better state. It was as if some blight had struck this little corner and returned it to its natural state, the sole remaining relics of its interlude of human habitation being these crumbling dwellings.

Though we were only yards now from the site of the crossing gates we failed to get there directly. Deep mud and impregnable whitethorns forced us to take the longer route round by the shore. On the road at last, we said goodbye to Moyasta for here ends that townland and also the jurisdiction of Moyasta Station. We now stood in Bawnmore, and were surprised to find from our map that it is possible to walk the shore at high-tide mark for the best part of a mile along one of those little footpaths that were once so extensively used but which are now almost forgotten. It might well have made an interesting excursion, but our priority at that moment was to find someone who could give us some information about the area, for as well as Bohaunagower we had just noted on the map a cluster of oddly named ecclesiastical ruins a quarter of a mile to the north: Kilnamanorha and Tobarnamanorha (whether the burial ground and well of the golden women or the women of prayer, even John O'Donovan was unsure).

But people are scarcer than corncrakes in this part of Bawnmore, and we walked a substantial way north, even to the main road, before we cornered a man who could help us. A gatekeeper was killed one time at Bawnmore crossing, he said, but the details of when and how he could not remember. The mysterious Bohaunagower yielded up some of its secrets. There was a little quay at the place indicated on the map, where boats of up to 40 tons, but more often cots, came to load turf for Limerick. Many times in his youth, over sixty years ago, he watched as many as fifty boats busily at work there, where now there is no sign of any activity. If we kept a sharp eye out near Blackweir Bridge, he assured us, we would see the bones of one of the cots in the mud. The Bothán itself was a mere shelter for boatmen, but how it came to be associated with goats was something he had never heard. Of the quaintly named ecclesiastical ruins nothing more remains than a lonely graveyard without access road or proper enclosure. It is known locally as Kylebeg, and no burials have taken place there in many years, since the new cemetery at Lisdeen replaced it. His description of it reminded us of the graveyard at Kilclehaun, which has suffered a similar sad oblivion.

Having put our minds at rest on the more outstanding of our queries, we made our way back to the ruined cottage to continue through Bawnmore. Our beginning was auspicious, along a fine stretch which presented no difficulty. The bay sweeps in a long shallow curve towards the line here, and for most of the way to Garraun crossing, three-quarters of a mile away, we were never more than a stone's throw from the water. Off to the south-east we could clearly make out the low broken fragments of the 1860s embankment at the mouth of the bay, and directly south, across the slob, traces of the ill-fated line stand out in Termon and Leaheen, though it needs a practised eye to distinguish them in their present decayed state. We were later to walk all that remains of this old line from the valley below Termon school, past St Senan's Well in Termon East, to where it meets the tide opposite Ilaunbeg, and in those 2 miles we found only one culvert intact. It was shockingly difficult going along that southern shore, the line far more eroded and overgrown than the West Clare, but worth the trouble if only to see the huge cutting where Kilnagalliagh shoulders out into the bay. Standing in the rushes that carpet its floor, one might well believe that this was cut out by no mortal hands but was, in fact, the great trench that anciently separated the territories of Fuaim na hAdhairce and Carthainín Mac

The one remaining culvert on the ill-fated 1860s line, at the boundary of Termon East and Leaheen. (Illustration: M. Lenihan)

Caoidhearn, two gigantic rivals who divided west Clare between them. Fuaim, who lived at Lisheencrona, near Doonaha, was singular in that a great horn grew from his forehead; hence his name.[4] Mac Caoidhearn has given his name to Querrin, a little village 2 miles to the south-west, and his dwelling, Cathair Ó Caoidhearn, is still to be seen near Clarefield House, 1½ miles east of the village.

Needless to say, two such people could not co-exist peacefully, and they lost no opportunity of attacking each other. Fearsome though Fuaim's horn was, it eventually turned out to be his undoing. The story goes as follows: He was an extremely heavy sleeper and was even in the habit of lying on a bed of furze in his fort. One night Carthainín made a more determined effort than usual to murder him, but succeeded only in wounding him, whereupon the mad-dened Fuaim jumped up and pursued him. The attacker ran for the great dividing trench and jumped across safely, but poor Fuaim, in trying to do likewise, fell short and his horn became embedded in the opposite bank. Carthainín, seeing him temporarily helpless, rushed down, cut off his head and buried him in the trench. After this good night's work he became the sole proprietor of all west Clare.

In more recent times Doonaha was the birthplace of another giant, but of a different sort. This was Eugene O'Curry, who was born here in 1794 and went on to become one of the best-known Irish scholars of the nineteenth century. For several years he worked with John O'Donovan on the Ordnance Survey and later became professor of Irish history and archaeology in the new Catholic University of Ireland.[5] A great deal is owed to him by all who hold things Irish dear, and as a token of his native county's regard for him, the old Mangan forge near Lisheencrona, a short way to the north of Doonaha village, has been restored and two plaques erected there in his memory.

Kilnagalliagh, 'the church of the nuns', was founded by St Senan, but of its subsequent history not a great deal is known. Some of the nuns, together with monks from Scattery, are reputed to have been drowned in the Shannon by the Cromwellians, while others were shipped off into slavery in Barbados.[6] Whether there was a connection between these nuns and the 'mná órtha' of Bawnmore it is not possible to say, but the proximity of the sites – no more than a mile apart – makes it impossible that they would have been unfamiliar with each other.

South of Kilnamanorha we ran into serious difficulty when the line slipped out of sight under a vast heap of bushes, and we were left to make our way as well as we could through a little field by the bay where wind-stunted blackthorn ruled, viciously tough. There was no possibility of getting on to the line along here, and for a time it looked as though we might have to travel along the shore, so swampy and reedy did the field become. Step by step we had to beat our way through, and when at last we reached the line again, it was at the entry to a substantial cutting, but one so choked that the best we could do was cross the way and pick our steps along its northern lip. A hillside path carried us out beyond the end of the cutting and into level ploughed land where the shadow of the line was visible as a darker green stroke through the grey-green of the field around. Better again, through the next hedge we could discern the cottage at Garraun crossing, 44¾ miles from Ennis, for the gap where the trains passed had not been closed. From that distance, the cottage – nestling low on the down side – appeared to be in reasonable repair, but a closer look revealed a scene of disarray, both inside and out. An old black overcoat, frosted over with mould, still hung at the back of the kitchen door, but it was the only thing left in its accustomed place. If a few calendars and Mass cards lying amid the other debris were a true guide, the house had been occupied up to 1984, but what cataclysmic occurrence overtook the owner at that time remained hidden from us. Whatever it was, the elements have had free rein since and have done their worst. It is an exceptionally exposed site here, as bad as Carrowncalla no. 1, and high-water mark is only yards from the wall of the little yard, so it is not entirely surprising that it, like Bawnmore, should have been abandoned to its fate. We pulled the shaky door to and walked on, leaving this little bit of the past to its own mouldering peace, its own silence.

Between this cottage and Blackweir Station, very little walking on the actual line is possible, so overgrown has it become. It was with regret that we passed here without being able to distinguish the features of the line, for it was on this very stretch that a number of accidents occurred, though happily without any deaths or serious injuries. One such happened on 18 August 1892 – a trying day indeed for all those people whose only wish was to get speedily from Kilrush to Kilkee. First, there was an hour's delay to the train at Kilrush, and as if this was not bad enough, an unusual jolting was felt about half a mile from Blackweir. The train was stopped and it was discovered that the engine wheels and also the wheels of some of the carriages were off the permanent way. But the passengers knew nothing of this until they were released, for it seems that the carriages were locked on both sides – surely a dangerous practice, if the report was correct.[7] After this misfortune, they all had to make their own separate ways

Blackweir Station, 1952
(Photo: Irish Railway Record Society, no. 10155)

to Kilkee. Who could blame them if their opinion of the West Clare that evening was slightly jaundiced?

Ten years later, on 22 June 1902, a very similar accident happened here when an inexperienced driver swung into a curve too fast and derailed the engine. The fireman escaped injury, but the driver in jumping clear cut his head badly. He was brought to Kilkee, where the doctor who attended him promptly ordered two glasses of whiskey for the patient, one to drink, the other to disinfect the wound. The sixty passengers were more fortunate. None of the carriages was upset, and the most they suffered was a walk to Kilkee.[8]

Until the station-house itself comes into view, the only other building of note along here is Shannon View, an eighteenth-century house situated on rising ground a few fields north of the line. It was once the property of Colonel Crofton Vandeleur and is still standing though inhabited.

At 45½ miles from Ennis, Blackweir was the only halt on the Moyasta–Kilkee run. In the early days of the railway all trains stopped here, but at the turn of the century it was downgraded to a flag station, where drivers stopped only if requested. This is clear from the

ENNIS TO KILRUSH AND KILKEE

Distance from Ennis	DOWN TRAINS	Sectional Running Pas.	Gds.	WEEK-DAYS 1		2 PAS.		3 Goods D.E.		4 PAS. D.T.		5 PAS. D.T.		6 PAS.	
				arr.	dep.	arr.	dep.	arr.	dep.	arr.	dep.	arr.	dep.	arr.	dep.
Miles				a.m.	a.m.	a.m.	a.m.	a.m.	a.m.	a.m.	a.m.	p.m.	p.m.	p.m.	p.m.
—	ENNIS ... ¶ W ●	0	0	...	...	...	...	...	8 00	...	11 00	...	4 20	...	...
1½	LIFFORD	...	...	...	...	...	...	C.	R.	C.	R.	C.	R.	...	...
6¼	RUANE ... N	...	...	...	...	...	...	C.	R.	C.	R.	C.	R.	...	...
8½	COROFIN H ... ¶ + W	19	26	...	...	...	...	8 30	8 40	11 20	11 21	4 40	4 41	...	...
11¾	WILLBROOK H ... N	...	...	...	...	...	...	C.	R.	C.	R.	C.	R.	...	...
14	CLOUNA ... N	...	...	...	...	...	...	...	...	C.	R.	C.	R.	...	...
15¾	MONREAL ... N	...	...	...	...	...	...	...	...	C.	R.	C.	R.	...	...
18½	ENNISTYMON ... ¶ W	26	32	...	...	...	...	9 16	9 35	11 47	11 48	5 07	5 09	...	...
19½	WORKHOUSE L C	...	...	...	...	...	...	...	...	C.	R.	C.	R.	...	...
20½	LAHINCH ... ● ¶	6	6	...	...	...	...	9 45	9 50	11 55	11 57	5 16	5 18	...	...
22½	HANRAHANS BGE. ...	...	...	...	...	...	...	...	...	C.	R.	C.	R.	...	...
25	RINEEN ... N	...	...	...	...	...	...	...	...	C.	R.	C.	R.	...	...
27	MILTOWN MALBAY ¶ W ●	16	17	...	...	...	...	10 11	10 26	12 15	12 16	5 36	5 37	...	...
29½	ANNAGH NO. 2 ... N	...	...	...	...	...	...	...	...	C.	R.	C.	R.	...	...
31½	QUILTY H ...	10	12	...	...	...	...	10 42	10 47	12 28	12 29	5 49	5 50	...	...
32½	KILMURRY H ... ¶ +	3	4	...	...	...	...	10 55	11 00	12 33	12 34	5 54	5 55	...	...
34½	CRAGGAKNOCK H	3	6	...	...	...	...	C.	R.	12 38	12 39	5 59	6 00	...	...
37½	DOONBEG H ... ¶ +	6	8	...	...	...	...	11 22	11 30	12 46	12 47	6 07	6 08	...	...
39½	SHRAGH ...	...	...	...	...	...	...	C.	R.	C.	R.	C.	R.	...	...
43	MOYASTA JCTN. H ¶ † + W	13	15	...	...	...	...	11 49	11 56	1 01	1 07	6 22	6 24	...	...
—	BLACKWE R H ... N	...	...	...	...	...	...	To		C.	R.	C.	R.	...	...
48	KILKEE: ... † ●	7	15	...	...	...	...	Kilrush		1 15	...	6 35	...	...	...

Sectional Running (Passenger) refers only to steam trains.

KILRUSH TO MOYASTA AND KILKEE

Distance from Kilrush	DOWN TRAINS	Sectional Running P. G	WEEK-DAYS 13 PAS.		14 PAS.		15 PAS.		16 Goods		17 PAS. M.T.T.F.		18 PAS.		19 PAS.		20 PAS. W.S.		21 PAS.	
			arr.	dep.	arr.	dep.	arr.	dep.	arr.	dep.	arr.	dep.	arr.	dep.	arr.	dep.	arr.	dep.	arr.	dep.
Miles			a.m.	a.m.	a.m.	a.m.	p.m.	p.m.	p.m.	p.m.	p.m.	p.m.	p.m.	p.m.	p.m.	p.m.	p.m.	p.m.	p.m.	p.m.
—	KILRUSH † W ●	0 0	...	8 00	...	...	...	...	...	1250	...	1 25	...	1 45	...	4 00	...	4 45	...	...
4	MOYASTA JCN. H † W +	7 12	8 08	8 20	...	...	1258	1 07	41	2 08	1 53	...	4 08	4 12	...	...	4 53	5 05	...	6 24
6¼	BLACKWEIR HALT N	...	C.	R.	...	...	C.	R.	...	...	...	...	C.	R.	...	...	C.	R.	C.	R.
9	KILKEE † ●	7 12	8 28	...	...	...	1 15	...	...	...	...	...	4 20	...	...	...	5 13	...	6 35	...

†—Train Staff and Ticket Stations.   C.R.—Stops when required.

† –Train Staff and Ticket Stations.   C R. – Stops when required

KILKEE AND KILRUSH TO ENNIS

Distance from Kilkee	UP TRAINS	Sectional Running Pas.	Sectional Running Gds.	7 arr.	7 dep.	8 PAS. D.T. arr.	8 PAS. D.T. dep.	9 Kilrush Goods arr.	9 Kilrush Goods dep.	10 M.T.T.F. PAS. D.T. arr.	10 M.T.T.F. PAS. D.T. dep.	11 W.S. PAS. D.T. arr.	11 W.S. PAS. D.T. dep.	12 PAS. D.T. arr.	12 PAS. D.T. dep
Miles				a.m.	a.m.	a.m.	a.m.	p.m.	p.m.	p.m.	p.m.	p.m.	p.m.	p.m.	p.m
—	**KILKEE †** ... ●	0	0	...	...	...	**8 05**	...	...	...	**1 45**	...	**4 45**	...	...
—	BLACKWEIR H N	...	...	...	...	C.	R.	...	...	C.	R.	C.	R.	...	...
5	MOYASTA JCT. ¶ H † + ●	6	13	...	...	8 13	8 15	1 41	2 08	1 53	1 55	4 53	4 55	...	...
8¼	SHRAGH	...	...	...	...	C.	R.	C.	R.	C.	R.	C.	R.	...	...
10¼	DOONBEG H ... ¶ +	14	18	...	...	8 26	8 28	2 30	2 35	2 06	2 07	5 06	5 07	...	...
13½	CRAGGAKNOCK H ...	8	8	...	...	8 35	8 36	C.	R.	2 14	2 15	5 14	5 15	...	...
15½	KILMURRY H ... ¶ +	6	6	...	...	8 42	8 43	2 53	2 58	2 21	2 22	5 21	5 22	...	...
16¾	QUILTY H	2	4	...	...	8 46	8 47	3 06	3 11	2 25	2 26	5 25	5 26	...	...
18½	ANNAGH NO. 2 ... N	...	...	...	...	C.	R.	...	...	C.	R.	C.	R.	...	...
21	MILTOWN MALBAY ¶ W ●	9	20	...	...	8 56	9 00	3 35	3 50	2 35	2 36	5 35	5 38	...	...
23	RINEEN ... N	...	...	...	...	C.	R.	...	...	C.	R.	C.	R.	...	...
25¾	HANRANANS BRIDGE ...	...	...	...	...	C.	R.	...	...	C.	R.	C.	R.	...	...
27½	LAHINCH ... ● ¶	17	16	...	...	9 20	9 22	4 10	4 30	2 55	2 56	5 57	5 58	...	...
28½	WORKHOUSE L. C. ...	...	...	...	...	C.	R.	...	...	C.	R.	C.	R.	...	...
29¼	ENNISTYMON ... ¶ W	5	6	...	...	9 28	9 31	4 40	5 10	3 02	3 03	6 04	6 05	...	...
32¼	MONREAL ... N	...	...	...	...	C.	R.	...	...	C.	R.	C.	R.	...	...
34	CLOUNA ... N	...	...	...	...	C.	R.	...	...	C.	R.	C.	R.	...	...
36¾	WILLBROOK H N	...	...	...	...	C.	R.	...	...	C.	R.	C.	R.	...	...
39¼	COROFIN ...+ ¶ W	20	32	...	...	9 58	10 00	5 46	5 52	3 30	3 31	6 32	6 33	...	...
41½	RUANE ... N	...	...	...	...	C.	R.	...	...	C.	R.	C.	R.	...	...
46¼	LIFFORD	...	...	...	...	C.	R.	...	...	C.	R.	C.	R.	...	...
48	**ENNIS** ... ¶ W ●	12	24	...	...	10 20	...	6 20	...	3 50	...	6 51	...	...	...

KILKEE TO MOYASTA AND KILRUSH

Distance from Kilkee	UP TRAINS	Sectional Running P.	Sectional Running G.	22 PAS. arr.	22 PAS. dep.	23 arr.	23 dep.	24 GOODS arr.	24 GOODS dep.	25 PAS. arr.	25 PAS. dep.	26 PAS. arr.	26 PAS. dep.	27 arr.	27 dep.	28 PAS. W.S. arr.	28 PAS. W.S. dep	29 PAS. arr.	29 PAS. dep.
				a.m.	a.m.	a.m.	a.m.	p.m.	a.m.	p.m.	p.m.	p.m.	p.m.	p.m.	p.m.	p.m.	p.m.	p.m.	p.m.
—	**KILKEE†** ... ●	0	0	...	8 45	...	...	...	...	...	...	...	1 45	...	...	...	4 45	...	6 05
2¾	BLACKWEIR H ... N	...	...	C.	R.	...	...	...	...	...	...	C.	R.	...	...	C.	R.	C.	R.
5	MOYASTA JNC. H † W +	7	13	8 53	8 55	...	...	...	1156	...	1 11	1 53	2 01	...	...	4 53	...	6 13	6 35
9	**KILRUSH †** ... W ●	7	12	9 03	...	...	...	1215	...	1 20	...	2 10	...	...	...	...	...	6 43	...

†—Train Staff and Ticket Stations. C.R.—Stops when required.

† – *Train Staff and Ticket Stations,* C.R. – *Stops when required.*

timetable for June 1903 and others that followed. The platform still remains intact, on the down side, and the original station-building, a plain, single-storey structure, also stands, parallel to the line and now restored to its original state with only minor external alterations. A large dwelling house has been added at the Moyasta side, and the two blend together extremely well. The glowing accounts we had been hearing of it along the way were certainly borne out by this very pleasing development.

Close by, a handsome five-arched stone bridge spans the upper reaches of the bay, and just off the road at its north-eastern parapet is a small quay, used extensively during the heyday of the turf trade, but now semi-derelict. A hundred yards downstream, the skeleton of the cot *Maggie Anne* lies in the mud, just as the man in Bawnmore had said. Much of the same mud was planted with rice grass in the 1930s as a means of reclaiming the slob, and while it has very successfully done its work of preventing erosion, it can hardly be said to have provided local farmers with the bonanza which many of them seem to have expected.[9]

A few minutes was all it took to see the sights at Blackweir, after which we returned to the line to continue our journey, passing as we did so a now-disused corn mill. An old woman in the house next door provided us with a sketch from the past of summer excursion trains, twice each Sunday, packed with holidaymakers from Limerick. A single fare from the station here to Kilkee was threepence, but most locals were not to be lured by the new-fangled mode of conveyance, and preferred to walk or cycle the 3 miles, it seems. Perhaps the accidents already alluded to, or the routine smashing of the station gates which this station was notorious for, unnerved them. Even as late as 1960 Blackweir continued to attract occasional notice, mostly on account of some misfortune or other. In that year, one of the railcars stopped here and 'began to tick like a clock but would not move', an occurrence considered newsworthy enough to be picked up by an English newspaper.[10] God be with the uncomplicated times that used to be in it!

Across the road from the station, the line is now being used as a working road, and with no obstacle to slow us we soon left the mill and its garden behind and were in open country again. Clearly to be seen under our feet was the clinker and the coal ash laid with the ballast a generation ago. To the south, the tidal creek swings away at right angles to the shore and disappears amid the reeds, while the line curves gently to the right. Our only difficulty along here was at a shallow cutting of 150 yards' length which was flooded, but we were able to pick our steps through it. At its western end, the land drops away sharply on both sides, and immediately and quite unexpectedly a bridge lay before us, its fine masonry at least 15-feet high. There are no parapets here, and as we looked cautiously over the girder-faced edges we saw that it was stone-lined, even to its floor, where the stream that forms the boundary with Lisdeen townland flows.

A large turning-place has been levelled out beyond this, or perhaps a site for a house. It would serve the latter purpose admirably, as it gives a fine view of the valley at the point where the creek separates into two distinct channels. All along here the line runs at field level, and only a narrow strip of rough land separated us from the slob at any time, a strip we soon had to avail ourselves of, for at this point our long, clear walkway ended, swallowed up by the bushes. Here it was, too, that we made a new acquaintance: a type of electric fence we had not seen – or felt – before, a nylon rope interwoven with metal strands. Oddly, though, it was suspended no more than 18 inches from the ground. How it would have delighted the heart of our friend W. R. Kenny, who in 1887 created such a stir by his complaints about the inadequacies of the line, one of which, he claimed, was that his livestock (especially hens and geese!) were constantly wandering on to the permanent way *under* ill-fitting gates.

Down on our left we had lost sight of the creek once more. The map showed us why: it runs parallel to this portion of the line at least halfway across the valley and continues in that course until an arm of it swings back to the line at the next culvert, a quarter of a mile off. But we could see the levees that contain it, running in a roughly crescent shape south of us. The line itself, it seemed, was the only solid ground in this part of Lisdeen – even the higher land to the north looked suspect. But though the map shows it as quite a straight run from Blackweir to Kilkee, the reality for a walker is somewhat different. Several curves block a forward view, and it was at the actual turning point of one of these that the whole of Lisdeen and Termon opened up before us, giving us more of interest to take in in a few moments than we had experienced in the whole section since Blackweir. First, and immediately to hand, was a most peculiar electric fence strung high above a pair of crossing gates, at least 6 feet off the ground, allowing us to walk comfortably underneath. Farther off, lower into the valley, was a conglomeration of colours that looked very like a dump, while in the distance were low hills like sand dunes (as well they should be, for the Irish name for the area is Dumhach, 'a sandbank'). All these struck us simultaneously, emphasising the saucer shape of the land here in Lisdeen at the highest reaches of ordinary tidal waters.

Three hundred yards off, an old man, having stared at us, went back to work, as we crossed yet another culvert and started towards him, passing en route the site of the forty-sixth milepost.

He pointed to various landmarks: Lisdeen churchyard – 'The finest graveyard in Ireland. Dry!'; the property south-west of it called The Retreat,[11] where The O'Gorman Mahon once lived – he who bested the Keanes in the matter of where Lisdeen Church should be built (the upshot being that that family are said to have never darkened the door of a church again); Termon school, now closed, across the valley; the dump, a short way off and just south of the line; the green earthen bank slightly beyond; that, he said, was the remainder of the first railway line built in west Clare, and he pointed out its intended route through the slobland to where it resumes on the higher ground to the south-east and continues out of sight on its way to Kilnagalliagh. He knew that it had never been finished: 'The contractor got broke. You see, if the engineer had brains enough they'd succeed, but they closed it from the two sides out at the tide an' the current brought it away.'

He told us of the Emergency, too, and of the burning of a public house in Garraun by a turf-fuelled county-council steam engine which was scattering sparks in all directions.[12] As for the West Clare, he missed it, he said. "'Twas great company, you know. Men, now, that'd be in the bog, they'd know they had enough done when they'd hear the whistle o' the train going down at six o'clock. There was no watches in the country that time, you can be sure.' This was known far and wide as 'train time', and it was not only people who reacted to the whistle. Many farmers still recall that their cows and calves would begin to become restless as soon as the train was heard, the former to be milked, the latter fed. But he was glad to be able to say that no one, in his lifetime, was killed or injured by a train here. 'A cow o' mine got killed one time, all right, but, sure, it could have been a human being.' The sentiment seemed typical of the man, and on that note we left him to get on with his fencing, grateful for his help.

We had gone hardly a hundred yards when we came to the first of two culverts shown clearly on the map. The line was so near to field level here that we were able to climb down and take a close look at the workmanship. It was worth the trouble. The stonework is massive but elegant, and the passage is floored with smooth flags – obviously to lessen the chances of blockage and prevent undermining of the foundations.

From here we had an unimpeded view along the line as it rose gradually past the 1860s bank and entered a deep cutting just beyond, and there was the added attraction that this was probably all that separated us from a prospect of Kilkee. We accordingly moved quickly, admiring the excellent state of preservation of the long, low embankment we were on, convinced that here at least it would be quite feasible at minimum cost to lay down a portion of the track again, should it ever be desired to do so. We had nearly reached the dump when we came to the second culvert, again a noteworthy piece of building with a scenic little pool at its downstream exit which even the presence of the dump so close at hand cannot detract from. This last we passed with only a remark on how coincidental it was that our journey had begun with a view of Doora dump as we left Ennis Station and was now ending almost within sight of this one.

In minutes we had crossed a third culvert and 20 yards south of us was the sheered-off edge of a grassy bank as high as the one on which we stood. Chisel-ended, it is more a ramp than a bank at its cut-off point, and as we followed its outline we noted how it and the West Clare line gradually drew closer together until they met at the entrance to the cutting. This was a landmark we were determined to see at close quarters. The engineer who looked down into the valley from here in 1864 probably uttered a groan of anguish at the task that faced him. For the proposed course of his line makes it all too apparent why it was never completed with the resources available at that time (about £35,000): it would have had to run by the side of the creek through the actual slob itself. The siting of the South Clare a few hundred yards north three decades later made all the difference, since its bed was at least on dry land.

We started towards the cutting, a backward glance showing us 'Fionn Mac Cumhaill's goalposts' in a dead-straight line to the south-east. At the top of a slight rise we entered Lisdeen cutting, but were prevented from passing along its floor by the flooded state of the ground. Only a little ledge worn by cattle along the left-hand side enabled us to make our way forward without any detour. It is a long-drawn-out affair, Lisdeen cutting, only coming to an end well beyond the nearby level crossing. We came to the usual palisade of sleepers and a road to nowhere important. But it was important to us. For we had reached the third-last stop of our journey, Lisdeen crossing, 46¾ miles from Ennis. Though the cottage was in good repair, it appeared not to be occupied. Built on the down side, on the edge of a little 5-foot-high cliff, it has no back garden and very little at the front. In this almost wholly treeless flat countryside, it cannot have been the most comfortable of places to be stationed in winter.

We easily avoided the mud and water of the remainder of the cutting, and began the gentle descent from the line's summit in Lisdeen, across wide-open fields towards the townland of Dough and the site of the final milepost, the forty-seventh. Approaching from this direction we were taking Kilkee unawares, for there it stood, its arms around Moore Bay and its back towards us. It gave us a vague sense of being thieves creeping up on an unsuspecting victim. The Kilrush–Kilkee road swings very close to the line at the boundary of Lisdeen and Dough, and through the drizzling rain we could make out the motorists, comfortably driving by only a field north of us. Looking down the incline from Lisdeen, we found it hard to believe that there was one last intervening crossing between us and the station, so near at hand did the town seem. But so there was: Dough level crossing, just over 47 miles from Ennis and 700 yards from the terminus.

Little has changed here since 1961. The cottage, on the down side, still displays its original timber-work, windows and roof, and we had hopes that it might be occupied by the last gatekeeper. But in that we were disappointed. Yet the old man whose home it is was welcoming, and being a native of the district, he was able to tell us much concerning the area round about.

He remembered well the last days of the West Clare. Many people in this part of the county never expected that it would be closed down, so much a part of everyday life had it become, and even when it was they assumed that it would reopen in a short time. 'They found out their mistake in a few weeks after closing it. Sure, the few lorries they put on the road to replace it couldn't do a quarter of the work 'twas doing. I tell you, only that the rails were took up so fast they'd have it opened again. 'Twould be still passing that door there.'

A few tenacious souls cling yet to that forlorn hope, but not this old man. Of the line itself he had little to tell, since there were no accidents or other events of note along here, but on other topics he was not without words, particularly the Good People, and he knew more about Biddy Early than is usual this far west.

As we left, Kilkee was framed for us by the walls of a hugely wide cutting 200 yards away, but we had gone no more than a quarter of that distance when we were faced with a hiatus again – the line had vanished, been chopped off and removed. But we quickly found it, just at the point where a culvert cuts underneath. Through the cutting several large buildings stood head and shoulders above the rest, the church and convent among them, but our immediate attention was for the cutting itself. So wide is it that little of the small hill it sliced through now remains, and one would naturally think that there must have been two or more lines of track here, a notion reinforced by the distance between the side fences, at least 30 feet, though Ordnance Survey maps or old photographs do not suggest that this was so. But looking ahead now, we could at last observe in detail what we had been looking forward to all those winter days since our first steps out of Ennis Station nearly six months before: the final gentle slope into Kilkee yard and station.

First one boreen and then another we passed in that last 300 yards, as well as their concession gates and the site of the first signal post. We paused at none of them, intent now only on the final goal and anxious, too, for a possible respite from the rain. As we huddled in the first of the station buildings – a well-preserved stone shed on the down side – to protect our maps from the drizzle, we discovered that it was the former engine shed, now serving as a garage, and that almost directly opposite, on the up side, had stood the signal cabin, which was demolished soon after the line closed. Despite this and the elements, we had reason to be delighted, for we were in the precincts of Kilkee Station, line's end, 47½ miles from Ennis. Here, on 9 October 1890, the first sod of the South Clare Railway was turned by Mrs Grace Reeves, wife of R.W.C. Reeves of Besborough. A somewhat different scene than we looked out on must have been presented by this place at 1 p.m on that sunny autumn Thursday a century ago. A large flag-bedecked platform was erected for the big occasion, and the Kilkee Fife and Drum Band 'discoursed appropriate airs through the town', putting the population in a humour befitting the occasion. At least a dozen clergy (of the three main local persuasions) graced the stand, including Fr Quinlivan, parish priest of Kilkee, who had done so much to make the line a reality. Mr Reeves, in the concluding words of his speech, said that the line would open up communication with the outer world and that they would no longer be, as they had been up to then, at the back of God speed – a sentiment which was received with loud cheers. A select group then retired to Moore's Hotel, where they were further entertained and feted by the contractor, W.M. Murphy.[13]

Kilkee Station, 1952. (Photo: Irish Railway Record Society, no. 10156)

Before venturing out into the rain we took in the scene before us. A hundred yards away, on the up side, was the station-house itself in a well-paved yard, but surrounded by what appeared to be chalets. Old photos show that one siding led to the turntable, which was sited only yards from where we were now standing, in front of the engine shed; a second to a large building (probably the goods' store) directly east of it; and that the main running road and passing-loop joined near the signal cabin. But, as in every other station, there is nothing to show this today. A quick inspection confirmed for us that of this terminus of the South Clare the only remnants are these two buildings, both constructed in 1891. The water-column, the 3,800-gallon tank, loading-bank, 23-foot-4-inch turntable and goods' store have gone the way of all the others.

How similar it all is to the scene at that other terminus, Miltown Malbay. And yet it is at least immeasurably better than the state of Kilrush. Here at least the station-house is in an excellent state of preservation, though since it is being leased out as flats it probably has been internally altered. A long, two-storey, three-chimneyed building, it is immediately recognisable from its red-brick window surrounds, but even more so from the long verandah supported by its eight wrought-iron pillars, still intact and well maintained. The stone edging of the platform is here, too, but now at yard level since the line has long been filled in, and we were in the process of carefully meas-uring it when a woman from one of the flats interrupted us. We told her our business and she said many tourists come here doing much as we were now doing, so she had become accustomed to answering queries. We were invited into more comfortable surroundings, the stationmaster's parlour, now the living-room of a modern-looking apartment.

Over a badly needed cup of tea, the station in its twilight years was pictured for us through the recollections of this woman and her husband who, though they had spent many years in England, had kept these treasured memories. We heard of the loading of cattle on fair days, the arrival and departure of throngs of tourists in the holiday season, but most effectively conveyed of all was the complete casualness of the whole thing, the taking for granted of the supposition that since it was part of normal everyday life it would continue to be so for ever. Alas for unthinking faith! The writing had been on the wall for the West Clare since the end of the Emergency, but only a few perceptive souls could read it. But that is long-forgotten wisdom today, and we tempered our regrets by taking to the streets while we still had light to see the town to some advantage.

Kilkee is by no means a large town. Moreover, it is easily recognisable as a resort by its windy streets and the many lodging houses which line nearly every one of them. The area has a longer and more inter- esting history than is immediately obvious, though the town itself dates only from the end of the eighteenth century. Above all else, it is distinguished by its fine position, at the head of the sheltered inlet called Moore Bay. The Duggerna Rocks, extending across a large portion of the mouth of the bay, protect it from the full force of the Atlantic, and it was the resulting quiet waters within that drew the gentry here in the early nineteenth century, particularly those from Limerick, since Kilkee was the nearest safe watering place to Kilrush, the terminus of steamer traffic on the lower Shannon. With the build- ing of summer lodges began the growth of the town, and by 1840 it was a substantial size and regarded by better-off Limerick people as their 'home from home', a custom that has continued right up to the present day, though on a much broader social base. Considering this, it was natural enough that in 1819 John Scanlan, seducer of the Colleen Bawn, when it became noticed that she was missing, should have claimed that she had gone to Kilkee to his sister.[14] Even yet the tradition lingers on that they actually honeymooned in the town.

The prosperous classes brought their morality with them, as can be seen from the proclamation issued in August 1833 that forbade male bathing on the strand after 10 a.m, behaviour that was reckoned to be a great annoyance to 'Females, who are, by such indecent exposures, prevented from exercising on the Beach'.[15] Needless to say, the 'problem' did not go away; it merely moved to the Pollock Holes further west, and for decades these remained an all-male preserve, but quite acceptable because they were out of sight.

Only the Famine brought the jollity of the Kilkee 'season' temporarily to a halt, for the parish of Kilferagh, together with the rest of the Kilrush Union, suffered horribly from the effects of hunger, disease and evictions. By 1850 things were at a low ebb, and in an effort to lend some cheer to an otherwise gloomy time, Mr Dickson of Merton Lodge, one of the few Limerick proprietors to visit the town that year, kept his yacht lit up in the bay and arranged a fireworks display.[16] During those same awful years, Summer Lodge, owned by Jonas Studdert, a local magistrate, was used as a hospital. Studdert, a somewhat priggish and officious man, came to wider notice three years later when he caused Fr Comyn, the local parish priest, to be brought before the Kilkee petty sessions for obstruction arising out of a political celebration in the town during that summer of 1853. The case, which was too obviously actuated by personal spleen, was dismissed by the presiding magistrates.[17]

It was this same Fr Comyn who did much to aid the rescue and comforting of the survivors of the *Edmond*, an emigrant ship bound for America, which was wrecked in the bay on the night of 19 November 1850. Through the bravery of a number of local people and coastguards, 100 of the passengers and crew were saved, but ninety-eight were drowned, most of them women and children.[18] Ever since, the unfortunate place has been known as Edmond Point.

Half a mile from the town, just south of Diamond Rocks and

under Look Out Hill, is a little bay where another wreck is remembered in a name. This was the *Intrinsic* of Liverpool, which perished here with all hands in January 1836 while crowds stood helplessly by on the cliff. The woman who prayed on the sinking deck is still remembered locally, as is the detail that when the ship finally went down, a seagull snatched something from the water, then dropped it in mid-flight, whereupon it was blown ashore by the gale and found to be a woman's glove. But if the *Edmond* and the *Intrinsic* are the best-known casualties of this coast, many another ship has come to grief here, too. Since the time of the Spanish Armada, each passing century has seen the toll mount, and in the nineteenth century, when traffic round the Irish coast probably reached a peak, scarcely a decade went by without a new addition to the grim tally.[19] The sea claimed its share of victims in other ways, also. Three miles down the coast, at Goleen Bay, five people were drowned on 25 May 1888 when a tidal wave swept over the rocks where they were picking seaweed. The same wave caused casualties all the way from Kilkee to Kerry.[20] And even today, in an era of immediate communication and speedy assistance, no year passes without a few more drownings on what has aptly been called 'this iron-bound coast'.

Even if one has no interest in things historical, one could hardly fail to be impressed by the many splendid views along the coast road south-west of Kilkee. Most visitors prefer to see it in fine weather, but it is, if anything, more thrilling during a storm, when the waves exploding up from the rocks fling their spray even to the road, giving a real sense of excitement and danger.

Five hundred yards from the cliffs can be seen Bishop's Island, also known as the island of the hungry bishop, and when one considers how inaccessible the place looks, the name is hardly surprising.[21] But that someone once lived there seems to be proved by the existence on it yet of a building known as St Senan's Oratory. And up to the mid-1920s, large inscribed flags were to be seen there, as well as a holed standing stone. Farther on towards Goleen Bay is the site of Dunlicky Castle, built by the McMahons at a strategic point across a narrow neck of land on to a promontory. Very probably an ancient fort existed at the same place, but neither it nor the castle has survived, though many descriptions of the latter, as well as some photographs, are extant, together with accounts of buried treasure protected by some fearsome spectral guardian.[22]

Legends aside, the living conditions of the vast majority of the people of the combined parish of Moyasta (Carrigaholt) and Kilballyowen (Cross) – which cover the whole peninsula – were truly deplorable in the early nineteenth century. In 1822 the population was close to 12,000, and substantially higher by 1841, at which time seventy per cent of those living in the western half of the parishes dwelt in one-roomed mud cabins and cultivated tiny plots of ground. In such circumstances there was no reserve, no margin of safety, when bad times came. And they came frequently: famine in 1822, cholera in 1832 and general misery and deprivation throughout the hungry 1830s. Nothing stood between the people and utter helplessness except their priests, and even these could do little to soften the oppressions of nature and the landlord system. However, two more forceful and energetic men could hardly have been found than those who held the office of parish priest here from 1817 to 1878.

Malachy Duggan – known as 'Father Parliament Malachy' because of his visit to London in 1824 to give evidence before a parliamentary inquiry into disturbances in Ireland – was appointed to the parishes in 1817 after his predecessor had been killed by a fall from a horse. For the next three decades, in the face of conditions which we nowadays would hardly associate with even the most deprived of Third World countries, he led his people, but in spite of all his life's unremitting slavery on their behalf, he had to witness their wholesale destruction by starvation, eviction and emigration during the Famine. He himself died in May 1849 of cholera contracted while ministering to the sick, his life's work seemingly in ruins about him. He is buried in Carrigaholt Church.[23]

His successor, Fr Michael Meehan, had much experience of the same conditions that occupied the last years of Fr Duggan's life. He had spent eleven years as a curate in Kilrush, and saw at first hand the terrible events there from 1847 onward. Little wonder that he was no friend to most landlords or their agents. One of the best known and most efficient of these latter at that time was Marcus Keane, of Beech Park, Ennis. So expert was he at the task of squeezing impossible rents out of impoverished tenants that he was engaged by several of the landlords in Kilrush Union to do for them the ugly business that they would not soil their own hands with.

Within a year of Fr Meehan becoming parish priest of the combined parishes on the peninsula in 1849, he was faced with a challenge to his authority and religion that could not be ignored. For in 1850 the Irish Church Missions, a zealous Protestant proselytising organisation, came to this afflicted part of Clare, with encouragement from Marcus Keane and his brother, Henry, who lived at The Cabin, Loop Head. Their stated purpose was the education of children, and three schools were opened, at Kilballyowen, Doonaha and Kiltrellig. But within a short time it became obvious that more than education was involved – that in fact it was no more, no less, than Souperism, a feature of so many other places during these famished years, an attempt to buy a change of religion with the promise of food.

Fr Meehan's early efforts to counter the activities of the proselytisers culminated in the famous 'cursing' episode at Cross Chapel on 28 September 1851, when, it was reported, 'he quenched the candles and rung the bell', and then proceeded to curse most virulently all those people who had sent their children to Kiltrellig school.[24] Fr Meehan denied that he had gone so far as to curse anyone, but the matter made big news at the time, and so it was no surprise that, a short time later, he was refused a site for a church and school in Kilbaha.[25] No doubt it would have been an acknowledgement of defeat for the Keanes, whose summer residence, Doondalhen House, was just south, and within sight, of the village, to have to look out on a Catholic chapel where they intended no Catholics to be.[26]

Fr Meehan was hardly being provocative in seeking to build a church at Kilbaha. Ever before the proselytisers had chosen the place as one of the locations for their activities, he had celebrated Mass here in a farmhouse each Sunday, until he was given notice to quit by Marcus Keane, who then locked up the building and left it idle. For some time, Mass had to be celebrated in the open air, until such time as Fr Meehan hit on the idea of a portable wooden chapel, the famous 'Ark', which soon became known in many parts of the world as a symbol of resistance to religious repression. But his problems were far from over. Though he placed the 'Ark' on the public road at the crossroads leading to Kilbaha quay, in order to be outside the landlord's control, he was prosecuted by the Keanes for creating a nuisance. He won the subsequent court case, but the harassment continued until 1857, when a site for a church was finally given, but only because Marcus Keane needed to secure a favourable election result for the son of one of his chief customers, the Marquis of Conyngham.[27] But even before this date, the tide had turned against the proselytisers, and most landlords and magistrates – practically all Protestants themselves – had distanced themselves from their activities, regarding them as more trouble than they were worth.

Of Henry Keane, there is little more to be said, but Marcus, 'the stringent and successful collector of rents', made news again some years later when his body was stolen from its place of temporary burial and dumped by persons unknown while his mausoleum was a-building. Only after several years were his remains found. It is doubtful whether many tears were shed for him in the parishes of Kilrush Union. Beech Park, the family home just outside Ennis, Doondalhen and The Cabin are all uninhabited ruins today, whereas the little wooden 'Ark' is still intact in Moneen Church, near Kilbaha.

But it would be unkind to leave the impression that this part of Clare had little to recommend it other than past misery, degradation and struggle. There is a brighter episode worth telling, and from Kiltrellig, too, the site of one of the Mission schools that caused so much trouble. Here, a mile east of Kilbaha, is the holy well of St Cuán – a monk of the Celtic Church – the water of which was carried by fishermen in their canoes to ward off misfortune.[28] But the most interesting story is told not of the virtues of the well itself but about the man for whom it is named. Cuán and another monk were walking by the shore one day when they spied a lovely woman bathing her 'snow-white' feet in the sea. The manly Cuán remarked on what fine legs she had, whereupon his companion replied, "Tis a sin for you to be talking like that'.

'Faith, we'll see if it is,' replied Cuán, indignant. He lifted up a flagstone. 'If this sinks, what I said was a sin. But if it floats it wasn't.'

He threw it into the water and it floated. But to prove his point to his prudish friend, he stepped onto it and sailed off around Loop Head. On the journey he met with an accident, but though the stone was cracked it did not sink, and he later returned to Kiltrellig, where the flag can still be seen to this day.

As we made our way back, near darkness, along O'Connell Street we turned right, into Railway Road, for there was one last visit to make. It was to a man living a mere shout from the station. We had been told that he had an excellent knowledge of the South Clare Railway and many memories to share, anecdotes to recount. And he was, if anything, even better than we had hoped. His grandfather, he told us, was a fireman on one of the first trains – if not the first – into Kilkee Station in 1892, and a man who, though he was sensitive to Percy French's criticisms of the West Clare, often himself would joke about it in stories such as the following: 'A train is crossing Sragh when suddenly there are sounds of screeching brakes and pounding feet. An American tourist on board hails a red-faced guard: "Say, is anything the matter?"

"'No, sor. Only a cow on the line."

'The train moves off, but ten minutes later they screech to a halt once again. More running feet. The American calls the guard: "Don't tell me there's another cow on the line."

"'No, sor. The same one.'"

On a more serious note, he told us of the proposed extension of the South Clare to Carrigaholt in 1892, while the euphoria of the line's opening was still fresh. The plan never came to anything in spite of the fact that there was a large fishing industry there at the time. He also made the undoubtedly valid point that without the railway, Kilkee would have suffered a great decline in tourism during two world wars. Motor cars had made their first appearance in the town on 15 August 1901, in the course of the 'Great Motor Tour' – and almost frightened to death some of the older inhabitants, who thought they were the *cóiste bodhar* – but it was not until the 1960s that such transport came within the grasp of common people.[29] In the meantime, the West Clare continued to make the town a lively place every summer, from the mêlée on the platform, where young boys attempting to earn a few pence jostled with the porters hired by the various hotels to carry the visitors' luggage, to the scene on Railway Road just before the six o'clock train, as those who had come down from Ennis and intermediate stops for a day's drinking rather than to take to the sea now staggered back, good humoured and singing, towards the station.

It was all a world away from the dark and silent Railway Road that we too soon stepped out into on that blustery, wet March night in 1988. We also faced the station, but only briefly, before turning left at Percy French Estate. For the salt sea-wind was already bringing tears to our eyes. It was better to move on briskly for Moyasta, before we began to imagine, sentimentally, that the elements were trying to tell us something.

Because we knew that, really, there was nothing more to tell. Never again would a train arrive at or depart from this place for, like it or not, 'Kate Mac' is no more.

Yes. The West Clare is dead.

Long live the West Clare Railway!

Postscript 1999

In the Introduction to the first edition of *In the Tracks of the West Clare Railway* in 1990 I pointed out how rapidly the Irish landscape is changing in recent times and how much this is interfering with physical remains such as those of the West Clare Railway (pp. 8-9). In order to bring the reader up to date with developments in the years 1990–99 I have revisited as many parts of the line as possible. And yes, there have been changes, most of them of a negative nature while a few show a growing awareness of the value of tradition and things historical. The attempt to reopen a section of the line at Moyasta on which a refurbished engine 5C would run during the tourist season is one of these latter. But any sensible person would have to question the viability of the actual plan. Surely it would have made more sense to use the funds to reopen part of the line between two centres of population, and the obvious choice would have to be Ennis–Corofin. Yet that has recently been made almost impossible by the building of a new housing estate at Lifford crossing on the northern edge of Ennis. It seems that those in charge of planning in the Ennis area have not considered that the West Clare Railway might have anything to contribute to Clare tourism. This is a pity in light of what has been achieved in similar circumstances in Tralee – the integrated development of railway, Blennerville windmill and restored ship-canal shows an enlightened use of amenities for the benefit of town and tourists alike.

The following are the main changes to what is left of the fabric of the West Clare line in the past decade: at Ennis Station not a great deal has physically altered since we first began our railway walk here in September 1987. The station precincts have not grown smaller but appear so since new houses press in closely all around. There are now two abandoned locations in the yard where engine 5C formerly stood, the latest having been evacuated in April 1996 when this much-loved – and latterly black-painted – relic was removed, in spite of some local opposition, to Moyasta where it still stands, pending its use on the relaid Moyasta–Kilkee section of the line.

At Lifford crossing a new housing development named Aughanteeroe was built on the site of the line in 1997. One of its larger dwellings now dwarfs both crossing cottage and adjacent ESB sub-station (p. 42). But things are not quite as bad as they appear from the main road, for the houses have been arranged in such a way that the former track bed is now a path between two rows of these dwellings. One may stand at the ESB station, look across the main road towards St Clare's School and see the track run straight and in its wonted way; turn around, face west, and one is looking along what was a cutting when last I attempted to walk here in 1987. In early 1999 I travelled here again, noting now what I then could not. Gone are all the briars and undergrowth (p. 44). It is so easy to walk here now that I was at Fergus no. 2 Bridge within a few minutes. It is presently at the outside edge of a communal green space and a tarred path leads on to it. But oddly the approach is completely unprotected. Perhaps in an estate as new as this there are no young children yet, but when there are this will be a dangerous amenity indeed, for it remains as we experienced it on that September day in 1987, solid, intact but treacherous because of the gaps between the girders. One hopes that no future accidents here will lead to demolition of this fine structure.

Across the river here nothing has changed. The same bushes, ten years older, stronger. I would not like to be trying to force my way through them now.

Corofin Station is, without doubt, the most finely preserved of all remaining West Clare Railway buildings, and in the years since we called here (p. 81) the owners have spared no effort to further restore and improve it. Much credit to them for their loving care. It is appreciated by all railway enthusiasts.

A large house has been built on the western side of the road near Cullenagh Bridge (p. 116), directly on the line, a hundred yards of which had been cleared away, beginning abruptly from the very stonework of the bridge. The whole structure still stands, but sooner or later the deck will have to be removed since the underside is in poor condition and the supporting girders are corroded, even holed, in places. But when this becomes necessary care will hopefully be taken to allow the stone abutments to remain, for they are a notable landmark and often photographed.

At Ennistymon on a single day in early February 1999 was destroyed one of the most visible of all West Clare Railway buildings – namely, the goods' shed. Perhaps it was in the way of a new house just built nearby, or maybe the road needed to be widened at this, the eastern entrance to the town. Whatever the reason, Ennistymon has lost one of its monuments and the place from which much of the trade of this whole region emanated for well over half a century. Its stones have been used to build the new wall adjoining the Telecom building and day hospital.

At the site of Madigan's Bridge just opposite the derelict house a short distance beyond Skerritt's garage, I paused to get a photo and suddenly realised that on my 1988 visit I had made a mistake (p. 128). Then I thought, for whatever reason, that no trace of the bridge remained. Now I saw that in fact the base of both abutments survive, to a height of five courses of masonry.

Just beyond Workhouse Halt the large area in process of preparation for building in 1988 has indeed been built on. It is now a playing pitch, blocking the line at this point.

At Lahinsey no. 2 crossing one of the surprises of this 1999 trip awaited me: the crossing keeper, still here after all those years. How I missed her in 1981 I don't know, but I did. And I missed something special – for she vividly recalls her time as gatekeeper here, the various engine drivers and their foibles, problems with unruly farmers at the gates, and the change over from steam to diesel: 'The diesel'd be on top o' you an' you wouldn't hear it if there was any bit of a breeze. But the steam engine, you'd hear it a mile away.'

Apart from Ennis, Lahinch and its environs have changed most in the past decade (though that claim might be disputed by Kilkee, which has practically doubled in size in recent years). A huge amount of building has occurred in the fields facing Lahinsey no. 2 crossing. Lahinch Station building itself was demolished in 1991, and the site is now occupied by a mini-estate of twelve houses. Only a few hundred yards of the line survive within the environs of the village, south of School Road crossing. Ocean View Park for caravans now occupies the site of the line to within a hundred yards of Creg Bridge. From the intervening plot of waste ground I looked south over the remnants of the bridge, glad to see the fine embankment stretching into the distance. That at least has remained undisturbed.

Perhaps the month of February is not a time to see places at their best in Ireland. That would certainly apply to the Moyasta I witnessed in February of 1999. It was rain-washed and woebegone. The station building and its surroundings looked desolate. Even engine 5C, standing silent in the siding that was once the Kilrush branch, seemed forlorn. Across the platform, on the Kilkee side, exposed to the elements, stood a small locomotive with a passenger carriage attached. Built in 1958 for transporting Bord na Móna staff and equipment about the bogs, this tractor unit has travelled widely, from Clonsast to Cahir to Dromod to here.

Nothing was moving. Not a single person did I meet on this visit to Moyasta. There is, however, evidence in the surrounding area of work having been done, particularly north of the junction, on the Sragh side. Here sleepers and rails have been relaid for perhaps 400 yards and the fencing restored for a distance of almost three-quarters of a mile, and here it is that the little engine and its carriage ply their trade in the tourist season, though the view here, as ever, is anything but inspiring: rushes and bogland. The Kilkee branch has received practically all the attention, though rails have been laid only as far as the Kilrush–Kilkee road. Beyond this, the track bed has been cleared of overgrowth, ballasted and fenced for almost a mile west of the 'Red Bridge', which has been repainted. If the Moyasta–Kilkee section of the line is eventually reopened, as proposed, it will be an expensive enterprise, and only time will tell if passenger traffic in the tourist season will be sufficient to make it a going concern.

Perhaps it would have made somewhat more sense to try to reopen the Moyasta–Kilrush branch. For in the years since I last visited that town a great deal has changed, and for the better, particularly at the station end. Gone is the rubbish dump that defaced the area beside Leadmore no. 2 level-crossing cottage (p. 249). It is now as clean and level as a town park, and an unimpeded view of the station is possible from several hundred yards away.

Kilrush marina, which was then only in its planning stage, is now in full operation and has brought life back to the creek, though hardly to the same extent as when Turf Quay, Customs Quay and Merchants' Quay were in their heyday. Close by, a Scattery Island interpretative centre has been opened, and across the creek, beside Doherty's timber yard and the site of the removed railway bridge (p. 256), is a new activity centre.

Near the Scattery Centre a workman pointed out to me an overgrown space between two houses where once stood a wooden dwelling that seems to have been for the use of railway personnel and in which at least one former stationmaster lived.

The engine shed still stands, as does Leadmore no. 2 cottage, though the latter has suffered much in the intervening decade. The '1891' stone plaque is gone, many slates are missing and the timber-work is rotting. A pity this, in view of the improvements all round it.

On the landward side of the road to Cappagh pier, a great deal of house building has been going on, and only two green fields remain. Cappagh, in fact, is now part of the town.

At the right-angle in this same road, on the final lead-up to the pier, an RNLI station has recently been built on the line, and just beyond it a playground, opened officially on 1 July 1996.

These, as of March 1999, are the most obvious changes to what remains of the West Clare Railway line.

Annageragh Bridge

Engine 5C being removed from Ennis Station to Moyasta, April 1996.

Postscript 2008

For this edition of *In the Tracks of the West Clare Railway*, I visited, between November 2007 and January 2008, all fifty-two of the former manned road crossings of the West Clare. It was a most instructive journey as a measure of the way the development of Ireland has proceeded in the past decade.

Building of new houses is everywhere to be noted, especially in the vicinity of practically all of the towns and villages along the line – Ennistymon, Lahinch, Kilrush and Kilkee, to name but the most obvious. Yet the appropriateness, even the long-term sustainability, of some of these developments, is very questionable, and time may prove that they are, as the West Clare was, a thing of their era, no more. The railway, at least, spread permanent employment for three-quarters of a century to communities over its length. But these new developments ...?

Taking them as we find them now, two shore-side examples – Lahinch and Kilrush – are instructive. Lahinch appears to have expanded haphazardly, the main aim of developers being, it would seem, to build on every possible clear space, whereas Kilrush seems to have picked itself up from its dishevelled state of only a few years ago and now looks positively attractive, having rediscovered the potential of its position at the meeting-point of the Shannon and the ocean. Its great days as a working port may be over, but it has not been slow to appreciate the potential of tourism and various leisure industries, as its busy new marina demonstrates.

The relative decline of farming in recent years has, ironically, helped protect the remnants of the West Clare earthworks, since it is scarcely worth the expense of removing them now that any expected return would hardly repay the effort.

Something else I discovered was that there would appear to be odd anomalies in the planning processes. For example, some owners of parts of the former line have been forced to modify their building plans in order not to obstruct what was once the track bed, whereas in other places new houses are being built unhindered on the same former line.

On a positive note, quite a few of the crossing cottages which were empty and run down on my last visit are now restored and either rented, lived in as family homes or used as summer houses. Being stone-built, they are now listed structures, I was told time and again – sometimes resentfully. In such cases, it was reasonable to suppose that demolition would have been the preferred option.

Sad to report is that only five of these cottages are still lived in by their original keepers – that is, the actual people who opened and closed the gates – though several others are still owned by family members. This is a fact hardly to be wondered at since it is now almost half a century since those long-vanished gates were closed for the last time.

Starting at Ennis, the following, in brief, is the condition today, in 2008, of what was once the West Clare Railway line and its close environs.

Ennis Station, though it is now again an arrival and departure point for rail passengers from Limerick as opposed to being hardly more than a bus depot in 1999, is still unsatisfactory, only a shadow of its once-busy self. There is nothing written and scarcely any physical remnants to remind visitors or passengers that the West Clare ever had a presence here, which seems a pity. Kilrush has not been neglectful in this regard.

Between Ennis and Corofin, if things are not too much worse than previously, they are certainly no better. Yet, as I walked the straight embankment between Fergus no. 1 Bridge and Corovorrin (Tulla Road) Bridge on 11 November 2007, I was taken aback by … the absence of any rails at all! This was the stretch that once accommodated both broad and narrow-gauge lines. The West Clare was forty-seven years gone. That much I knew. But where was the main line?

Only shortly afterwards did I discover that, as part of the reopening of the first portion of the 'western rail corridor', as far as Athenry

Junction, all this line was being relaid. I can only applaud that, and hope it will be seen through to its conclusion.

East of Corovorrin Bridge, the 'gaunt, skeletal' remnants of Toureen House (pp. 39-40)have recently been rebuilt, and it is now once again a family home. But Brookville (p. 43) has not been so fortunate. It is now derelict.

The wreckage of Shaughnessy's Bridge is still where it was, in the very same condition, as is the long straight stretch to Lifford crossing, where the last gatekeeper still lives.

And Fergus no. 2 Bridge remains, as solid as ever, the approaches now fenced sensibly, though not so securely as to keep active young people away from its treacherous allurements. The only practical solution here will have to be the restoration of the deck or demolition of the whole structure. Anyone who has observed the bridge closely will know what an absurdity the latter option would be if such a thing as a real Ennis urban plan exists. We can only hope it survives.

In fact, what is remarkable in this vicinity is that despite the huge expansion of Ennis in all directions in the past decade, there has, thankfully, been relatively little in the way of destruction or even obstruction of the West Clare track bed east or north of the town. This can not be said of Ennistymon, Lahinch or even Kilrush.

Drumcliff road-bridge was removed in 2002. In wet weather it had become an obstacle to funerals to nearby Drumcliff cemetery, one of which a short time before had to be rerouted by the very narrow bridge at Ballyallia. This, in part, seems to have decided its fate.

Erinagh crossing (p. 51) is the same as we found it in 1987, no longer recognisable as a railway structure.

Nor was Ballygriffey very impressive, even though it seems to have become quite a picturesque rural retreat for those discontented with urban living. There was no railway information to be gleaned there on 14 November, though, so I pressed on.

Ruan Station is, as before, in fine condition, its owner fully aware of its historic past.

At Laurel Vale crossing, beside Macken Bridge, I met again the excellent and humorous former keeper of these gates, one of the five such remaining on the whole line. And she was still of the firm opinion that in spite of all the good times, working for CIÉ was akin to a form of slavery, especially for the women involved, since it was they, mainly, who opened and closed the gates, often at outlandish hours. It was certainly no nine-to-five job.

All three cottages between here and Corofin Station still exist, but revealed nothing of railway lore. Of these, Cragmoher no. 2 is at present in a very run-down state, but I was assured locally that it was shortly to be 'done up'.

Corofin Station, as always, is in pristine condition, but Minihan's, next door – the former watering place of so may West Clare crews – is no longer a public house. It was, on this occasion, in a gutted condition, in the process of being renovated and converted into a private dwelling. A fine building it looked, too, even in this stripped-down version of its former self.

From Corofin station to Ennistymon, there have been changes, yes, but no very serious damage to the line.

Roxton crossing cottage was also being renovated as I passed. It is still owned, I was told, by the family of the last gatekeeper.

Newtown cottage is now unoccupied and has been for sale of late.

Willbrook, too, seemed not to be occupied, though still in good condition. At Clouna, I was told a humorous – and very likely true – story of the time, in 1953, when a petition was being organised locally to have a halt established here. The names of people who had been dead for years were included on the list. And it succeeded, for in 1954 the halt became a reality.

Russa Bridge was scarcely recognisable as a structure that a train could ever have passed under. But at least one thing had not changed hereabouts: the difficulty of the terrain. It was as wet and cold as I recall it twenty years ago (pp. 110–113).

A pleasant surprise awaited me at Knockdrummagh crossing. The woman who tended the gates all those years ago was still there and welcomed me. Not alone that, she generously allowed me to borrow and copy an old photo of the crossing which I had not seen before (pp. 118).

Ennistymon river-bridge remains not much changed, but near Piodar's Bridge much house building was in progress, as is the case of late in many parts of the town. Nothing odd about that, one might say, in this modern Ireland of ours. What I did find odd, though, was that the back gardens of some of these new houses intrude onto the riverside embankment that leads to the bridge.

The metalwork of the bridge is showing inevitable signs of wear and tear, but the stone abutments are now decorated with a whole new generation of graffiti (p. 128). Gone is poor Sid Vicious. Like many a pop idol before and after him, he has had his day.

On the short section between Ennistymon and Lahinsey no. 1, there is little new to report, but from there to Crag Bridge, practically every trace of the line has been obliterated. Lahinch goods' shed was demolished several years ago. In fact, nothing now remains of the West Clare within the precincts of the former station yard. School Road (Crag) crossing cottage still stands, tastefully restored and modified, and a little stretch – perhaps 150 metres – of track-bed survives on the Ennistymon side, leading to a new house built directly on the line. At the other side of the crossing, a domestic garage obstructs the way.

In short, if, twenty years ago the growth of Lahinch posed an obstacle to any possibility of ever reopening the line, it is far more of an obstacle today.

From 'the Major's Bridge' at Moy to Miltown Malbay there has been little destruction except for a short piece at the northern side of Downes' Bridge, the site of a new house. All the other bridges, embankments and cattle-passes are still as they were in 1999.

Miltown Station was for sale when I called on 23 November, but the owner was at home. She was kind, helpful and allowed me to examine what railway memorabilia, some if it most informative, was still in her possession.

Flag Road cottage was occupied, as was Breaffa. The cuttings that caused us such trouble hereabouts in 1988 have been cleaned or filled in. In fact, it can be said of Miltown and its hinterland that in general a sensible mix of old and new has been preserved. Yes, there have been modern housing developments and other changes, but not of such a concentrated nature as to obliterate the best of what remains from former times. Respect for tradition is a part of everyday life in this part of Clare, and even though the Darling Girl Festival may have gone the way of the Festival of Finn in Corofin, the Willie Clancy Summer School continues to thrive, attracting visitors from all parts of the world.

Annagh no. 2 cottage is beginning to show the effects of not being lived in, but at Emlagh occurred one of those little incidents that stick in my mind. As I was examining the crossing cottage a local man pointed out to me a metal part of the failed 'fly-swat' wind electricity generator I had noted all those years ago (pp. 175–6). It now supports a nearby wire fence.

At Quilty East cottage I was welcomed and, as at Miltown, allowed to examine – even borrow – documents relevant to the West Clare.

Quilty Village has not changed greatly, nor the station-house. The church porch is still home to its 'Leon' display, and a further reminder of that episode is the large new Leon Centre, opened in 2007. Fishing may not be a livelihood here any more, but a spirit of enterprise has obviously not deserted the place.

King's Bridge (p. 184) still looks impressive, though at water level its stonework is beginning to be undermined. Sullivan's Bridge, on the other hand, appears to have been repaired, for there is now no sign of the damage to its abutments that I noted in 1988 (p. 185)

Kilmurry station, as previously, is in good hands. Not alone is it in excellent condition but the owners have relaid a short length of the line in its original position, constructed from West Clare rails dug up in the station yard. It is worth seeing.

At Cloonadrum, the kind people who helped us in our time of need all those years ago were still in residence, and as hospitable as ever. Good people don't change.

The Annageragh Bridge abutments are as majestic today as ever, but the crossing-plank downstream is gone, time rather than any human malice being the culprit. Happily, nearby Kilclehaun graveyard (p. 194) is now walled, tidied, and St Brendan's well restored to what it must have looked like in its heyday.

Craggaknock Station appears lonesome today, not one of the more memorable places I visited on this trip, for reasons I was unable to discover.

Clahanes cottage has been sold several times since West Clare days, but remains in good condition, though presently unoccupied.

To the west of it, the seaward bank of the freshwater Lough Donnell was breached by winter storms late in 2007, and unless repairs are carried out soon, great damage is certain to be done to the lake's flora and fauna.

At Caherfeenick no. 2, Mrs. O'Donnell, the last gatekeeper, is still in residence and had many interesting details to relate about her work here. And yes, she had heard of Tom Shanahan's death, another link broken with the past of this place.

Caherfeenick no. 3 ('Lendrum's gates' as I heard it referred to only very recently) has been completely rebuilt. The cottage we saw in 1988 was, I was told, 'letting in the water' (from below) and was demolished five years ago. The new building, though, is a fair replica of the original. And the occupants are the same family we met in 1988. A surprise awaited me here: none other than a picture of Captain Lendrum, who met his death at this place in 1920. It was a sobering moment, to see at last the face of the man I had heard so much about on my travels. My response, I fear, was what might have come to many others in the same position: 'Wasn't he a fine-looking man.' And he was, there in his spotless uniform. It was my only comment, for who was I to try to interpret grim deeds of the past, from whichever side they came.

With thanks I passed on to Caherfeenick no. 4. A building site it resembled, the cottage roofless, though in process, it seemed, of being incorporated into an adjoining larger house. It appeared, just then, an uninspiring sight.

Clearly visible from Caherfeenick and especially from the Skivileen river-bridge (now thankfully clear of debris) is the huge new Doonbeg golf resort facing White Strand on the south-eastern shore of Doughmore Bay. It promises to be a great boost to the economy of this area.

Doonbeg station-house is still in good condition and inhabited, but just beyond it, a house has been built on the line in the former station yard. The goods' shed was destroyed by fire early in the new millennium, and the remnants of it stand roofless.

In Sragh there was evidence of further land reclamation, and several more culverts have been removed, leaving the line more fragmented than on my previous visit. But the Doonbeg river-bridge still stands, though part of its deck is holed and care is needed when passing there.

Moanmore crossing cottage (p. 222) has been completely restored, maybe even rebuilt. It could not be more different from the scene of dereliction we witnessed twenty years ago. Other signs of renewal I noted in this boggy region, including, as before, houses being constructed on the solid foundation of the line. But there are still many abandoned properties hereabouts, a silent reminder of depressed times in the not-so-distant past.

Not a great deal appeared to have changed in the vicinity of Moyasta station and platform. There was a distinct appearance of disuse about the place on the three occasions I visited it in January 2008. What rolling stock was there looked somewhat the worse for wear, some of it rusted and shabby. Quite clearly, some kind of shelter is needed for this machinery, especially in this salty environment. And engine 5C, absent now for some years for repairs, is still not back.

But quite a bit of work has been done on the western (Kilkee) side, towards the 'Red Bridge'. Rails have been laid to the bridge itself, and the line cleared almost as far as Moyasta no. 5 crossing. But the road-crossing of the N67 has still not been completed, though the rails extend to both edges of the road.

Taylor's pub is now Clancy's, and the West Clare items on display have dwindled to a dozen or so old photos in the lounge.

The former Loop is today in a far worse state than on my last visit. Only one of the twelve cottages (p. 209) that once formed a little village here, remains, and that ruined and roofless.

Something positive to report, though, is that crossing cottage no. 3 has been refurbished, but of its small platform I could still find no trace.

To the north of the river and west of the main road, my wish of 1988 (p. 261) has come to pass: a little park has been laid out here, com-

memorating P.J. Crotty and Ellen ('Nell') Galvin, two well-remembered musicians of this place. It is a tasteful development, a pleasant
stopping place for tourists and local people alike in fine weather.

In the 5 miles from Moyasta to Kilkee, my latest travels revealed the
following: Moyasta no. 5 cottage is changed out of all recognition. It
has been extended and is a modern-looking dwelling now. But far more
interesting than any matter of bricks and mortar was the story that the
present owner had to tell. She and her husband, after years in England,
bought and modernised this cottage. Why? Because she grew up in
Bawnmore cottage, at the next crossing. But even more of an attraction
back to this area was the fact that her father, who was gatekeeper in
Bawnmore, was born in Garraun cottage, two stops away. This triple tie
to these cottages is unique today in all of the line's length, particularly
since the Taylor connection with the railway in Moyasta (p. 225) has
been broken.

Bawnmore cottage is almost totally ruined today, its remnants as
well as the line here inaccessible in a wilderness of whitethorn, as they
were in 1988.

Garraun cottage, lonesome as ever, is even more forlorn now than
when I last saw it. The four walls still stand, but most of the roof is
gone, as is nearly all of the stone porch that sheltered the front door
from winds from the nearby bay. Why a cottage was ever necessary
here, since the road seemingly leads to nowhere, is the obvious question
that anyone who might visit this place must ask. And it was answered
for me locally: this lonesome boreen was once a busy route for turf
deliveries to the boats that loaded Limerick-bound cargoes all along
this northern edge of the bay.

Blackweir Station is much as it was in 1999, but Downes' corn mill
across the road (which ceased operations in the mid-1970s) is gone,
replaced by a tastefully built commercial development that specialises
in eco-tourism.

Not a single person did I manage to meet here, though I called to
all of the buildings adjacent to Blackweir Bridge.

At Lisdeen, the dump is no more. It is now a recycling centre and waste transit point. At the crossing, nothing has greatly changed. The cutting and cottages are as they were in 1999. No one was at home, but it has been restored and is, I was told, for rent.

Dough cottage has been altered, extended, but there was no one home there, either, so I passed on to journey's end, the station-house at Kilkee.

And here, to anyone with eyes to see, appears in concentrated form the dilemma of modern Irish development. The station-building – patently a structure of distinction and character – has been allowed to decline to a shabby condition, isolated in a welter of new houses (most of them still apparently unlived in).

The engine shed has followed the goods' shed to oblivion, and every other trace of what was once a busy railway yard has been replaced by very typical, undistinguished modern housing.

To approach Kilkee from this side today is hardly an inspiring experience.

From Moyasta to Kilrush, there have been very welcome improvements in that all four crossing cottages – Carrowncalla nos. 1 and 2 and Leadmore nos. 1 and 2 – have been renovated and all are lived in except the first. The fact that the access road to this latter from the N67 is in poor shape is probably no encouragement to permanent residence here.

The portion of the line between Leadmore no. 1 (Shanakyle) crossing and Leadmore no. 2 is very different now than in 1999. A short distance beyond the sewage-treatment plant (p. 246), the tarred roadway that up to here was once the line veers to the right towards the creek and the marina lock-gates. From this divergence point, the line ahead is very overgrown and difficult to travel.

The former seaweed factory is closed now, its site and buildings converted into a timber yard. Traces of the track bed still survive here, but one has to search carefully to find them.

What was not difficult to find, however, was the high wall blocking the cutting to the rear of the houses facing on to Merchants' Quay. There was, as previously, no passing here. All I could do, since I was curious to know what might now lie behind it, was detour onto the Shanakyle road. And there, from the field overlooking the cutting, I saw that the coal yard (p. 248) was gone, that space now a neglected, overgrown wasteland. A wrecked car lay there, and far worse, the fine stone engine shed, though still standing solidly, looked very much the worse for wear, with many slates missing.

In fact, from this cutting to Cappagh pier the remnants of the railway are few and scattered indeed.

The station-house is there, certainly, and is once more a dwelling, for two families now. Its eastern gable, which was disfigured by a large door during the building's days as a truck garage, has been restored. But the fine triangle of clear ground between it, the marina and Leadmore no. 2, which common sense might suggest should be preserved as a public amenity, is now under pressure of commercial development, despite the fact that the future of some of the similar recent developments in the town is uncertain because of the deflation of the property bubble.

Glynn's mills, on 13 January 2008, when I visited, were swathed in what looked like plastic sheeting. The building was in the process of being transformed into apartments, I was told by a passer-by. But at least the imposing façade, recognisable from so many photos of the past century and more, is to be retained.

A short distance from the station, where the railway bridge diagonally crossed the creek (its fine abutments remain), there is now a footbridge leading directly to an activity centre, and to the right of this is a boat yard, obviously an appendage of the marina. This was the space occupied by Doherty's timber-yard on our 1988 visit.

As then, few traces of the line now remain along the Cappagh road. In fact, the only visible reminder that trains ever passed this way is the stonework surrounding the site of the turntable at the pier head (p. 257-258). Luckily it has been preserved; otherwise the West Clare Railway here would be not a legend only but a myth. And whatever else it may have been, it was certainly never that.

Cullenagh Bridge, April 1999.

Ennistymon Goods' shed, 24 January 1989.

Notes

Part I: Historical

1. Saturday 4 February 1961.
2. The 4.20 p.m passenger train from Ennis to Kilkee was cancelled and buses substituted. See *Irish Times* and *Cork Examiner* of 1 February 1961.
3. One railway worker I spoke to claims that he heard a bus driver actually encouraging people to use the bus, saying that the train would not get them to their destination at all.
4. That station-houses were repainted in 1960, and a section of line replaced, several hundred yards in length, near Ruan in the same year, seem to support this view – unless one is to believe in some large and expensive conspiracy to fool public and workers alike!
5. Ignatius Murphy, 'The Kilrush–Kilkee Railway and Reclamation of Poulnasherry Bay', *The Other Clare*, vol. 6, 1982, p. 16.
6. Ibid. p. 17. But note also the *Clare Journal* of 26 March 1849, and 2 April 1849, which berated the gentlemen of Clare for their lack of interest in ensuring that the proposed branch line from Limerick to Galway should pass through the county, whereas their Galway counterparts were suitably active in this matter.
7. In July 1866 a case of traverse in the matter of Kilrush and Kilkee Railway Company came to court. A Mr Shannon was claiming £600 compensation for land that was to be taken by the railway in Leaheen and Kilnagalliagh. The company was offering £200. See the *Clare Journal*, 12 July 1866.
8. *Munster News*, 29 May 1869, 25 August 1883.
9. *Clare Saturday Record*, 6 March 1886, and L. Hyland, 'Twilight of the West Clare, 1961', p. 1 (pamphlet distributed on the day the line closed).
10. Ignatius Murphy, 'The Early Years of the West Clare Railway', *The Other Clare*, vol. 11, 1987, p.6.
11. *Clare Saturday Record*, 3 December 1887.
12. Ibid. 6 March 1886.
13. Ibid. 21 May 1887.
14. Ibid. 27 February 1886, 6 March 1886.
15. Ibid. 5 June 1886.
16. H. Fayle, *Narrow Gauge Railways of Ireland*, London, Greenlake Publications Ltd., 1946, republished 1970, S.R. Publishers Ltd., p. 78.
17. *Clare Saturday Record*, 21 May 1887.
18. Ignatius Murphy, 'The Early Years of the West Clare Railway', *The Other Clare*, vol. 11, 1987, p. 7. For a copy of the advertisement see *Clare Saturday Record*, 2 July 1887.
19. Within a few weeks of the opening, cattle wagons had also to be used since the existing carriage stock was unequal to the demand. See *Clare Saturday Record*, 30 July 1887 and *Limerick Chronicle*, 2 August 1887.

20. *Munster News*, 11 October 1890.

21. *Clare Journal*, 16 May, 19 May 1892.

22. Information supplied by Martin Boland, Kilkee.

23. Patrick M. Taylor, 'Are You Right There Michael, or How to Give Co. Clare Tourism a Boost', *Irish Independent*, 13 November 1975.

24. Ignatius Murphy, 'The Early Years of the West Clare Railway', *The Other Clare*, vol. 11, 1987, p.9.

25. See, for example, *Clare Journal*, 3 August 1896.

26. H. Fayle, *Narrow Gauge Railways of Ireland*, p. 79.

27. Ibid. p. 79.

28. Ibid. p. 81. These cars, nos. 395 and 396, were found to be not powerful enough to handle the gradients on the West Clare section and were used for a few years on the more level Kilrush–Kilkee run.

29. Of all the carriage works only a carpenters' shop, employing three men, was left by 1941.

30. J.H. Connolly, 'The West Clare Railway' (paper read to South-Western Group, Institute of Transport , at Ennis, 28 October, 1965), p.5.

31. Ibid. p.6.

32. L. Hyland, *Twilight of the West Clare*, 1961, p.6. The Irish Railway Record Society also possesses a photograph (no. 11163) which shows coach 9C at Kilrush in September 1954. Though obviously on its last legs it was still being used.

33. Fergus Mulligan, *One Hundred and Fifty Years of Irish Railways*, Belfast, Appletree Press, 1983, p. 167. The diesel locomotives were not so lucky. CIÉ's efforts to sell them came to nothing and they lay rotting for years at Inchicore before being scrapped at last around 1970.

Part II: The West Clare Railway

Day 1

1. *Clare Journal*, 9 April 1891.

2. Ibid. 18 January 1897.

3. *Clare Saturday Record*, 21 May 1887.

4. T. Kelly, 'Ennis Courthouse', *The Other Clare*, vol. 5,1981, p. 20.

5. *Clare Journal*, 2 December 1858, quoted J.B. Pratt, who presented the Engineer's Report: 'the line is now in good running order from Limerick to Clare Castle. The portion between Clare Castle and Ennis has been formed and fenced and the permanent way laid on the greater part of it. All the piles for the Fergus bridge have been driven and the iron superstructure has been constructed and is in a course of erection. Six stations have been completed and the terminal station at Ennis has been contracted for on favourable terms. Goods and cattle platforms are in course of erection at the principal stations.'

6. Fergus Mulligan, *One Hundred and Fifty Years of Irish Railways*, p. 57

7. *Clare Saturday Record*, 7 May 1887.
8. Hugh Weir, *The Houses of Clare*, Whitegate, Ballinakella Press, 1986, p. 209.
9. *Clare Journal*, 28 January 1889.
10. Maurice Mullins, Inagh.
11. S. Spellissy & J. O'Brien, *Clare County of Contrast*, Ennis, 1987, p. 25.
12. *Clare Journal*, 8 March 1888.
13. But see Gerald O'Connell, 'Stephen Joseph Meaney' in *Dal gCais*, no. 5, 1979, pp. 115–16.
14. Maurice Cuffe, 'The Siege of Ballyally Castle', in Alan Bliss, *Spoken English in Ireland*, Dublin, Dolmen Press, 1979, pp. 106–8.
15. *Cabhail*: ruined shell of a house.
16. Brian Ó Dálaigh, 'The Old Urban Boundaries of Ennis', *The Other Clare*, vol. 12, 1988, p.27.
17. G. O'Connell, 'Cutting on the River Fergus at Ballyhea near Ennis', *The Other Clare*, vol. 3. 1979, pp. 25-6; *Clare Champion*, 19 April 1985.
18. The parish of Barefield is officially 'Templemaley, Kilraghtis and Doora'.
19. See my 'Survey of Otherworldly Clare, Part 4', *The Other Clare*, vol. 12, 1988, p. 46.
20. Ibid. p. 49.

Day 2

1. Rev. P. White, *History of Clare and the Dalcassian Clans*, Dublin, Gill & Son, 1893, p. 208.
2. *A History of the Parish of Inagh and Kilnamona*, Ennis, 1965, p. 34.

Day 3

1. James Frost, *The History and Topography of the County of Clare*, reprinted Cork, Mercier Press, 1973, pp. 140, 697.
2. *Clare Saturday Record*, 26 January 1889.
3. See Katherine Simms, 'The Battle of Dysert O'Dea', *Dal gCais*, no. 5, 1979, p. 65.
4. *JRSAI*, vol. 30, 1900, p. 418.
5. See *Ordnance Survey Letters*, Co. Clare, vol. 1, pp. 144–6 (pp. 52–3 in typescript copy).
6. Spellissy & O'Brien, *Clare County of Contrast*, p. 74.
7. Michael Mac Mahon, *A History of the Parish of Rath*, Clare Archaeological & Historical Society, 1979, p. 55.
8. Ibid. pp. 68, 72.
9. Weir, *The Houses of Clare*, p. 91.
10. See David Brooke, *The Railway Navvy*, Newton Abbot, David & Charles, 1983, p. 19.
11. Maurice Mullins, Inagh.

12. Seán Ó Súilleabháin, *Legends from Ireland*, London, Batsford, second edn., 1981, p. 153.
13. For example, 'Feis Tighe Chonáin': see *Transactions of the Ossianic Society*, 1854, vol. 2 (Dublin 1855).
14. Mac Mahon, *A History of the Parish of Rath*, p. 81.
15. Among the useful books and maps on this region are: G. Cunningham, *Burren Journey*, 1978, and *Burren Journey West*, 1980, Shannon Western Regional Tourism Organisation; F. Donaldson, *The Burren Flowers*, no. 13, Irish Environmental Library Series, Folens. nd; J.M. Feehan, *The Secret Places of the Burren*, Cork, Royal Carbery Books, 1987; E. Fox, M. Leonard and P. O'Dowd, *Ó Ghaillimh go Ceann Boirne*, RTC, Galway, 1978; M.A. Keane, *The Burren*, Eason, no. 30, Irish Heritage Series, 1983; W. Nolan, *North-west Clare Today/Tomorrow*, 1977; G. O'Connell (ed.), *The Burren: a guide*, nd; E. Rynne, *Burren for the Archaeologist*, UCG, nd; K.K. Tratman, *The Caves of North-west Clare*, David & Charles, 1969. The most useful of the maps of the region are: various Ordnance Survey sheets; T.D. Robinson's 'The Burren' (1977), and the latest rambler's guide published by Jeff O'Connell and Anne Korff.
16. Kevin J. Browne, *Eamon de Valera & the Banner County*, Dublin, Glendale Press, 1982, pp. 176–7
17. *Clare Journal*, 27 August 1900.
18. Jim O'Neill, Clarecastle.
19. *Irish Times*, 1 February 1961.
20. Block-post: a station at which the electric token staff system (ETS) operates.

Day 4

1. Weir, *The Houses of Clare*, p. 36.
2. Mac Mahon, *A History of the Parish of Rath*, p. 71.
3. *Transactions of the Ossianic Society*, 1854, vol. 2, p. 63.
4. Mac Mahon, *A History of the Parish of Rath*, p. 86.
5. Sharon Gmelch (ed.), *Irish Life and Traditions*, O'Brien Press, Dublin 1986, p. 106.
6. Weir, *The Houses of Clare*, p. 236.
7. *Clare Champion*, 24 January 1931.
8. Mac Mahon, *A History of the Parish of Rath*, p. 17.
9. Mrs Harbison, 'Mysterious Murder at Applevale', *The Other Clare*, vol. 7, 1983, p. 27; also *Clare Journal*, 24 January 1831.
10. See also Weir, *The Houses of Clare*, p. 27.
11. Maurice Mullins, Inagh.
12. *Glaise*: a little stream.
13. Mac Mahon, *A History of the Parish of Rath*, pp. 26–7.
14. *Clare Champion*, 29 December 1978.

Day 5

1. *Clare Journal*, 19 September 1892.
2. *Claíochán*: the trace left on the ground by a sod wall ('ditch') which has been removed.
3. See, for instance, *The Other Clare*, vol. 9, 1985, p. 26.
4. *Clare Champion*, 4 July 1942.
5. Jim O'Neill, Clarecastle.
6. *JRSAI*, 46,1916, p. 112
7. GSR, 'Appendix to the Working Time Table', 1 March 1935, p. 29.
8. *Clare Journal*, 6 February 1888.
9. *Cuaird*: a visit; the custom of visiting neighbours' houses at night to play cards, tell stories or exchange gossip.
10. *Clare Saturday Record*, 23 November 1901; *Clare Man*, 21 June 1902.
11. But see the version of these events given in Browne's *Eamon de Valera & the Banner County*, pp. 113–14.
12. For differing tallies of the casualties inflicted in this engagement compare Browne, *Eamon de Valera & the Banner County*, p. 119 with Mac Mahon, *A History of the Parish of Rath*, p. 79.
13. *Clare Journal*, 21 February 1910.
14. Weir, *The Houses of Clare*, p. 283.
15. Evidence of Mr Hopkins, Locomotive Supt., West Clare Railway, at the hearing of *French V The West Clare Railway Company* at Ennis, 15 January 1897, *Irish Independent*, 13 November 1975.
16. *Clare Journal*, 18 January 1897.
17. *Clare Man*, 30 August 1902.

Day 6

1. *Clare Journal*, 30 January 1888.
2. Ibid. 9 February 1888.
3. See, for example, *Clare Saturday Record*, 1 November 1902.
4. He was one of the very few TDs to protest vehemently at the line's closure. See *Sunday Review*, 30 October 1960.
5. Spellissy & O'Brien, *Clare County of Contrast*, p. 95; *Ireland's Own*, 31 March 1989, p. 32; Weir, *The Houses of Clare*, pp. 118–19.
6. Mac Mahon, *A History of the Parish of Rath*, p. 72.
7. Seosamh Mac Mathúna, *Kilfarboy* (nd), p. 47.
8. Msgr. John T McMahon, *Ramblers from Clare & Other Sketches*, Sydney nd, pp. 171–2, quoted in *Clare Association Yearbook*, 1988, p. 13.
9. Browne, *Eamon de Valera & the Banner County*, p. 182.
10. Frost, *The History and Topography of the County of Clare*, pp. 108, 110.
11. Wm. Shaw Mason, *A Statistical Account or Parochial Survey of Ireland*, vol. 1, Dublin, 1814, p. 494.
12. *Clare Champion*, 1 August, 1936. For the bad weather see *Clare Champion*, 1 August 1942.

13. See Conrad Arensberg, *The Irish Countryman*, New York, Natural History Press, 1968, p. 40. Shaw Mason gives the location of Cill Stuifin as 'near the mouth of the Shannon, in the centre of the bed of it.' See vol. 2, p. 491 of his *Statistical Account or Parish Survey of Ireland*, Dublin, 1816; see also Francis J. Litton: '"Cill Scoithín" alias Killstuipheen', *Dal gCais*, no. 5, 1979, pp. 87-8; *Clare Journal*, 16 November, 1854.

Day 7

1. See, for example, *Clare Champion*, 12 June 1987.
2. Weir, *The Houses of Clare*, p. 201.
3. Mac Mathúna, *Kilfarboy*, p. 112.
4. Ibid. p. 110; Weir, *The Houses of Clare*, p. 190; Shaw Mason, op. cit. vol. 1, p. 501.
5. Shaw Mason (op. cit., vol. 2, p. 443) states that Clahansevan Castle, near Loop Head, was used for the same nefarious purpose.
6. *Clare Journal*, 30 January 1888.
7. Mac Mathúna, *Kilfarboy*, pp. 97–8.
8. For the words and tune of this ballad see Colm Ó Lochlainn, *More Irish Street Ballads*, London, Pan, 1978, p. 142.
9. Mac Mathúna, *Kilfarboy*, pp. 85–6.
10. For a short description of this and similar incidents see Richard Bennett's *The Black and Tans*, London, NEL, 1970.
11. Weir, *The Houses of Clare*, p. 131.
12. *Clare Journal*, 27 December 1888.
13. *Clare Champion*, 31 August 1946.
14. Weir, *The Houses of Clare*, p. 191; Shaw Mason, op. cit., vol. 1, p. 485.
15. Samuel Lewis, *A Topographical Dictionary of Ireland*, London, 1837, vol. 2, p. 371; Shaw Mason, op. cit., vol. 1, p. 481.
16. Mac Mathúna, *Kilfarboy*, p. 12.
17. See *Clare Journal*, 29 January 1885.
18. Mac Mathúna, *Kilfarboy*, p. 80.
19. Ibid. p.10.

Day 8

1. Weir, *The Houses of Clare*, p. 80.
2. Ibid. p. 61.
3. Mac Mathúna, *Kilfarboy*, p. 53.
4. Weir, *The Houses of Clare*, p. 188.
5. Mac Mathúna, *Kilfarboy*, p. 11.
6. Written in the early twentieth century by Thomas Hayes, Miltown. The late Tom Lenihan was one of the few people who could sing the song in its entirety in recent times.
7. Weir, *The Houses of Clare*, p. 253.
8. GSR, 'Appendix to the Working Time Table, 1935', p. 145.
9. *Clare Champion*, 3 September 1955.

10. *Clare Saturday Record*, 6 March 1897.
11. *Clare Journal*, 12 January 1899.
12. Ibid. 10 August 1896.
13. *Cond*: morsel, crust.
14. Recalled by the late Nicholas Brody, Kilmurry.
15. Weir, *The Houses of Clare*, p. 78.
16. He died at Formby, Lancashire, in 1920 and is buried there.
17. Browne, *Eamon de Valera & the Banner County*, p. 117.
18. Spellissy & O'Brien, *Clare County of Contrast*, p. 53.
19. *The County Express*, Ennis, January 1985.
20. Weir, *The Houses of Clare*, p. 103.
21. T.J. Westropp, in *Limerick Field Club Journal*, no. 3, 1905–08. pp. 1-5.
22. Weir, *The Houses of Clare*, pp. 241–2.
23. *Dal gCais*, no. 8, 1986, p. 121.
24. Ibid. p. 111.
25. Weir, *The Houses of Clare*, p. 170.
26. Mac Mathúna, *Kilfarboy*, p. 57.
27. *Clare Champion*, 20 August 1955.

Day 9

1. Vouched for by Mr Tom Shanahan, who served here before his transfer to Doonbeg
2. For much useful information on this subject see Hugh Brody, *Inishkillane*, Harmondsworth, Pelican Books, 1974.
3. Henry Boylan, *A Dictionary of Irish Biography*, Dublin, Gill & Macmillan, 1978, p. 266.
4. *Clare Journal*, 8 July 1858, 6 April 1874.
5. Probably the first proposal to use weed killer rather than gangs of men as heretofore was made in 1915. See *Clare Journal*, 7 June 1915.
6. From this deed comes, no doubt, the castle's unenviable reputation. See Shaw Mason, op. cit., vol. 2, p. 442 and T. Crofton Croker & Sigerson Clifford, *Legends of Kerry*, Geraldine Press, 1972, p. 16.
7. *Clare Champion*, 13 September 1941.
8. Weir, *The Houses of Clare*, p. 198.

Day 10

1. *Clare Journal*, 30 March 1874.
2. Ibid. 27 April 1874.
3. Ibid. 4 May, 11 June 1874.
4. Spellissy & O'Brien, *Clare County of Contrast*, p. 54.
5. Weir, *The Houses of Clare*, p. 182.
6. *Clare Journal*, 16 May 1892.
7. Headlines like that in the *Clare Champion* of 9 August 1941 ('Two Weeks' Coal') became commonplace from this time on.
8. How great that traffic may have been, though, particularly in the early

nineteenth century, can be gauged from Shaw Mason's claim that turf 'to the value of upwards of £10,000 is sent annually from this and the neighbouring bogs.'

9. *Munster News*, 5 July 1893.

10. *Limerick Chronicle*, on 27 August 1896 and on other occasions, found Moyasta Junction a rather confusing and worrying place for passengers. It claimed that they were never quite sure whether they would have to change or sit tight.

11. *Irish Times*, 1 February 1961.

12. Shaw Mason (op. cit., vol, 2, p. 415) calls it 'Poulanishery Bay or Oyster Cove'.

13. Ibid. p. 416.

14. Shaw Mason claims that such vessels could earn about £200 a year at this trade.

Day 11

1. *Clare Journal*, 26 July 1888.

2. *Munster News*, 22 August 1888.

3. *Clare Journal*, 11 March 1889.

4. Ibid. 23 August 1888.

5. The work of Robert French, the photographer in question, is now part of the Lawrence Collection in the National Library.

6. Ignatius Murphy, 'The Vandeleur Evictions – Kilrush 1888', *The Other Clare*, vol. 4., 1980, p. 38.

7. Ibid. p. 39.

8. *Clare Saturday Record*, 3 April 1897; Weir, *The Houses of Clare*, p. 164

9. *Clare Man*, 1 November 1902; *Clare Saturday Record*, 1 November 1902.

10. Ignatius Murphy, 'The Kilrush–Kilkee Railway & Reclamation of Pounasherry Bay', *The Other Clare*, vol. 6, 1982, p. 16. Accompanying the article is a photograph of this bridge.

11. *Clare Journal*, 17 December 1849. As early as 1816 Shaw Mason had sounded an ominous note regarding this operation: 'The Ferry at Carnacalla near Kilrush requires a second and safer boat than that at present used there'.

12. Weir, *The Houses of Clare*, p. 125.

13. Shaw Mason, op. cit., vol. 2, p. 439; Frost, *The History & Topography of the County of Clare*, p. 82.

14. The very name 'Scattery' is of Viking origin. See 'St Senan's Fifteenth Centenary', a supplement to the *Clare Champion* of 24 June 1988, p. 5.

15. Shaw Mason, op. cit., vol. 2, p. 492.

16. Ignatius Murphy, 'Father Mathew', *The Other Clare*, vol. 9, 1985, p. 5. See also *JRSAI*, 38, 1908, p. 399 for an interesting note on the 'station-stone from Scattery and its fate after the suppression'.

17. Spellissy & O'Brien, *Clare County of Contrast*, pp. 179-81 has a useful short account of the island's history.

18. Ignatius Murphy, 'Capt. A.E. Kennedy, Poor Law Inspector, and the Great Famine in Kilrush Union, 1847–50', *The Other Clare*, vol. 3, 1979, p. 22.

19. *Limerick and Clare Examiner*, 4 September 1850.

20. So great was traffic between Carrigaholt and the Continent at one time that, as Shaw Mason (op. cit., vol. 2, p. 431) reports, when the Earls of Thomond wrote to their noble relatives here they sometimes directed their letters to Carrigaholt, near Spain.

21. *Clare Journal*, 16 January 1899.

22. Long before the Famine it was seemingly one of the most sought-after burial-places in the county, from the belief that all bodies buried there were miraculously conveyed under the bed of the river into the holy ground of Scattery. See Shaw Mason, op. cit., vol. 2, p. 441.

23. Ignatius Murphy, 'Capt. A.E. Kennedy, Poor Law Inspector, and the Great Famine in Kilrush Union, 1847–50', p. 17.

24. Ignatius Murphy, 'The Vandeleur Evictions – Kilrush 1888', p. 38.

25. Weir, *The Houses of Clare*, p. 216.

26. This seems to have been a problem here always. See Shaw Mason (op. cit., vol. 2, pp. 485–7) for details of proposals to deepen the harbour in the early nineteenth century.

27. *Clare Champion*, 19 May 1989, 10 November 1989; *Irish Press*, 5 January 1990.

28. Ignatius Murphy, 'Capt. A.E. Kennedy, Poor Law Inspector, and the Great Famine in Kilrush Union, 1847–50', p. 20.

29. Weir, *The Houses of Clare*, p. 46.

30. Ignatius Murphy, 'Capt. A.E. Kennedy, Poor Law Inspector, and the Great Famine in Kilrush Union, 1847–50', p. 22.

31. Ibid. p.23.

32. *Limerick Reporter*, 4 December 1840.

33. For a delightful account of how Senan got his name and how St Senan's Lake was formed see Shaw Mason, op. cit., vol. 2, pp. 438-9.

34. See W. McLysaght & Sigerson Clifford, *The Tragic Story of the Colleen Bawn*, Dublin, Anvil Books, 1964.

35. James T. McGuane, *Kilrush from Olden Times*, Clódóiri Lurgan, 1984, p. 81.

36. 'The Passing of the West Clare', *Irish Times*, 1 February 1961.

37. Irish Railway Record Society photograph, no. 10439.

38. Contrast this with Shaw Mason's (op. cit., vol. 2, p. 425) account: 'The view of the town and harbour is truly delightful at sunset on a summer's evening when Scattery Road is crowded with shipping and upward of two hundred herring-boats issue together from the neighbouring creeks.'

39. James T. McGuane, *Kilrush from Olden Times*, p. 73.

40. See Seán Marrinan, 'The Shannon Boating Tragedy of 1893', *The Other Clare*, vol. 7. 1983, pp. 35-6.

41. G.M. Hopkins, 'That Nature is a Heraclitean Fire and of the Comfort of the Resurrection' in W.H. Gardner (ed.) *Poems of Gerard Manley Hopkins*, Oxford, 1968.

Day 12

1. A proposal was made in the late eighteenth century to cut a canal from Poulnasherry Bay to Doonbeg Bay, but nothing came of it. See Shaw Mason, op. cit., vol. 2, pp. 475–6.
2. *Clare Journal*, 9 June 1904. Moyasta made front-page headlines on several occasions up to the time of the line's closure, usually for the wrong reasons. See, for example, *Clare Champion*, 10 February 1940.
3. *Irish Builder*, 15 January 1885, p. 22.
4. Spellissy & O'Brien, *Clare County of Contrast*, p. 68.
5. Henry Boylan, *A Dictionary of Irish Biography*, p. 257.
6. Spellissy & O'Brien, *Clare County of Contrast*, p. 68.
7. *Clare Journal*, 22 August 1892.
8. *Clare Man*, 28 June 1902.
9. Early in the eighteenth century Mr. Van Hoogert of Querrin and a Dutch company were also hopeful of recovering much land from the slob. See Shaw Mason, op. cit., vol. 2, p. 476.
10. *Irish Times*, 1 February 1961 carried the report.
11. Weir, *The Houses of Clare*, p. 226.
12. The plaintiff in the subsequent court case was awarded compensation of £800. See *Clare Champion*, 25 July 1942.
13. *Clare Saturday Record*, 11 October 1890.
14. McLysaght & Clifford, *The Tragic Story of the Colleen Bawn*, pp. 28, 45.
15. For a reproduction of this proclamation see Béaloideas (Journal of the Folklore of Ireland Society), vol. 56, 1988, p. 95.
16. Seán Marrinan, 'The Wreck of the Edmond at Kilkee', *The Other Clare*, vol. 3, 1979, p. 33.
17. Ignatius Murphy, 'Father Michael Comyn', *Dal gCais*, no. 8, 1986, p. 16.
18. Seán Marrinan, 'The Wreck of the Edmond at Kilkee', p. 34.
19. Seán Marrinan, 'Some Shipwrecks near Kilkee', *The Other Clare*, vol. 4, 1980 p. 35.
20. *Clare Journal*, 28 May 1888.
21. For the legend of the Hungry Bishop see T.J. Westropp, 'Kilkee and its Neighbourhood' in *NMASJ*, vol. 2, 1912, p. 228 and vol. 3, 1913, p. 38 ff.
22. Ibid. See also Seán Marrinan, 'The Tower Houses of South-West Clare', *The Other Clare*, vol. 8, 1984, p. 41.
23. Ignatius Murphy, 'Fr Parliament Malachy', *The Other Clare*, vol. 10, 1986, pp. 38–45.
24. *Clare Journal*, 6 October 1851.
25. *Limerick Chronicle*, 14 October 1851.
26. Weir, *The Houses of Clare*, p. 106.
27. Ignatius Murphy, *Fr Michael Meehan & the Ark of Kilbaha*, Ennis, 1980, p. 13.
28. Bairbre Ó Floinn, 'The Lore of the Sea in County Clare', *Dal gCais*, no. 8, 1986, p. 111.
29. Seán Marrinan, 'The Motor Car Comes to Clare', *The Other Clare*, vol. 9, 1985, p. 62.

Index